VOICES
FROM THE
SUMMIT

VOICES FROM

The World's

THE SUMMIT

Great Mountaineers on the Future of Climbing

ADVENTURE PRESS

NATIONAL GEOGRAPHIC
WASHINGTON, D. C.

In association with
The Banff Centre for Mountain Culture

TABLE OF CONTENTS

FOREWORD

DR. GRAEME MCDONALD, BERNADETTE MCDONALD,
AND JOHN AMATT

25 years ago, 450 people gathered together in the small Rocky Mountain village of Banff, Alberta, to view some exceptional mountain films. It was that special quiet season between the frenetic activity of a short intense summer in the Canadian Rockies and the much longer winter to follow. This fledgling one-day gathering had a name: the Banff Festival of Mountaineering Films. Little did the organizers and audience members know that they were launching an annual tribal gathering of the Banff Mountain Film Festival, which now attracts thousands of people to Banff each November and carries extraordinary moving mountain images to tens of thousands more through its global tour.

The Festival was originally conceived as a "community" event, and it remains true to its roots. The only thing that's changed is the scope of the community. Climbers, adventurers, filmmakers, authors, photographers, and others who are passionate about the mountains come from every corner of the globe to experience this annual celebration of the spirit of adventure.

The Festival is the flagship program of The Banff Centre for Mountain Culture, which promotes understanding and appreciation of the world's mountain places by creating opportunities for the international mountain community to share experiences, ideas, and visions. Because the 25th anniversary of the festival coincided with the start of the new millennium, a challenge emerged to do something that would be adequately meaningful.

The personalities connected with the 25-year history of the festival are a formidable group. In the world of mountaineering, the best men and women have passed through these festival doors. These individuals have three things in common: They hold esteemed positions within the global mountaineering community, they are passionate about mountain places, and they have all appeared as guests at the Banff Mountain Film Festival. They represent the extended Banff Festival family.

Each has been asked to project into the future of mountaineering, based on their experiences. Some of these individuals are public personalities, widely published and well known. Others are known and revered only among the mountaineering cognoscenti and are intensely private individuals. The geographical, cultural, and generational scope of the contributors to this book is immense, ranging from Japan to France, media superstars and national heroes to relative unknowns, and 90-year-old veterans to a teenager.

Voices from the Summit and the Banff Mountain Film Festival give substance to an otherwise virtual community of men and women whose lives are focused on mountain places. This volume brilliantly captures the visions and the visages of more than 30 of the most accomplished members of that community, and provides a rare opportunity to experience the passions, the tensions, the thrills, the collegiality, and the respect these individuals share with each other.

Projecting the future of mountaineering is a grand and perhaps overly ambitious objective. To provide a focus for this book, numerous topics important to mountaineers were chosen, and the authors were asked to contribute based on their experiences and their passions.

The Alps are the birthplace of alpinism, so it was natural to begin in this vertical playground and testing ground. New trends have repeatedly established themselves in Europe before moving to North America, and the Alps continue to be a training arena for Europeans preparing for the Himalaya. Himalayan climbing is clearly one of the most vital topics in any examination of the future of climbing. This mountain range has presented some of the most profound challenges and has seen some of the greatest mountaineering achievements in the past 50 years. For such a significant subject we have included three perspectives: from the first historical achievements through the golden age and on to today's lightweight, leave-no-trace approach. The Himalaya have also provided a particular form of motivation for climbers—collecting. Whether through first ascents, new routes, difficult grades, 8,000-meter peaks or the Seven Summits, the collectors of mountains and mountain experiences set their sights on tick-lists of climbs. For complex and sometimes controversial reasons, collecting created a framework for these climbers to structure their mountaineering careers.

Two areas of specialization have emerged that deserve their own examination: rock climbing and ice climbing. The rate of technical improvements on rock and ice is increasing exponentially. Media interest is high, competitions are booming, and careers are blossoming. All of the climbers writing on these topics are visionaries in their sport.

Mountaineering history is full of heroic figures, commanding respect decades after their careers have faded. Climbers speak eloquently and respectfully about the characters who have stood out as their mentors, and some of those who had mentors have become role models themselves. Each of the contributors to this topic has moved into that realm.

Ethics is about making choices and, when applied to mountaineering and adventure, can ignite an emotional response in anyone who has a passion for wild places. The issue of ethical adventure is a complex one, and is very important to people in the mountaineering community.

In the year 2000, some might think there are no wild places left to visit. But three mountaineers are inspirational in their creativity in identifying the last frontiers. Other climbers have that rare ability to stand back and observe dispassionately with words or through a camera lens; their perspective as critical observers is important for any community as intense and focused as mountaineering. And great climbers, like Sir Edmund Hillary and Reinhold Messner, offer a Himalayan perspective simply from the vast breadth of their experience. All of these voices are represented in this collection.

Throughout the essays, stylistic and moral issues, disagreements, and frustrations emerge. The current wrangling over "commercial climbing," and the debate about whether anyone can credibly purport to be responsible for anyone else in the nocuous atmosphere at 29,000 feet, both echo throughout this book, as they do wherever mountain people gather these days. The recent death toll on high mountains has been nothing if not disconcerting, and we have from time to time wondered ourselves whether we have presented too much celebration and too little sober consideration of what happens when mountaineers push their skills and endurance to the limit— and beyond. In several of the essays that follow, some of the most accomplished climbers on Earth wrestle with the issue of responsible climbing from a number of perspectives. So, even in its emphases and in its preoccupations, *Voices from the Summit* is a startlingly lucid reflection of the state of the mountain community at the turn of the millennium.

This volume is a tangible legacy of the past 25 years of the Festival. It is a tribute to all who made the Festival what it has been: the filmakers, audiences, sponsors, and the incredibly committed staff. Above all, it is a rare and unique collection of the very personal thoughts and memories of an exceptional group of people. What they all have in common is their passion for the mountains. And that's what this book is about.

Exploratory Steps

Sir Edmund Hillary

I was born in Auckland, New Zealand, 80 years ago and spent my first 14 years on a farm. I was a small and rather lonely child, but sinewy and strong. I gained most of my pleasure from reading a multitude of books on adventure. I was a great dreamer too, walking dozens of miles on the tough country roads with my head in the clouds.

In my last year at high school I went with a winter party to Mount Ruapehu. It was the first time I had ever seen snow. For ten days I skied and clambered around the snowy mountainside; it was the start of my love for snow, ice, and mountains.

I struggled through my exams at high school and, at 16, went on to university. For some reason I proved absolutely hopeless academically at this level, and I didn't pass a single exam. Maybe I was just too young and immature. In any event, I proved that you don't have to be a genius to get on reasonably well in life; I have since received seven honorary doctorates.

In the winter of 1944 I was in the Royal New Zealand Air Force training camp in the Wairau valley of Marlborough. Dominating the hills to the south was the massive snow-covered summit of Mount Tapuaenuku—a remarkable sight. I didn't have much climbing experience and couldn't get anyone to go with me, so I determined to climb it alone. I was now much larger and stronger—six-feet-two-inches tall and weighing 190 pounds.

On one three-day weekend I heaved my hefty load onto my back and set off along the narrow gravel road up the valley. After a couple of hours I reached the nearest sheep station and asked rather nervously if I could use a spare bunk in the shepherd's quarters for the night. The owner's wife invited me inside, fed me generously, and offered me a comfortable shepherd's bed.

I was away very early the next morning, prepared to hitchhike up the valley. Traffic was negligible on this lonely road, so I only managed to get two short lifts and had to walk at least 15 miles. The few people I met tried to discourage me from going on, but the snow-covered peaks were looking even more tremendous. At 2:30 p.m., somewhat footsore, I reached the Hodder River, where I had to leave the road for the mountains.

I climbed down from the road and commenced the uneven plod up the shingle riverbed. Soon I was in the depths of a gorge, fording the river through freezing cold water, winding backward and forward. The shadows were lengthening when I reached the Shin hut.

I didn't rest very much because the hut was full of fleas and mice. The sky was dark and the air very cold as I groped my way across the riverbed and up the side of the main ridge. The early morning light found me already high above the hut, grinding slowly upward with a heavy frost crunching under my feet. As the sun rose, warming me a little, I started to appreciate the glorious morning.

I reached the snow line at 4,000 feet and plugged steadily on...only 5,000 feet to go. At 7,000 feet, heavy cloud came over the peak and snow fell quite heavily. I pushed on, but heavy snow was everywhere now, along with a great deal of knobbly ice. A strong cold wind had sprung up as I worked my way very slowly up to the Pinnacle at 8,800 feet. I was in a spectacular position; below me to the east I could see the blueness of the sea stretching all the way to Wellington.

I set off again and the climbing became a lot harder. I had to make my way across the side of the Pinnacle—a tall rock tower—and I was very much aware of the steep drop on my right. I cut hundreds of steps in the icy surface and felt isolated and a little frightened, but I was exhilarated, too! I was glad to get off the traverse, reach the slope beyond, and then head upward once more. The slope was steep and all the rocks were festooned with great bulges of ice.

I crossed an easy flat section but was now half blinded by drifting snow. I fumbled my way upward for quite a distance until there was nowhere else to go, and I realized I must be on top.

Turning downward, the slope to the saddle was slippery and unpleasant with soft snow sliding everywhere. But the traverse along the Pinnacle was much easier when I couldn't see the big drop because of the dense fog. To my relief I came out of the cloud at 7,500 feet and began the long trudge down the ridge. I was very tired and knew I hadn't a hope of getting down before dark. It got dimmer and dimmer and finally as black as pitch. I reached the place where I thought I should drop off the ridge, but I couldn't be sure. Then I stumbled over a rock that I seemed to remember stumbling over in the morning. I decided to go straight down and tumbled and slid over steep snow grass slopes, hoping I wouldn't find a bluff in the dark. My guess proved right and I reached the riverbed without striking any difficulties. I staggered across to the hut feeling dead weary. I'd been going for 14 hours. Food held no interest; I just crawled into my sleeping bag, and neither the fleas nor the mice kept me awake this time.

I set off again at 4:00 a.m.—somehow I had to get back to camp that day. I shuffled down the river in the dark and felt much happier when I reached the road. At least now I had a chance of getting a lift. For six hours I tramped down the shingle road and covered at least 20 miles. There wasn't a single vehicle going in my direction. I met two cars coming up the valley and both stopped to pass the time of day and to cheerfully inform me that I'd become a common topic of local conversation. The betting had been that I'd be dead by this time; they almost seemed disappointed!

Finally my luck changed when a truck came down the valley and the driver willingly offered me a lift. I reached camp late in the evening—dirty, unshaven, and very tired but excited. Despite my lack of experience I had climbed a decent mountain. I believe I was the first person to make a solo winter ascent of Mount Tapuaenuku.

I had become physically robust with plenty of energy. Any spare time I could get I headed for the mountains, and as my skill increased, I made a number of first ascents on the great peaks and ridges in the Southern Alps of New Zealand. Like most New Zealand climbers, I became accustomed to backpacking huge loads over remote glaciers and ridges to tackle new approaches to the mountains, and I became a rather useful snow and ice climber too.

My thoughts started turning to the Himalaya and four of us gathered what little funds we could and headed off to the Gawhal Himalaya in 1951. We were rather pathetically equipped, but full of energy and motivation, and we succeeded in climbing six new mountains from 21,000 feet to nearly 24,000 feet in elevation. Our success attracted attention in the United Kingdom, where the famous climber Eric Shipton had permission to reconnoiter Mount Everest from the Nepalese side. He invited two of us to join his four-man party, so we dashed after him across a monsoon-flooded Nepal and caught up with the team in the village of Dingla.

I was thrilled to meet Eric Shipton—one of the most heroic figures in my life—and we quickly became very good friends. Together we climbed the great ridge of Pumori and were the first to look up the Khumbu Icefall into the Western Cwm. We could see up the Lhotse Face and realized that there was a potential route to the summit from this direction. Our small team climbed the dangerously unstable icefall, peered into the Western Cwm, then retreated with the determination to return the following year, fully equipped for an assault on the summit. But, alas, on our return to Kathmandu we discovered that the Swiss had permission for two expeditions in 1952—one pre-monsoon and one post-monsoon. We knew they would have a formidable party.

The Everest Committee in London sensibly decided to also send a team into the Everest area in 1952 to test oxygen equipment and gain more experience. My fellow New Zealander George Lowe and I climbed together and quickly proved we were the fittest team in the party. Our most exciting challenge was to cross the Nup La Pass, a tiny notch in the ridge to the east of Cho Oyu protected by the mighty icefall of the Ngojumba Glacier. It had never been attempted before.

We left the village of Khumjung accompanied by three of our permanent sherpas: Angputa, Tashi Puta, and Angje. Although not great mountaineers, they were hardworking and loyal. We made our way up the beautiful Gokyo Valley, past the sparkling Dudh Pokari Lake. We dropped from a great moraine wall onto the smooth lower stretches of the Ngojumba Glacier and followed the glacier to where it swung sharply to the left and the ice was broken and contorted. It took us some time to penetrate through this area, and we finally climbed up onto a smooth crest. The view ahead was unbelievable. Towering over us on the immediate left was the enormous face of Cho Oyu and to the east of it, in one great sweep, stretched peak after peak, culminating in the summit pyramid of Everest nearly 20 miles away. The valley ahead was crammed full of an enormous icefall tumbling thousands of feet down in a ruin of shattered ice. The icefall was split in the middle by a great rock buttress and high in the far distance we could see a dip in the ridge—the Nup La.

We tried the right-hand icefall without success and then spent six hours on the great rock buttress in the center of the face. Boulders were rattling down and we were lucky to escape with our lives.

Later the same afternoon I went for a stroll with Angputa to the left side of the glacier, looking for a possible route. For most of the way we passed a 1,000-foot-high ice wall that we knew was impossible to climb. Then, as we approached the left side of the valley, I saw with quickening excitement a rounded sweep of moraine sneaking up above the icefall. The going was easy and seemed very safe. We carried on a little farther and my excitement grew. Despite the rows of crevasses and ice walls above us, the route looked difficult but not impossible. As

darkness fell, we hurried back to camp and told George our good news.

We left at 6:30 a.m. George and I reached the farthest point of the previous day in excellent time. George was a little reluctant to call the way ahead an easy route but agreed it had possibilities. We roped up, put on crampons, and made our way upward. This was the work we really loved: hacking our way up icefalls, crossing shaky snow bridges, and descending down into crevasses and out the other side. At first we were being forced to the left toward broken and impassable ice; then a lucky snow bridge led us back to the center and somewhat easier ground. At 10:30 a.m. we cramponed on to a snowy knoll and saw in the far distance the Nup La, a 19,400-foot dip between two great 24,000-foot buttresses. The way ahead looked promising, so we returned and prepared a camp to be carried in the next day.

The next morning was unusually mild. We discovered that an avalanche had wiped out part of our track and that all the snow bridges were softened by the warm conditions. We reached my farthest point and George led off across the murky expanse of the snow plateau. In the soft snow conditions we broke through into crevasse after crevasse. When I heard a shriek from Tashi Puta and turned to see only his head peeping above the snow, we decided to stop for the day.

While George set up camp I took the Sherpas back over our route to collect supplies on the far side of the closest of the big crevasses. We climbed down into it and then out again and collected our loads. Once more I descended into the crevasse and started over the much softened bridge. Suddenly there was a *whoomph* and the bridge and I dropped into the crevasse. Instinctively I threw my cramponed feet against the far ice wall and thrust my pack against the other. And there I hung suspended. We duly extricated ourselves and returned to a somewhat demoralized camp.

Despite our fears, we were determined to carry on and were greatly encouraged next morning when it was much colder. We wove our way through a series of open crevasses and then came over a crest and saw a smooth gully running in the direction we wanted to go. Above it was a long slope sweeping toward the Nup La itself. Nothing could stop us now. We raced up the hill and, to our immense joy, reached the rocky crest of the pass. I had never felt a greater sense of achievement. In those days, of course, we had no climbing harnesses, front-point crampons, curvers, pitons, carabiners, or jumars. But we swung our long-handled ice axes with mighty enthusiasm.

In the late afternoon the clouds lifted, and we were able to look down the Rongbuk Glacier and see the mighty summit of Everest. Fit and acclimatized, we spent a marvelous five days in Tibet. We raced down the West Rongbuk Glacier, hacked our way through the giant ice spires of the main Rongbuk Glacier, and looked with trepidation at the Rongbuk Monastery ten miles away down the valley, now controlled by Chinese soldiers. We reached the site of the Base Camp for the prewar British expeditions, with its debris of batteries and rusty tins, and rushed up the East Rongbuk Glacier to the foot of the North Col. It was wonderful to look up those long slopes where so many famous British climbers had struggled toward the summit. We camped at 21,000 feet and next morning started the long and arduous day to reach well up the West Rongbuk Glacier.

I crawled out of our tent at 5:30 a.m. and was horrified to see that the sky over Nepal was black as night, with ugly clouds surging up and writhing about the summits. We literally ran up the rest of the glacier, and in just over an hour we were back on the Nup La. Below us great clouds were sweeping over the icefall, which was already covered by thick fresh snow, and we could hear avalanches thundering down the cliffs. We quickly worked out our technique: We would use 200 feet of rope; I would go down first to test the ground; George would follow next with a tight hand on my rope; and the three sherpas would follow George as the final check. So, in that order, we headed across the treacherous plateau. When I sank into a crevasse George pulled me out; this happened time and again. Somehow, despite the blanketing snow, I was able to steer a reasonable course, although we had to find our way over dozens of crevasses before, to our great relief, we reached the two large crevasses and scrambled our way in and out of them again. Six inches of fresh snow were on the lower icefall, and at times we completely lost our route. By experience, good luck, or plain determination, we battled our way down. It was an emotional moment when,

through the blizzard, I caught a glimpse of the strip of moraine, and I knew we were safe at last. The Nup La was behind us; we had completed one of the most exciting challenges I had ever attempted. It had been close: One false move or a moment of inattention and our bodies would have remained down a crevasse forever.

The Swiss put in two mighty attempts on Mount Everest that same year. Pre-monsoon, Raymond Lambert and Sherpa Tenzing climbed up the Southeast Ridge before being turned back at 28,000 feet. Post-monsoon, strong winds made high climbing almost impossible, and the Swiss had to give in. Our turn came in 1953.

John Hunt proved an excellent leader and our team spirit was exceptionally strong. Tenzing and I reached the South summit, and I hacked a line of steps along the corniced summit ridge. We reached the 40-foot step, and I wriggled and jammed my way up the crack between the rock and the ice cornice. Tenzing joined me and I led on again, continuously cutting steps. Above us to the right was a rounded snowy dome. After only a few more whacks of the ice ax Tenzing and I were on top of the world. I had built up a very close relationship with our Sherpa companions who contributed so much to our activities. I admired their toughness and great sense of humor. I have never felt sorry for them despite their tough environment and the lack of benefits that we just take for granted.

In 1961, I decided to do the thing the Sherpas wanted most—to build a school in Khumjung village. I raised the necessary funds and we constructed the school on a flat area of an empty valley nearby.

The opening ceremony was a remarkable occasion. The head lama and his musical entourage carried out the official blessing, and I was invited to cut the ribbons and open the door. The 40 pupils had bare feet and scruffy clothes, but their rosy cheeks and sparkling eyes were irresistible.

I started getting petitions from other villages—some of them five or six days away by foot. I am proud of the fact that we just didn't go into a village and look around and say, "You need a school or a medical clinic!" We always responded to the wishes of the local people, and they contributed a considerable amount of free labor too. We've supported them now for nearly 37 years.

With the financial help of people from all around the world, we have built more than 30 schools, 2 hospitals, 12 medical clinics, a dozen freshwater pipelines, bridges, and 3 mountain airfields. We have even rebuilt a number of Buddhist monasteries. The local people wanted these things, and we have responded to their requests.

There have been vast changes in mountaineering since we climbed Mount Everest in 1953. The technical equipment has become much more sophisticated, and so has the skill of many of the climbers. Clothing is more protective, food is better, hardware much more professional, and oxygen equipment far more efficient. As a result, a climber can move much more quickly over dangerous ground.

But still, severe weather or avalanches can prove disastrous. Foolish decisions are frequently made, and more and more people die.

I am sad that the traditional sense of personal responsibility seems to have faded a little and that camaraderie and leadership are now far less important. We have entered an era where it is every man for himself, particularly above 8,000 meters (26,284 feet). Concern about the welfare of your companions seems to fade as the air gets thinner. There are exceptions of course, but perhaps not so many as there should be.

And then there is the commercialization of climbing: So many ascents have become just conducted tours. If you have a spare $65,000 plus a couple of well-paid experienced guides, three or four tough Sherpas, and a bit of luck with the weather, you can climb this great mountain Everest with a fair chance of success. The peak is shackled with 60 aluminum ladders, thousands of feet of rope, and a beaten track leading upward. Even the Hillary Step near the summit usually has a choice of three separate fixed ropes to climb.

You can stand on the summit being generously photographed and then happily descend the mountain and return home, confidently expecting a ticker tape parade. One proud lady complained to me that her son had been to the summit of Everest and only received two inches in the local newspaper. There are obviously some advantages in doing these things first.

Perhaps I am being a little harsh. To reach the summit of Everest is a considerable achievement even if you are led by the hand, but it is hardly mountaineering in the best sense of the term.

I had always regarded George Leigh Mallory as a heroic figure. He brought Mount Everest to the notice of the world, explored most of its routes, and finally disappeared when heading for the summit on the north side. What happened to him has always been a puzzle. Did he die before reaching the summit or on the descent? Nobody knows, and to me it has been of small consequence: He was still a great man.

But now an expedition has made a great effort and discovered Mallory's body after 65 years. They have searched it, taken personal items and specimens, photographed it extensively, and sold the terrible pictures to almost every newspaper and magazine in the world. I have found the photographs revolting; surely this heroic figure should have been left in peace. Who cares if Mallory reached the summit? He was certainly not successful in reaching the bottom again. I have to admit I despise this most recent expedition for their completely heartless approach.

I believe that our expedition in 1953 was the lucky one. We had to pioneer the route and tackle the problems. We established our own tracks and made our own decisions. We were a strong team: If a problem arose, we all expressed a view; if a decision was necessary, it was made by our leader John Hunt and we followed it through. We were chosen for the many difficult tasks we had to perform according to our skill and fitness, and a backup team was always ready in an emergency. We were a good team; of that there can be no doubt! And we succeeded without loss of life. That's a fairly good recommendation.

Sir Edmund Hillary was guest speaker at the Banff Mountain Film Festival in 1994 and is honorary chairman of the International Advisory Committee of The Banff Centre for Mountain Culture.

While Hillary became a household name around the world after his 1953 ascent of Mount Everest with Sherpa Tenzing Norgay, he has always insisted that his triumph be shared with all mankind, and to the betterment of the people of Nepal and the Himalaya. He has devoted a major part of his life to this humanitarian end. Hillary has helped build more than 30 schools, 3 airfields, 2 hospitals, and 12 medical clinics in Nepal, and funded a 10-year reforestation program in Sagarmatha National Park.

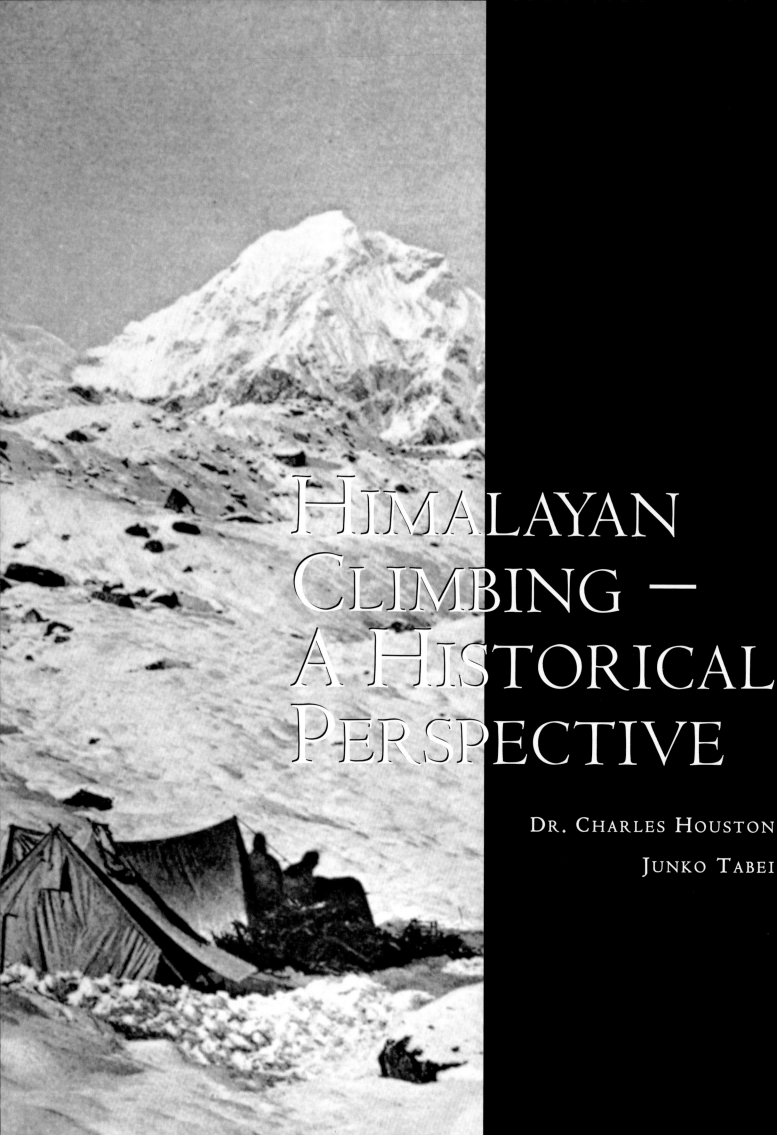

Himalayan Climbing — A Historical Perspective

Dr. Charles Houston

Junko Tabei

THE HIGH THINNE AIRE

DR. CHARLES HOUSTON

Five thousand years ago a lone man died during a storm high in the Alps; his body was found by chance in 1991 and carefully studied. He was about 45 years old and was dressed for mountain travel. Because some of his arrows were missing, archaeologists suggest he was trying to escape from pursuers. Why had he gone there? How did he regard mountains?

I won't try to answer this. My interest is in exploring attitudes toward mountains, rather than the motives that led some of our ancestors to climb them, though this may be a feeble difference. How did people feel about the immense and beautiful but forbidding and dangerous masses of rock and snow that towered over them? How may those who follow us feel?

Throughout history our forebears have looked to mountains with awe, fear, and reverence. For some, these incredible masses of rock and perpetual snow and ice were, and are, sacred—the homes of gods and goddesses, and not to be profaned. Adam's peak on Sri Lanka is said to show on its summit the footprint of the first man. In Mongolia, Bogdo-ol means "mountain of god." The Chinese Tien Shan mountains are called the "celestial mountains." But Kinabalu is "the mountain of the dead" and Kilimanjaro, "mountain of the snow devils." On the highest Andes we find ancient altars and relics of sacrifices made to the mountain gods, often to persuade them to send water and thus life to the lands below. Fujiyama (Fuji-san) means "everlasting life" and is a place of pilgrimage for many Japanese. Noah landed on Ararat, and the ancient Greek and Roman gods lived on Mount Olympus and Mount Ida. Moses brought sacred precepts down from Mount Sinai and died on Mount Pizgah.

In the Himalaya some mountains are holier than others, and thousands of the devout make long and difficult pilgrimages to them as they have for centuries. One of these, Kailas, is sacred to Hindus as the paradise of Shiva, and to Buddhists it is the cosmic center of the world. Nanda Devi is the home of the goddess Nanda, consort of the Hindu god Shiva. Many believe that climbing these mountains violates their sanctity; some few of our contemporaries have respected this and paused short of the summit. The mightiest, however—Everest, "Goddess Mother of the World"—has been attempted by thousands unable to resist the lure. One can hope that those who truly love mountains will learn to approach them with respect and reverence.

Twenty-three hundred years ago Alexander crossed mighty ranges, driven by his ambition to conquer the known world. His armies regarded mountains as obstacles—neither beautiful nor sacred. Centuries later the Muslim hordes swept across Asia and over Himalayan passes to ravage much of Europe. They, too, saw the high

Himalaya as hostile barriers to be overcome.

Envoys and traders from China confronted terrible dangers from cold and high elevation and heard tales of dragons as they ventured westward. Marco Polo's attitude during his long journey eastward was one of intense interest and curiosity, and he left a fascinating record. But he and later travelers made trade their purpose and saw mountains as dangerous—not sacred—objects.

So, too, in the 17th century, were they viewed by Buddhist priests who suffered as they crossed the ranges seeking converts. Jesuit missionaries moved eastward with their religion. They began mapping Central Asia and describing the people and the flora and fauna as they charted routes through high passes. Their motives were not only practical but also driven by an attitude of curiosity about what lay on and beyond those snow-crowned mountains. As was happening in other ranges, some travelers sought food, gold, gems, or the treasures of lost civilizations. The concept of climbing for pleasure was far in the future.

The attitudes of awe and reverence and worship of mountains was slowly eroded by pragmatism. Great armies had no time or use for the sacred peaks; traders sought material profit; and for missionaries, making converts to Buddhism or Catholicism brought rewards in the hereafter. Some of the older Asian religions faded as European culture spread. Slowly the sanctity of the high places was eroded.

At the same time, curiosity increased. In the western world Empedocles is reputed to have tested his immortality by leaping into the crater of 10,000-foot Mount Etna (he died). The adventuresome Peter, King of Aragon, climbed Pic Canigou just to see what lay on top; he is said to have encountered a fearsome dragon. Descriptions of alleged encounters with dragons were common for hundreds of years, even into the 18th century in the Alps. Petrarch climbed Mont Ventoux (6,263 feet) purely for pleasure. In 1555 Dr. Conrad Gesner wrote the first book to celebrate the joys of climbing, *On the Admiration of Mountains*, and vowed to climb a mountain every year. He even obtained a rare permit to climb Mount Pilatus (6,962 feet), seeking Pontius Pilate's ghost.

Practical need led the Jesuit Montserrate in 1590 to make the first crude map of the great ranges; this was the basis for d'Anville's large *Atlas of China* in 1737. Both relied on sketches drawn (usually secretly and in grave danger) by missionaries, who made extraordinary crossings between China and India during the 17th century. For the purpose of trade the East India Company commissioned maps of crucial areas of India, extending this major effort into the fringes of Nepal and Tibet from 1800 to 1830 with the Great Trigonometric Survey of India.

As this massive effort advanced, many very high peaks and passes were identified, and when the height of Everest was determined in 1852, explorers expanded the surveys, and serious mountaineers took notice. The reclusive W. W. Graham was among the first to visit many parts of the Himalaya "more for sport and adventure than for the advancement of scientific knowledge," as he wrote in 1883.

By the middle of the 19th century exploration of the high ranges had become deadly serious as Russia and Britain played the Great Game to determine who would control the riches of India. Many faintly famous and even more unknown men bravely traveled farther and higher than anyone had gone before, describing the basic geography on which later generations based maps (some remarkably detailed) of large areas of the great ranges of Asia. Some died of exposure and others were captured and executed, but from the intrepid survivors came much of today's detailed knowledge of the high Himalayan passes. These men were driven both by adventure and patriotism.

As the 20th century began, great pioneers such as Younghusband, Longstaff, Graham, and the Bullock Workmans climbed higher and higher and some began to appreciate the problems of altitude, illness, and cold. But they, too, were exploring and climbing for curiosity and pleasure rather than fame or fortune. This would come later.

By 1920 scores of wonderful mountains in the Himalaya and the Karakoram had been surveyed and a few dozen had been climbed. Tibet and Nepal were closed to foreigners, however, and Everest had been seen only from a distance. The second highest peak, K2 or Godwin Austen, had been attempted, as had Kangchenjunga and Nanga Parbat. High-altitude mountaineering attracted the daring explorers. Soon some attitudes began to change: In 1939 one climber attempting K2 remarked, "if we make this we're set for life."

During the golden age of Alpine climbing (1850-1885) every Alpine summit had been reached, and mountaineering was a popular recreational sport with unwritten ethics and codes of conduct. Those few who wrote books and the many who described their climbs in various journals were amateurs. But a young British physician changed this and may be credited for starting that golden age.

Dr. Albert Smith had become interested in mountains as a child, he said, and as a young man he visited the little-known village of Chamonix several times and gave a few lectures describing his journey. He tired of medicine, turned to writing and acting, and in 1851 climbed Mont Blanc and took up lecturing as a career. In seven years he gave some 2,000 talks to large audiences in London, of course without slides or film, but illustrated with huge painted canvases. This brought him fame and fortune as perhaps the first climbing entrepreneur. More importantly in the long run, first dozens, then hundreds of men and women took up climbing in the Alps for sport. At first with professional guides but later, as their skill and experience increased, without them.

A handful of other climbers gave talks and wrote books; their audiences sought dramatic stories and literary style. But for several decades no one approached Albert Smith's popularity.

After Everest had been clearly identified, mountaineers longed to attempt it. In 1921 Tibet allowed a small British expedition to examine the Tibetan side, and in the next 17 years several British teams struggled toward that high summit

A rimpoche reflects on an afternoon prayer walk against the dramatic backdrop of Ama Dablam.

in the small window of time between the end of winter and the arrival of the monsoon. World War II halted most mountaineering, especially in Asia.

Nepal remained tightly closed to Westerners until early 1950, and soon the dramatic story of the ascent of Annapurna captured attention around the world. Later that year Tilman and I went to Everest and saw a feasible climbing route; it is now the "ordinary" way. The golden age of Himalayan climbing could appropriately be said to have begun in 1950, a century after the start of recreational climbing in the Alps. Ever since then, thousands of peaks large and small have been attempted, and hundreds have been climbed. But there are many more awaiting the enterprising. Hopefully we will know how to avoid the environmental degradation that could result from too great a rush.

Inevitably the second half of the 20th century brought to the Himalaya the changes in climbing techniques and attitudes that had evolved elsewhere. These included basic changes in ethics, standards, and the whole attitude toward mountaineering. Climbing experienced a tumultuous coming of age after its naive and happy childhood. Some may consider this evolution sad and unfortunate, but it is probably unavoidable. It is for us to help our sport to a healthy maturity.

The attitude toward danger has changed. In 1820 the death of three guides in Dr. Hamel's party in an avalanche on Mont Blanc caused great dismay and official inquiries. After four climbers were killed in the famous fall on the Matterhorn in 1867, Queen Victoria is said to have asked her ministers whether it would be legal for her to ban mountaineering because it was so dangerous! By contrast in 1934, when the morale of their large expedition disintegrated during a storm and three

> *Sadly, mountaineering, particularly big-time climbing in the great ranges, has changed as it has gone commercial. . . .The line between sport and professionalism has disappeared.*

famous Germans and six Sherpas died on Nanga Parbat, Hitler called the Germans heroes and gave them medals. This prompted British author R. L. G. Irving to rail against "nationalism" in mountaineering. The deaths of 13 expert mountaineers on K2 in 1986 were widely mourned, but 10 years later 12 men and women perished in a storm on Everest resulting in a worldwide media frenzy that only fueled the desire of more people to summit Everest "because it's there."

Accidents and death, whether from unavoidable storm or avalanche, or from self-serving ambition, bad judgment, or ill preparedness, make news today, sometimes big and profitable. The likelihood of death and disaster seems to be a fully acceptable part of today's often competitive, high-stakes game of mountain climbing.

Before World War II many considered the British Alpine Club the conscience of climbing and its implicit guardian. Use of artificial aids like pitons and even crampons was "not quite cricket." Jumars and carabiners and the current masses of metal were unknown and, when they first appeared, were frowned upon. Irving criticized this trend in "Mechanization and the Cult of Danger," a chapter in his excellent book *The Romance of Mountaineering.* The fellowship of the rope, a term denoting the dependence of each climber on his

companions, was traditional. To fall indicated inadequate ability rather than daring. Some brilliant mountaineers were ostracized ("not quite our kind") for disregarding a vague and unwritten code. Some of the best climbers went on book or lecture tours, but only certified professional guides made a living from the sport. At the same time, development and sales of mountain gear evolved into a hugely profitable industry.

Annapurna, spectacular climbs like those in Yosemite, and the extreme walls of the Alps and Andes changed much of this. Direct aids became essential; well-protected leader falls were common, even considered evidence of extreme difficulty. The envelope was pushed further and further. The more spectacular or dangerous a route, the more dramatic an accident or rescue, the more popular could be the lecture and book. In a few years, excellent climbers found that they could pay for their Himalayan adventures by writing and lecturing; a few were able to make a modest living from mountaineering.

Inevitably this spawned competition. True, this was not entirely new: Efforts to make the first ascent of Mont Blanc had led to furious controversy. Whymper had desperately tried to beat Carrel to the top of the Matterhorn a century later, and the British clung jealously to their exclusive access to Everest. Still, in general the race to be first on a summit or a new route was "sporting" until money entered the picture.

Climbing competitions were organized on carefully scouted rock faces; when prizes and prestige increased, these became international and attracted excellent competitive climbers. Quite logically, artificial climbing walls were built in mountaineering shops, gymnasia, and schools, and models were marketed for home use as well. The routes became more and more complex and difficult, and these artificial walls soon bred what might be called rock acrobatics, an activity with its own specialists. For some, the attitude of love for the total mountain environment gave way to the satisfaction—and the hormonal rush—of extreme gymnastics.

For those who preferred the mountains, big stories made for big books, big lecture fees, and famous faces and careers. "Conquering" a great mountain might lead to riches. Surviving a spectacular accident might be even more lucrative. The physical and emotional bond of the climbing rope was lost as unroped climbers, with or without jumars (ascenders), sped up and down miles of fixed ropes, often alone. Sometimes the long tradition of helping fellow climbers was violated when a party, intent on a summit, failed to respond to the desperate need of strangers and, in a few terrible instances, of members of their own party.

Something else changed. History is never complete, never accurate: Perception is reality, and different individuals often describe the same events quite differently. This has been true for as far back as we have historical records. Facts have a way of dissolving into myth. One asks, "What is the truth?" Some climbers and authors thought it was bad form to write about mistaken judgment, poor preparation, or personality conflicts on a climb or expedition. But others believed in candor (honesty they thought it) and described warts and all. History was often warped, or at least incomplete. The attitudes of many, especially on the greatest mountains, seemed to become more self-serving. The accuracy of some accounts, even their honesty, was more frequently challenged.

Money has become a big factor. With new equipment, boots, clothing, food, and more,

climbers faced increasing expenses. Some Himalayan countries began to charge high fees for permits to big mountains. Travel to far parts of the world became easier but much more costly. Consequently the expense of Himalayan mountaineering skyrocketed, and almost everyone needed sponsorship. Companies that made anything used on an expedition, such as clothing, tools, film, cameras, and many other items, became willing to donate goods or money in return for favorable testimonials. Sometimes this is done discreetly; sometimes it is blatant; sometimes the testimonials are even untrue as, alas, is so much of media advertising.

Sadly, mountaineering, particularly big-time climbing in the great ranges, has changed as it has gone commercial—like almost every other sport, from skiing to baseball, tennis, and all the others. Most games have been irreversibly changed by the opportunity for players and owners to make money, often an obscene amount. Money talks loudly. The line between sport and professionalism has disappeared, in the Olympic Games for example.

Today anyone with enough money can be taken to the top of almost any mountain and can broadcast live and in color around the world. There is money for those who become professional mountain guides or trip leaders. Organizations of professionals have held lucrative monopolies to lead parties on public lands like Rainier and Denali and on the major rivers. Like other athletes, many of the world's best mountaineers have made rewarding careers in writing, lecturing, and endorsing products. This isn't evil, but it is somehow unseemly for mountaineering. Not all have succumbed: Edmund Hillary, probably the best-known mountaineer of our century, returns his earnings to Nepal for schools, clinics, and other social programs. A few other greats do the same. Much of the spirit of climbing seems to have been contaminated—or has it?

As more and more people have gone to higher and higher mountains, the illnesses due to altitude have become better known. Long before high Himalayan peaks were first attempted, the severe and sometimes fatal mountain sickness occasionally experienced by mountain travelers was blamed on evil spirits, bad winds, minerals, and noxious exhalations from plants, minerals, or even, some claimed, from dragons. In the last part of the 19th century many climbers believed that to sleep a night above 20,000 feet would be fatal.

The real cause of mountain sickness was not known, but the earliest description, written by Jesuit missionary Acosta in 1590, suggested "thinne aire" might be responsible. The isolation of oxygen in 1775 and subsequent studies of its properties hinted that oxygen deficiency, not decreased barometric pressure per se, was the cause, though this was not proven for another hundred years.

By then, some hardy Himalayan climbers had gone as high as 22,000 feet and survived, feeling few ill effects. Various forms of mountain sickness were described. Then, the imperatives of air combat in World War II sharply increased interest and research in high-altitude physiology as it applied to aviation. By 1950, altitude hypoxia on mountains was more widely recognized and supplementary oxygen believed essential at great height.

Concurrently, several research projects, more experience, and ultimately the ascent of Everest without supplemental oxygen showed it was possible for people to survive there. Just recently a well-acclimatized Sherpa is said to have spent 27 hours on the summit breathing only the high thin air. An elevation of 29,000 feet may not be the ultimate limit for human survival, but it's very close.

The early apprehensions about extreme altitude are recurring for oxygen less climbs and are shaping the attitudes of climbers. Several dozen have summited Everest, and scores have gone almost as high, breathing only the thin air about them. Fragmentary evidence is beginning to show what some believed earlier: Repeated or prolonged exposure to extreme altitude may cause lasting brain changes. Some suggest it is an unacceptable risk to summit a great peak without breathing a bit of extra oxygen. This may be an overcautious attitude, but it's known that above 22,000 feet even a well-acclimatized individual does not think clearly or perform as well as necessary. At higher elevations this defect is more striking and can be (and has been) the cause of many tragedies. Furthermore, a few carefully done studies of climbers who have been very high frequently, or for many days, do show some minor neurological signs that may

persist for a long time after returning to sea level.

Until a few decades ago many climbers gave little thought to their impact on the physical environment. Trash and wastes were heedlessly dropped anywhere. Trees and brush were freely cut and burned, with no recognition that firewood could rapidly become very scarce in the harsh mountain setting. On the great rock faces, bolts and pins and fixed cables or ropes desecrated the mountains. Used or not, equipment was heedlessly abandoned.

Few climbers from the developed countries considered that such attitudes might be harming the economic and social structure as well as the physical environment of less advanced regions. Indeed, members of expeditions to remote ranges believed they were helping impoverished locals by paying small wages for their services or by giving out medicines en route. This may have been well-intentioned, but such short-term actions delayed local development.

Happily, many of these attitudes have changed. Some countries try with mixed success to halt reckless destruction of trees and bushes, and they try to control waste disposal by requiring expeditions to bring their own fuel and carry away their trash. Others have developed acceptable ways of local waste disposal. Individuals and groups have managed to remove and even recycle accumulated materials from some of the most spoiled areas. Organizations and individuals have built and helped to staff clinics and schools in remote areas, teaching the local people to assume the responsibility. In many regions fixed ropes, bolts and pins, and cast-off equipment are being removed. This happy change in attitude shows that visitors to the great mountains are beginning to respect the physical, social, and religious environment they are privileged to enjoy.

If it's true that the future mirrors the past, then we should be able to make educated guesses about where mountaineering will go in the next few decades, always assuming that we do not self-destruct sooner.

When the golden age of alpine climbing began about 1850, a few men and a very few women had climbed some of the smaller Alps—although 56 had summited Mont Blanc. Soon hundreds were swarming over peaks throughout Europe and abroad. Most engaged professional guides. At century's end all of the Alps had been climbed, most of them many times and often without guides. By the middle of the 20th century more and more difficult routes were done and Mummery's rueful remark was true: "Mountains go through three stages—first, an impossible peak; second, the most difficult climb in the Alps; and finally, an easy day for a lady." Today, of course, the ladies can do and have done whatever the men can.

Along with spectacular scenery and heart-stopping risks, mountaineers have found opportunities to earn money—sometimes a lot—from books, photography, and lecture tours. This will continue and will increase, and live television on extreme climbs will be the norm.

Professionalism is here to stay; guiding treks and expeditions will continue to be viable careers. As has happened in the Alps, there will always be amateurs who wish to be taken up even the greatest peaks at whatever cost. More handicapped individuals, more soloists, more winter assaults, and more remote ranges will attract attention. With the increased attention, we may find more thoughtful decisions about who is qualified to go to the utmost heights and whether, in the death zone, anyone is really qualified to be responsible for another. The death toll has been alarming, and climbers are asking hard questions. But who will answer them?

Countries that have great peaks within their borders recognize and happily demand the cash they can generate in peak and trekking fees. They justify this by claiming benefit to the national and local economy, which may or may not be exactly true. We can anticipate that this will increase, but not indefinitely. Already some countries are suffocating the golden goose.

Concern for the natural and social environment is increasing and will govern more and more Himalayan mountaineering. Already a few foresighted countries, in order to protect their heritage, are limiting the number of visitors they will admit. Some hope this practice will spread, if the smell of big money is not too seductive. A few uniquely sensitive areas have been closed for a time to allow them to recover.

As for risks, thrills, and endorphin rushes, these also are here to stay and will increase. More dangerous sports are becoming popular. Bungee jumping has extended to BASE jumping, which has the highest mortality and most serious injury rates of any sport. We can anticipate that as the current favorites pall, new risky games will be invented. Extreme sports will continue to get more extreme; skill levels will improve along with them.

We can anticipate more and more ascents in the known and yet to be explored Himalayan and neighboring ranges, and wherever else in the world there are great mountains. More difficult routes will be attempted, professionalism will expand, and Asian countries may increase permit fees but only to a limit, while others will restrict intrusions. Mountaineering, like skiing and a score of other sports, will attract those people who love the outdoor environment, as well as some who see it as a way to fame and fortune. Competitive climbing will be recognized as an Olympic sport. Medalists will join those in other sports, sometimes reaping rich rewards.

Mountaineering will continue to change along with all other human activities. Perhaps with one eye on the past and one on the future we can guide mountaineering and our lives to a better world.

Dr. Charles Houston—medical doctor, mountaineer, university professor, and author—was born in 1913. In 1936, he led a successful British-American expedition to Nanda Devi (26,250 feet) in northern India, and two years later he led the first American expedition to K2 (28,250 feet). In 1950, he was part of the first reconnaissance group to the south (Nepalese) side of Mount Everest. He returned to K2 in 1953 and to Everest in 1981.

Charles Houston first brought high-altitude pulmonary edema to the world's attention, and he has spent more than 50 years studying the mechanisms of the body's acclimatization to high altitude. He has written many books and scores of articles about mountain medicine and about his own climbs. His most recent revision of Going Higher: Oxygen, Man and Mountains *won the Mountain Exposition Award at the Banff Mountain Book Festival in 1998.*

GARBAGE ON THE GODDESS MOTHER OF THE WORLD

JUNKO TABEI

Known as Sagarmatha in Nepal and Chomolungma in China, the highest peak in the world rises to 29,035 feet. Unspoiled nature, geological significance, and unique Sherpa culture have all contributed to Sagarmatha National Park's designation as a world heritage site.

From the first attempt to climb Everest in 1921 until the 1970s, the numbers of expeditions to the mountain was severely restricted; only one climbing party per season was permitted from the Nepal side. As a result, only 27 parties climbed Everest during the intervening decades. In 1980, however, it became possible to climb from Tibet, and restrictions on climbing from the Nepalese side were relaxed so that the government could obtain more much needed foreign currency. In the 1980s, 144 parties mounted expeditions from the Nepalese side, and there has been a sharp increase in the 1990s; 303 parties have gone into the area in the past ten years. The local Sherpas' main occupations used to be farming and raising livestock, but these activities have now been replaced by guiding treks and portering for expeditions.

The increase in the number of mountaineers, along with innovations in mountaineering equipment, is causing a rapid increase in the amount of garbage left behind on the mountain—mostly equipment such as empty oxygen bottles, tents, and fuel cartridges. When the mountaineering population was still very small, garbage was not thought to be an issue. In recent years, however, it has emerged as a critical problem, with concerned voices rising from all directions. Along with the transformation of the Mount Everest region into a tourist destination, non-mountaineering visits have sharply increased as well. This trend has increased the need for lumber and firewood, and deforestation has become a serious environmental issue. In the face of these problems, the Nepalese government raised the park fee as a way of restricting mountaineers, but the visitor numbers show no signs of declining. A ban on climbing for several years was proposed but such a restriction would have a strong impact on the lives of the local Sherpa population and nothing came of it.

In 1975, I became the first woman and the 38th person to stand on the summit of Mount Everest. It was a struggle just to stay alive on that climb, and I left behind equipment including canisters, tents, and ropes. In those days, I did not have the slightest awareness that the abandoned equipment would eventually be regarded as garbage. If this lack of awareness persists today, it may be because of the inadequate effort to assess the effects of mountaineering on the environment.

The garbage situation at the South Pole made clear the devastating effects of unchecked dumping. The garbage problem caused by climbers at high elevations, however, is a problem that has arisen from the repetition of individual actions. Not much is known about the extent of the environmental damage in the Himalaya, and it is unclear where the responsibility lies. There is an urgent need for the situation to be documented and resolved. Despite this, there have been very few scientific studies conducted on the problem of garbage generated by high-altitude mountaineering.

This being the case, I collected data on past climbing parties and conducted a survey. The survey areas were Gasherbrum II near the Baltoro Glacier (1998), and Mount Everest Base Camp in the Khumbu area of Nepal. Using this data as a base and charting the types and quantities of equipment left behind by mountaineering parties, I was able to estimate the amount of garbage that is presently accumulating in the area. My ultimate aim is to clarify the extent of Mount Everest's climber-caused garbage problem and to contribute to the preservation of the park. By clarifying the effects of mountaineering on the environment, I hope to provide not only a new viewpoint on the merits and demerits of the interaction of people and nature but also an index for rethinking how mountaineering should be conducted.

Information was compiled on Mount Everest climbing parties and summiteers based on data from Tsunemichi Ikeda (of the publishing company Yama to Keikoku Sha, Japan) for climbs from 1921 to 1997, and from Elizabeth Hawley, a mountain journalist living in Kathmandu, for climbs from 1998 to 1999. The data were compiled by decade for the 1970s, 1980s, and 1990s.

The first person to attempt to reach the highest summit in the world was an Englishman, C. K. Howard-Bury, in 1921. Together with four other climbers and four scientists, he entered Sikkim via Darjeeling, advanced westward over the Tibetan Plateau, and attempted to climb Mount Everest. By 1938, British climbers had made seven more attempts. A total of 172 climbers and 265 Sherpas made up the parties during this time.

Prior to the reopening of Nepal in 1949, all of the climbs were undertaken from the Tibetan side. In 1921, 1922, and 1924, the oxygen equipment was inefficient and, at that extreme altitude, it was difficult to climb without supplemental oxygen. However, E. F. Norton, a member of the third party in 1924, was able to reach an elevation of 28,126 feet without supplemental oxygen. There is no record of whether discarded oxygen bottles were carried back out. This was a period during which the merits of oxygen were much debated, so it is unlikely that a large number of bottles were brought in and left behind.

In 1953, a team led by John Hunt, an Englishman, reached the summit for the first time from Nepal. In 1956, the Swiss, and four years later the Indians, repeated the ascent. That same year, a Chinese team also succeeded in reaching the summit from Tibet. In 1963, American teams reached the summit via the west and southeast ridges and completed the first traverse.

Prior to 1970, most of the successful ascents had been by the standard South Col route from Nepal, but in the decade that followed, a succession of climbs was undertaken from the Nepalese side using more difficult rock faces and ridges. Along with all of the footprints, each route was newly littered with equipment and food supplies, but climbing parties rarely mentioned the effects of discarded equipment on the environment.

In total, in the 48 years from 1921 to 1969, the number of parties to Mount Everest was 29. In the decade of the 1970s alone, the number of expeditions was 27, about the same number as in the previous ten years.

In 1979, the Chinese government opened up Tibet again, making it possible to climb Mount Everest from the north side. At first the Chinese Mountaineering Association announced a limit of one party per season, but the number of days at the base camp was set at around ten, allowing several parties to attempt the mountain in one season. The Nepalese government followed suit, and the restriction of one party per season was abandoned.

Summit successes continued by various routes, and Mount Everest began to be used as a stage for individual performances. Everest "firsts" or records received a great deal of attention with solo ascents, new routes, or the nth woman—attracting more climbers. Commercial expeditions grew in popularity. Because restrictions had been lifted in the 1980s there were 144 climbing parties, a 5.3-fold increase from the 1970s.

In 1993, on the 40th anniversary of the first

successful ascent, 294 people from 15 parties approached Everest and 81 people reached the summit in a mass assault. On May 10 of that year, as many as 40 people reached the top—more than the entire number of climbers who had succeeded between Sir Edmund Hillary's ascent in 1953 and my own in 1975. In reaction to environmental pollution and overcrowding, the Nepalese government raised the peak fee from $10,000 to $50,000, but this only led to an increase in commercial climbing. Because the fee was prohibitive for one party, international parties were formed and the costs were shared.

Evaluating the results of a detailed survey of Japanese parties during this period, and examining survey results from six parties that climbed in the spring of 1999, I was able to estimate the total amount of garbage and equipment left behind by the climbers and multiply it by the nearly 6,000 people who have attempted Mount Everest to date.

Abandoned oxygen bottles and other discarded equipment litter Everest's South Col at 26,200 feet.

I have concluded that an estimated minimum of 290 tons and a maximum of 1,115 tons of garbage have been left in the area. Based on the fact that an average of 304 people a year were attempting to climb Mount Everest in the 1990s, extrapolation reveals that the amount of garbage is increasing every year by between 15.5 and 60 tons.

At high elevation, the amount of urine passed by a person climbing is .5706 gallons per person per day, which is 1.5 times the normal amount. The average amount of time spent by climbing parties on Everest is about 50 days. The 1975 women's party had 15 climbers and 7 journalists, 22 people. The number of sherpas was 48. The number of sherpas for other parties, however, was about 1.5 times the number of climbers. Based on these figures, the volume of urine passed by climbing parties can be calculated at 162,356 gallons by climbers alone and 243,534 gallons by climbers and sherpas together.

In the Karakoram during the summer of 1998, 13 parties consisting of 109 climbers brought 101,210 pounds of food and equipment into the Baltoro region, in particular to Gasherbrum I and II. This amounts to 1,200 pounds per climber. On Baltoro Glacier expeditions, however, the party carries the porters' food. Therefore, including guides and cooks, 477 pounds of food and equipment were carried per person.

Porters were provided with fuel and stoves, but they preferred to walk to far-off forests to collect wood for a fire on which they would fry their *chapatis*. When asked why they did not use stoves, they answered that they preferred their traditional cooking method because chapatis cooked with fuel do not taste good. The porters who came to the base camp had no choice but to use fuel-powered stoves. But they wanted to get off the glacier as soon as possible and return to the trees. Because of this attitude, the number of trees is gradually decreasing, and the high-elevation juniper, which is slow to grow back once cut, is on the verge of extinction.

A survey was also conducted on the wild animals in the area, using pictures that were shown to villagers and sherpas alike. They were asked to indicate whether the animals that have been in the area in the past were still there or no longer present. In addition, they were asked to identify animal species that have increased in number.

At the Gasherbrum base camp, which is at an elevation of 17,060 feet, the number of crows and butterflies has increased. I have witnessed large numbers of crows attracted by food and observed butterflies flying around. A few porters said that they had seen bears and leopards a long time ago. Urdukas is the last green tract of land that the caravan crosses. The high-altitude porters and guides

> ~ Mount Everest is one of the Earth's great treasures, considered sacred by untold numbers of people. The protection of its natural environment is the duty of visiting mountaineers.

said that as a result of food being left behind here, the number of ibexes had increased. Several times from inside my tent I saw groups of ibexes leisurely walking on rocks far above. I was told, however, that wild yaks and tigers no longer exist here.

Because the Indian border is a mere 12 and a half miles beyond the Gasherbrum base camp, helicopters carrying army supplies are in evidence and telephone lines stretch along the glacier. These military activities and the increased number of climbing parties have obviously had a major effect on the wild animals of the Baltoro region.

At the Everest Base Camp, according to an SPCC report, 3,515 pounds of human waste from 13 climbing parties from 1996 to 1997 were transported and buried at Gorak Shep. Over the period from 1921 to 1999, an estimated total of 1,355,017 pounds of human waste has been excreted onto the glacier. It is conceivable that the amount of human waste is the same for the Baltoro area in Pakistan.

The number of trekkers visiting Sagarmatha National Park is also increasing, with over 20,000 visitors in 1998. For each trekker spending five days in the park, 7.8 ounces of garbage are created each day. On a ten-day trek, 10.8 ounces per person per day are created. This corresponds to 24 tons—67 tons of garbage each year. Appropriate countermeasures are necessary.

For the protection of the environment in high areas around Mount Everest, I believe it is necessary to make the following recommendations to the Nepalese Ministry of Tourism:

Form special parties to carry down garbage that has been left above the base camp.

Restrict the number of climbing parties that can enter the area each year.

Install a "control-tower camp" and toilets at the base camp for the climbing season. Station a permanent officer-in-charge from the Ministry of Tourism or an SPCC staff member at the camp, who will be in close contact with each climbing party and will work with them to clean up the environment.

In order to decrease the quantity of materials that each climbing party brings to base camp, install communications equipment in the control tower camp and allow climbing parties to make common use of them.

Temporary toilets installed at the base camp should be of the compost type, they would be taken down to a place with soil and reduced to their components. For this reason the toilet paper used should be completely biodegradable.

The permanently stationed officer should designate a campsite for each climbing party and check that members of the party sort the garbage from higher up and take it down.

Do away with the present liaison officer system, and have the permanently stationed officer at the control tower camp oversee the safety of each climb. Increasingly, expeditions are questioning the need for liaison officers, who often do not even come to the base camp. When surveyed, only one of eight Mount Everest climbing parties that climbed in the spring of 1999 responded that liaison officers were necessary.

In order to decrease the amount of garbage created by climbing parties and dispose of it properly, I suggest the following:

As a rule, food should be purchased in the area. The outside packaging of consumables from home should be removed at the time of packing.

The core of toilet paper should be removed to make it compact, and the paper should be used as packing material for boxes.

The number of fixed ropes, batteries, etc. should be carefully calculated according to the climbers' strength and objectives, and only the necessary amount should be brought in.

Extra food prepared for unpredictable circumstances such as bad weather should be calculated on the low side.

Chemically treated boxes should not be used for transportation. Boxes treated chemically are sturdy and can be used for the return journey, but if they are discarded in the area they cannot be burned. The packing material used for personal items to be carried back out, and that used for personal items to be consumed in the area, should be different.

Before the start of a climb, the climbing party should meet with the Ministry of Tourism and reach an understanding on the method of garbage disposal.

In addition to members of the climbing party, the accompanying sherpas, cooks, kitchen boys, and porters should all be encouraged to dispose of garbage correctly.

During the caravan, porters should be issued fuel and stoves and advised not to cut firewood.

At the base camp, the kitchen and toilets should be set up at designated places. Used toilet paper should be kept out of the toilets, thoroughly dried, and burned. Different toilets should be used for urine and excrement to facilitate cleaning up at the end of the expedition.

As a rule, everything carried up the mountain should be carried back down and taken out of the area. In the case of a climber not having the strength to do this, a sherpa should be hired to do the job, even if it means extra expense and time.

Each climber should carry down his or her garbage and burn it at the base camp. After attaining the summit, a climber should remove fixed ropes, tents, canisters, gas, etc.

Mount Everest is one of the Earth's great treasures, considered sacred by untold numbers of people. The protection of its natural environment is the duty of visiting mountaineers and the governments of the two countries on whose borders it sits. The International Mountaineering Federation, the Asian Mountaineering Federation, the Nepalese Ministry of Tourism, and national mountaineering associations should be informed of the quantity of garbage estimated to have been left on Mount Everest. We need to appeal to them to give due consideration to improving mountaineering practices so that we can preserve this wonderful park.

Japanese mountaineer Junko Tabei began climbing in earnest in 1962 after graduating from Showa Women's University with a degree in English literature. Since then, she has had a prolific mountaineering career, climbing more than 70 major peaks around the world.

She is best known as the first woman to summit Mount Everest (in 1975), but in 1992 she also became the first woman to climb the Seven Summits. The sheer volume of her climbing experience is astounding; after almost 40 years, she shows little sign of letting up. She directs the Himalayan Adventure Trust of Japan—an organization dedicated to the preservation of the mountain environment. She has received many prestigious awards and in 1999 was on the international jury of the Banff Mountain Film Festival.

HIMALAYAN CLIMBING – HIGH ACHIEVERS

GREG CHILD

DOUG SCOTT

THE HIGH COST OF A FREE RIDE

GREG CHILD

Climbing sure came a long way this past millennium. Climbs got harder and the sport became marketable. I wonder what is in store for climbers in this new millennium? Will I be shocked to see a newspaper headline reading, "Stop Press: AOL-Time Warner announced today the acquisition of Mount Everest; an offering of common stock soon to follow"?

No, I won't be surprised at all. I'll just be glad that I climbed when I did and that I got in a few new routes before the last unclimbed bit of cliff or mountain succumbed to our thirst for exploration. I'm sure that long before this millennium ends in 2999 every last ripple of verticality will have a route on it.

But seriously, it is incredible to look at our obscure little sport (climbers once cringed whenever climbing was called a sport) and track its progress through the ages, from the pre-commercial era to the age of professionalism.

People have been climbing up rocks and peaks ever since our hairy ancestors climbed down from the trees. Andean Indians made sacrifices and ritual burials on 22,000-foot summits centuries ago. The Anasazi built cliff dwellings that we still can't reach even with high-tech rock shoes. The Dogon people of Africa used caves in cliffs as burial vaults.

Okay, that gets us to 1786, when, to my way of thinking, the first modern climb was made. The

first ascent of Mont Blanc, the highest peak in the European Alps, was a truly modern ascent in that it was made for a cash bet—a presage of the corporate sponsorship, big-bucks guiding, and media-coverage that drove so many climbs of the late 20th century.

The sponsor was Horace Benedict de Saussure, a man so intrigued with the notion that it would be grand to see someone stand on top of that 15,771-foot snow giant that he offered a reward to whoever climbed it first. Two Frenchmen, Jacques Balmat and Dr. Paccard, went for the summit and the loot. The first truly professional climber-showman was also a Mont-Blancer. Englishman Albert Smith turned his 1851 ascent into an illustrated lecture using lantern-lit slides. The show ran for six years at the Egyptian Hall in Piccadilly. That ought to give the Everest IMAX film a run for its money as the longest running climbing show in history.

The first big media event in climbing this past century resurfaced as the last big media event of the climbing millennium. It was the expedition that gave us the handy phrase: "Because it is there." Of course, it was the 1924 British Everest expedition, on which George Mallory and Andrew Irvine disappeared high on the mountain. The mystery of whether they summited has tantalized us for decades. We still don't know the answer, but it came a step closer to resolution in 1999 when Mallory's body was found at about 27,000 feet. There has been much hand wringing over the media

> *...*There is nothing wrong with making a
> buck out of climbing. But climbers have to be careful now
> that climbing has become a hot property that the tail
> does not begin to wag the dog.

and live Internet coverage that showed images of his body, and over the contents of his pockets, which the climbers carted off and put on public display. But is that much different from digging up mummies? Speaking as a ghoul who once sold a photo of a climber's skeleton to *Life* magazine, and who herewith grants permission for my bones to be photographed if I croak in the hills (so long as my heirs receive 50 percent of all image sales), I believe that climbers run the risk of becoming part of the archaeology of a mountain. As such we forfeit our rights to privacy and become fodder for the high-altitude paparazzi of the third millennium.

A lot of great climbing was done all over the map in the first half of the 20th century, but Adolf Hitler put a damper on climbing development when he invaded Poland in 1939. Perversely, the Nazis were the first to latch on to climbing as a promotional vehicle to sell a product. When the four lads who made the first ascent of the Eiger North Face were paraded in front of Hitler, in 1938, the Nazis were using climbing to sell the sinister crackpotism of national socialism and, whether they liked it or not, the climbers were endorsing the master race. I have always been intrigued by the photo of Heinrich Harrer, Anderl Heckmair, Fritz Kasparek, and Ludwig Vörg posing beside the ice-eyed führer. They look as uneasy as sheep partying with a wolf, although recent disclosures show that Harrer was a member of the wolf's party.

The point of these digressions is to get us thinking about the role commercialism has played in climbing. We climbers have long teetered on a moral and spiritual tightrope. We are torn between diving into the glitzy mosh-pit of the buck-raking professional athlete or remaining amateurs, climbing in blissful obscurity, untainted by the grasping for filthy lucre.

Until very recently, no newspaper or magazine was interested in climbing unless the climb was Everest. Today, every newspaper and magazine is interested in climbing—so long as it is Everest. Okay, I exaggerate. The last 20 years have seen other mountains and rock-climbing slipstream behind Everest into mainstream popularity. It has become "cool" to be a climber. Advertising agencies have adopted climbing as a motif to sell products, and the exploits of a few climbers have become the stuff of stardom. Today, more and more climbers earn a wage as professional athletes with corporate sponsors, and from publishing and TV deals.

Okay, so what? you ask.

Well, not everyone agrees that making a buck out of climbing is good. When I returned from Everest a few years ago a little party was thrown for me. I noticed, however, that one friend was absent. The reason my friend didn't attend was because he felt I had sold out my principles. By then I was already a "professional" climber who had a contract with an outdoor company. In that person's eyes, I had climbed Everest solely to stick it on my résumé.

Worse, I'd used oxygen, a real cop-out. My friend was right. I did climb Everest in bad style, and I did do it to put it on my résumé. But that's a better reason than "because it's there," isn't it?

I once heard the great American big-wall climber Warren Harding remark that in his day—the 1960s—climbers used to dress "like fishermen" and nobody paid attention to them. But Harding started the drift to "cool" when, after his ascent of the Dawn Wall on El Capitan in 1970, he became a poster boy, advertising beer. Climbers have always cashed in on their fame: Sir Edmund Hillary has enjoyed a noble career that revolves around The Big "E." Reinhold Messner traded on his prolific Himalayan accomplishments to become a highly paid public speaker and endorser of products. Catherine Destivelle's slinky moves on limestone made her a bankable sex symbol for sponsors. By the nineties the X Games transmogrified climbing into televised competition, and climbers wore as many labels as racing car drivers. Climbing gyms brought the outdoors indoors and removed discomfort and risk for a membership fee.

But more than anything it was Jon Krakauer's best-seller that crowbarred climbing into the mainstream. This tale about being guided up Everest and expiring, titillated us all and inspired aspiring alpinists to covet discomfort and risk, proving at the same time that we watch climbing for reasons we watch Formula One racing: to see high-speed crashes.

Of course, there is nothing wrong with making a buck out of climbing. But climbers have to be careful now that climbing has become a hot property that the tail does not begin to wag the dog. Sponsorship and big-bucks guiding can drive climbers to push themselves into deadly situations if the climbers feel that success is expected to sustain their careers. The death on K2 of Alison Hargreaves, driven to accomplish her well-publicized goal of climbing the three highest peaks on Earth in a single year, and the deaths of Rob Hall, Scott Fisher, and their clients on Everest are untimely, tragic ends with a root cause: professionalism.

Any climber who has funded an expedition with a TV documentary knows there is no such thing as *cinema verité* on a mountain. The film is not about the climb; the climb is about the film. And now the digital age is upon us and our computers have real-time satellite links to expeditions. I went on one of these e-expeditions once. We carted so much weight in satellite phones, laptops, digital cameras, and batteries that we could barely move through the mountains. Ironically, the more connected we were to the outside world the less connected we felt to each other.

Meanwhile, the best climbers in the world, and the best climbs, are the ones you'll never read about or see on TV or on the Internet.

"Because it is there." When Mallory said those words in the twenties, he never intended the phrase to achieve the immortal status it enjoys today. In reality, he was trying to get away from an irritating journalist who kept asking him why he was going to climb Everest. Mallory lost his cool and blurted the phrase out as a dismissive, off-the-cuff remark. He had no idea why he was going to climb that mountain. Nor do I know why I climb. No one does. It's just there, that's all.

Eight-thousand-meter peaks, A5 big walls, and 5.13 sport climbs are all part of Australian Greg Child's climbing repertoire. It's no wonder that many consider him to be the most accomplished all-round climber in the world. He recently completed the first ascent of Pakistan's 19,000-foot Shipton Spire (a 36-pitch, 4,400-foot big wall), completed the first ascent of Lobsang Spire, and put up a new route on Nameless Tower.

In India, Greg has climbed the East Pillar of Shivling, a 50-pitch, mixed big wall and alpine ridge. He has summitted K2 without oxygen and climbed Mount Everest. Less known, but much admired by Himalayan veterans, was his climb of Gasherbrum IV in 1986, the first success on this difficult 26,000-foot peak in 28 years.

Equally impressive is Child's rare gift of writing. In 1987 he was honored with the American Alpine Club's Literacy Award for his prolific and insightful mountaineering literature, and in 1998 he won the Jon Whyte Award for Mountain Literature at the Banff Mountain Book Festival for Postcards from the Ledge. He has appeared at the Banff Mountain Film Festival as a guest speaker and twice on the international film jury.

FROM HERE TO THERE

DOUG SCOTT

At the dawn of this new century it is natural to look back upon what has been meaningful to give purpose to the future. Certain attitudes and traditions are worth preserving to illuminate the way forward with confidence and without hesitation, to avoid stumbling, and to keep from being side-tracked into blind alleys.

There has been such an increase in the number of people taking up climbing, coupled with the growth of information technology, that inevitably a rapid change has occurred in climbing values. As a result, climbing is going through a period of crisis. What was always valuable is in danger of being lost, but this crisis is also an opportunity for us to bring into sharper focus the reasons that people took to climbing mountains in the first place.

There is, in man, an essential paradox. On the one hand he seeks all the ways and means to make his life more comfortable, safe, and certain; but, on the other, he knows intuitively that only by taking risks and facing up to uncertainty is he going to stretch himself, go beyond himself, and arrive at that moment of truth when he can see more of the unknown around him.

Instincts for adventure, so deeply rooted over the past millennia as man evolved in the unpredictable, natural environment, now lie largely dormant. They are only given expression by chance or by design in an artificial way. The mountainside is such a medium when the climber concentrates his attention; he creates for himself heightened sensibilities and an awareness verging on the extraordinary, summoning up areas of his being that are normally hidden. These are times when a little light is let into our lives and we remember those climbs so illuminated. So profound are these moments, even if they last only for a few seconds, that they are savored with reverence. This is why every committed climber prefers to lead rather than follow. It is because these experiences are so profound that any diminution of the possibility of achieving them in the future causes consternation and even abhorrence among the regular mountaineering fraternity.

We come into this world, at heart, as primitive tribal hunters with a set of basic instructions to be creative, exploratory, resourceful. We are designed to investigate, organize, and create. Now we struggle to match our ancient, inherited qualities with the present situation of overcrowding. Will it all end up a human zoo, as Desmond Morris put it, like a "hideously cramped animal menagerie of the last century or a magnificent human game park."

Recently Greg Child, two Indian friends, Balwant Sandhu and Akhill Sapru, and I stumbled into the primary rain forest of Arunachal Pradesh. It was soon apparent that we were in an environment where we did not belong. We would not have made the 18-day journey through the forest to the peaks on the Indo-Tibetan border without the help of the indigenous Nishi tribesmen. We would not have managed a week on our own. As it was, we suffered typhoid fever, malaria, blood poisoning, torn tendons, festering sores from leeches and dim dim flies and a degree of despondency and helplessness not experienced on any other expedition.

Meanwhile, the Nishi, totally adapted to living on steep mountainsides covered in dense forests washed by incessant rain, displayed all the attributes and energy of real mountaineers.

They used, to ingenious effect, the forest cane and creeper to bridge torrential side streams and the thunderous Khurung River. Not having cattle to move, they preferred to take a direct line on the hillside, constructing ladders up rock steps rather than zigzagging. They were physically very strong, with exceptional balance, moving over the most precarious terrain with grace and an economy of effort that allowed them to cover in a day, barefoot and laden, what would take newcomers four or five long exhausting days without a load.

One young man came up to base camp with a letter Balwant had written between bouts of fever four days away down in the rain forest. By the time I had realized that the letter had been written that same morning the "postman" had gone melting back in the green! Not only were these people modest; they were also honest. Not a single item of gear was missing despite its being scattered along 150 miles of thick forest track, awaiting relays of porters to move it up to base camp.

Each evening, usually after dark, we would reach camp wet and exhausted only to find that the Nishi, before attending to their own needs, had our fire going with ample wet wood drying on a rack alongside. They had filled our water butt with fresh spring water, made a frame for our tarpaulins, and cut back vegetation to make a flat area for us to sleep on—all that after carrying a heavy and sometimes awkward load through creeper and thornbush, across innumerable side streams by slippery logs or slimy boulders.

Throughout this ordeal they remained stoically indifferent to the horrendous and often dangerous conditions of travel, where the slippery slope fell away toward monster cliffs above the Khurung River.

The Nishi not only were kind and generous in taking good care of totally inept strangers, they were also warm and spontaneous, producing laughter and amusement at every opportunity.

The lasting impression of them is one of being completely professional mountaineers. Small bands of hunters would suddenly materialize en route or in camp and vanish before we could organize a photograph of them. They wore thick homespun mosquito-proof jackets, carried lightly woven snug-fitting bamboo rucksacks and had woven bamboo sou'wester-shaped hats that overlapped capes of animal fur. Across one shoulder hung a sword (*dao*) and on the other a bow and quiver full of arrows. With strong bare legs and feet bleeding from leech bites, off they went with only rice and tobacco. They would shoot or trap wildlife on journeys that sometimes lasted a month beyond their forest village.

They seemed brilliant at living their entire lives on a "slant," as Verier Elwin put it and thus summed them up:

> A belief in the importance of truth, a hardness or moral and physical fibre, courage before impossible living conditions, the love of adventure and exploration, a fresh, candid simple attitude to life's problems are among the other qualities that the (Nishi) people have to give the world.

Time with the Nishi gives a snapshot of how all our ancestors presumably were for 200,000 years or so—a long time to have had the basic instinct of compassion for others. The same could be said of the Dani tribespeople of New Guinea and other remnants of hunter-gatherer nomadic peoples. They are, however, a dying breed.

The Labrador Naskapi Indian culture has disappeared within the past 50 years. The Naskapi were, until "civilized," taking guidance through life by making contact with the "Great Man" (*Mista'peo*). By paying attention to their dreams, they got to know the Great Man—their soul—better and they sharpened their intuitive faculties. The Great Man required that the individual told no lies, was not deceitful, and was open, kind, generous, and helpful to others. He helped them with their hunting and they became better at knowing the weather patterns and animal locations. For ultimate success, they needed to have respect for the animals they were about to kill and to perform prescribed rituals before and after eating the meat.

It seems to be universally accepted among anthropologists that primitive, uncivilized hunters are noteworthy for their "good behavior" until contact is made with "civilized traders," government officials, and the like.

It is hard to believe that man somehow contrives to be "good" for his survival. More likely something happens in the process of living a simple hunter-gatherer existence that engenders feelings of respect for self and compassion for all.

Hunting involves more than bringing meat home, and climbing is not simply ticking off another summit. Our ancestors knew what the Caribou Eskimo Igjugarjuk knew: "All true wisdom is to be found far from the dwellings of men, in the great solitudes; and it can only be obtained through suffering. Suffering and privation are the only things that can open the mind of man to that which is hidden from his fellows." In the process of climbing, the Himalayan climber especially experiences extreme discomfort and uncertainty for long periods of time, and he is at the limits of his endurance to such an extent that a change is inevitably effected in his state of being. It may be that, for a short time at least, he achieves a greater self-confidence and feels more consideration for others.

This state of being is likely to be more profound and longer lasting depending on how much of their physical and psychological burden the climbers are able to shed. The chances of achieving this are greater away from others, on a new route, in alpine style, with one or two friends, up a 6,000-meter (19,686-foot) peak rather than in siege style on a popular route up a peak of 8,000 meters, where every move is reported back home.

On the latter, the climbers are never completely committed to the climb. They not only remain physically connected to the bottom of the mountain by fixed ropes, but they also never really leave home in the first place because of all the media connections.

Today the pressure is unremitting. People are urged by the media, particularly TV, to want more of everything and to want it now! To get more sex, take Viagra, which is like taking Diamox to get to Everest Base Camp and back in ten days, or to go up Everest faster. To be more certain of the summit, someone is hired to fix the ropes and others to lead and make every decision on the way. In the long run "more" always means less of an experience. Better to wait your turn, serve your time, and enjoy the satisfaction of becoming a mountaineer at whatever level rather than going as a dog on a leash!

Most climbers climb through the different climbing games until they find the ones they can do best, or they go back to the ones that satisfied them the most.

The ultimate climbs have to be those done in good style, on new ground, up into the so-called death zone. Climbers who have earned the right to be there come as friends supportive of each other, in the spirit of cooperation rather than competition. They respect the weather and the place, prepared to await the moment when everything is right and everyone is in agreement as to when to go and where. For these people, going into the death zone can be the place they climb beyond ego and self-importance, and they come down more alive and aware of all and everything like never before.

Evolution, so it has been said, is the way back home to the primordial consciousness. Those going into the death zone will have a better idea of this. In the first century, Cicero said "that which has always fascinated man most is the unknown." This facet of human nature will keep climbing on course for another hundred years or more.

British climber Doug Scott has made 35 expeditions to the high mountains of Asia, reaching the summits of 30 peaks, half through first ascents and all by new routes or as first alpine-style ascents. Apart from his climb up the Southwest Face of Everest with Dougal Haston during Chris Bonington's 1975 expedition, he has made all his climbs in lightweight or alpine style.

He has climbed the Seven Summits, is president of The British Alpine Club, was awarded a C.B.E. in 1994, and received the Royal Geographical Society Patron's Gold Medal in 1999. He was the first guest speaker at the Banff Mountain Film Festival in 1982.

Himalayan Climbing — The Future

Kitty Calhoun

Mick Fowler

I wanted to climb in different parts of the world because I had numerous things to learn from varying environments. To be able to afford to travel where I wanted, I needed to get a sponsor or get a job as a guide. Sponsorship at that time was very limited, so I got work guiding in Alaska, Peru, and Nepal.

In 1986, Andy Selters and I had work in Nepal and Andy asked me to try a new route on the north face of Thalay Sagar. It is a 5,000-foot mixed rock-and-ice route and we wanted to climb it alpine style. We had 17 porters who accompanied us to base camp, and even that many seemed excessive to me. We had designed and built our own portaledge because the available ones were not light enough. We shared a single sleeping bag that zipped into an ensolite sleeve that, to this day, is still not made commercially. I was afraid of such an ambitious objective, but when we started the climb, I was able to focus on the moment and forget my fears. After four days of stunning climbing, we reached about 22,000 feet and snow started to fall. There, we were pinned down for eight days in our portaledge in a major storm. Spindrift avalanches poured over us every 30 minutes and racked our nerves. When it ended, we retreated.

I was very disappointed that we didn't summit. After months of soul-searching, I understood that if the summit was all-important to me, I would have attempted the standard route instead. I discovered that I could not compromise the style of climbing just to make the summit. To me, the means was more important than the end; the process of climbing more important than the summit.

Over the next ten years I led three more expeditions to the Himalaya and developed other views about alpine climbing. I realized that I enjoyed expeditions because I was able to focus on a single objective for weeks on end and I was able to escape from nuisances such as cars, phones, and money.

I began to understand that alpine climbing is like a game of chess. Success depends on my ability to take into account the weather, temperature, and snow and avalanche conditions. I must find a route, estimate the difficulty of a climb, and decide on a strategy that determines how much rope, rack, food, and fuel to carry.

I saw that the strength of the team is one of the most important factors in the success of the expedition. There is a synergy when teammates share similar levels of commitment to a common goal, tolerance for risk, and technical climbing ability—and when everyone is equally qualified, decisions are made democratically. Extra climbers are as much a detriment to success as too much gear. Risk may be substantially reduced by choosing routes with less objective danger and by attaining good judgment through experience. Although many accidents result from mistakes that could have been avoided, sometimes what happens just comes down to fate. I may have very different ideas about climbing than other people, but ultimately those personal differences do not matter. The only thing that really matters when considering our future as climbers in the Himalaya, is that we leave the mountains clean.

As I prepared to go back to the north face of Thalay Sagar in 1996, the climbing world, for me, had changed considerably. Enough sponsorship was now available that I only needed to guide part-time. In return for work on product development and promotion, I received equipment, clothing, and contract money. Additionally, companies involved with climbing began supporting expeditions through grants, and money became available through magazines, TV and video companies, and Websites. I submitted a proposal to The North Face, asking for money so that I might finish this still unclimbed route on Thalay Sagar. The National Geographic Society, which was looking for adventurous trips to support, heard of our proposal and agreed to sponsor us in return for photo rights.

Before I left the U. S., I received a call from our National Geographic contact. "We do not want our sponsorship to have any effect on decisions you make on the mountain. If you have good photos, we may still run the story even if you do not succeed," she explained. Because I considered the media to be generally interested in controversy and sensationalism, I was surprised to hear a comment that was so thoughtful and conscientious. Only a year earlier, Alison Hargreaves had died on K2. Some, wrongly I suspect, believed that pressure from sponsors or the media had clouded her judgment.

Increasing public interest in climbing has had, and continues to have, a tremendous impact on climbing and guiding. In the U. S., I think it started with Dick Bass's book about being the first American to climb the Seven Summits. People began to realize that, with enough money to pay for guides, and with fitness and determination, any goal could be attained.

In general, we have become a goal-oriented society with limited time. The Himalaya used to be the playground for experienced climbers; now they are mainly the working arena for guides. A few years after a surge in guiding 8,000-meter peaks took place, the Nepalese drastically increased peak fees. Subsequently, most expeditions to the Himalaya have been either guided trips or commercial ventures in which someone organizes a permit and does not provide a guide. The participants in both kinds of trips either do not have the experience or the time to put together an expedition of their own. This is great for guides and for business, but it has had a negative impact on time and energy directed toward new routes, at least on the 8,000-meter peaks, in the Himalaya.

This sentiment has been echoed by Christian Beckwith, editor of the *American Alpine Journal*. He writes: "The discerning reader will note that relatively little information on 8,000-meter peaks is recorded.... This is not indicative of a fall-off in the amount of activity on the world's highest mountains; as with other disciplines of climbing, the numbers of people on the 8,000-ers have gone up in the last few years, apparently increased, of all things, by the 1996 Everest tragedy and the ensuing media attention on mountaineering at the highest altitudes. Rather, the majority of ascents on 8,000-meter peaks in 1998 were via normal routes, and they were largely comprised of commercial expeditions.... Strong Himalayan climbers are trying to climb all fourteen 8,000-ers or are availing themselves of the opportunity to guide. The test pieces of a generation ago are becoming today's normal routes as more and more 'regular' climbers venture to the high Himalaya for 8,000-meter experiences of their own."

The influence of these factors on current climbing objectives and climbing style in the Himalaya is tremendous.

Today's public obsession with adventure, climbing, and risk has also led to an increase in media coverage. Within the last 12 months alone, several new "adventure" magazines—including *National Geographic Adventure* and *Outside for Women*—have sprung up. *Time* magazine just ran a cover story entitled "Why we take RISKS." In that article the writer said, "From extreme sports to day trading, thrill seeking is becoming more popular." The cover shot is of a sport climber. The explanation given for why we take risks is that "everyday life is too dull." In my mind, *Time* not only does not understand why we climb but also does not know what is extreme.

In a recent article in the *American Alpine Journal* about "climbing mania" and the legacy of the 1996 Mount Everest tragedy, Michael Chessler claims, "We were waiting for the tragedy to happen. We had the lights on and the cameras rolling.... In America, we measure success in dollars.... Therefore, the books and films directly related to Everest 1996 may have generated 150 to 250 million dollars in revenue. Now add just the additional revenue earned by tangentially related films and books like *Seven Years in Tibet* and *Endurance*, all the TV shows and magazines sold, the charitable contributions and speaking fees, the trinket sales and publicity tours.... This was a major international media and financial juggernaught that may have generated half a billion dollars in spending. That is why the media loves these tragedies so much."

To raise money to fund climbing trips, many climbers have turned to magazines, TV, and the Internet for sponsorship, and this has also altered what comes into the public's eye. The easiest climbs on which to shoot photos and get video footage are big-wall climbs, fixed with rope from bottom to top. Fixing the route almost guarantees success because you can bring enough food and fuel to wait out any storm. Sponsors love success, and I would hope that success sells just about as well as a tragedy. Unfortunately, it is very difficult to get good photos and video footage, or to appear live on a Website on an extreme alpine climb. So the public has a skewed perception about what is significant in climbing. As far as the public is concerned, climbing Everest is the ultimate in alpine climbing.

People are also preoccupied with "firsts"— such as first woman or first American. This is a good marketing gimmick, but unfortunately, the objective associated with the "first" is often not really visionary. As a judge for the Shipton-Tilman Grant, I have grappled with the issue of amateurs versus professionals. Today there are climbers who go on expeditions to make money by writing, giving slide shows, and performing on video and TV shows.

When I asked a mentor of mine, the great alpinist Mark Twight, what he thought of all these developments, he went off on a rampage: "Better physical condition and light gear are easy to come by. [But] it is the changes that must take place in the mind before attempting something genuinely new in the Himalayas.... This is why there are so few contenders for difficult routes demanding a huge level of commitment; certainly fewer than five percent of the total number of ascents. Besides, if you fix a big wall route, film crews can come along. Guaranteed success and media exposure make the sponsors happy. But I find the climbing boring, slow, and pointless. Film editors have to come up with ways to make watching paint dry entertaining—hence the sensational interpersonal conflicts, etc."

When I compare my past and current alpine climbing experiences in the Himalaya, I believe the media has had the greatest influence on the changes that have taken place. I do not think there have been huge changes due to better equipment, technique, or vision. There is still no light por-taledge on the market, many climbers continue to fix ropes on all but the least technical ground, and alpine gems that were first attempted more than 20 years ago are yet unclimbed. Now, however, the climbing market is growing and we can make a living while climbing. We can guide, write books or write for magazines, give slide show and lecture tours, or work for Websites, TV, or videos. We are accessible anywhere, anytime, via cell phones and laptop computers, which we can use to sell ourselves and our sport.

I don't want to give the impression that I believe the future of alpine climbing in the Himalaya is over. Although some claim that the tripling of peak fees for 8,000-meter peaks in

Nepal in the last ten years is a huge financial barrier for alpinists, there are more sources of sponsorship than ever before. It would seem that those sources would want to support expeditions of greatest interest to the public (e.g. Everest). But I have been able to get donations for smaller, unknown peaks, despite the fact that I do not have a perfect record of reaching summits.

Though some areas of technological development in equipment have lagged, there have been significant developments or improvements. In the last 40 years, synthetic clothing, plastic boots, and camming devices were introduced. Rock- and ice-climbing standards have increased from 5.10 and WI3 forty years ago to 5.14 and mixed Grade 9 today.

In view of such progress and resources, why do many of America's young alpinists prefer to fix big walls rather than engage in pure alpine climbing in the Himalaya? Is it because of the difficulty of getting photos and film in order to fulfill sponsorship obligations, or is it a lack of commitment?

Jack Roberts, best known for his alpine ascents in Alaska, thinks it is simply that Americans today have a different vision. He says: "What is limiting their commitment to a really lightweight style of climbing is their heritage of being American and having, as their heroes, big-wall climbers....There are always notable exceptions—Steve House for instance—but I think that because America has such a strong tradition of big-wall climbing, that this particular generation of climbers tends to emulate this and reflect it in the style of climbing they choose and in the goals they stack against themselves. Our heroes originate from Yosemite: Robbins, Chouinard, Bridwell, Middendorf, and these guys all embrace big-wall ethics. They aren't like Bonatti, Cassin, Maestri, Terray. They are alpinists in the American tradition. Our heroes are different and so our methods are different."

I wanted to verify this opinion, and so talked with young climbers who represent the future of climbing in the Himalaya. Jared Ogden is most known for his televised, fixed, big-wall ascents in Baffin Island and on Trango Tower. For Jared, the ideal climb in the future would be "new routes on high-altitude alpine walls with two-person teams, no fixed ropes, and no media attachments or responsibilities....The media does not represent the real value in climbing and does not further the development in style or speed." Why then, has Jared not pursued his ideal climb? "Because we wanted to climb (Trango) and it costs a lot of money. It is harder to get money from sponsors if you do not provide them with something. Videos are their favorite choice.... I feel like I've compromised myself for money, but I have to pay the bills. Not everyone understands that." Jared concluded: "It is fun showing people what it's like being up there for TV but I want to balance it out with the real thing—like when you are really committed on a route."

Steve House, whom Twight called "the Great White Hope" of American alpinism, is the other youngster whose opinion I sought. Steve replied: "I think of alpinism as having two separate but related branches. One emphasizes difficulty. These would be multi-bivvy projects that take on the biggest, most difficult objectives. This might include an Alpine big wall, or a route with lots of hard mixed climbing. The point is that the climbing is slow because it is hard".

"The other branch emphasizes style. Routes that stand out here are done super-fast with complete commitment to movement. Great routes have been done in both styles, but the development of alpinism as a whole, and therefore Himalayan alpinism, is dependent on the convergence of these two styles. In the future, we will be climbing the routes originally approached in the multi-day style, in the single-push fashion. Climbing hard; but with more efficiency, more speed."

"To me the great aesthetic of alpinism is that, at the heart of it, you're trying to solve the most complicated problem—a big high-altitude alpine face—with the simplest solution; the greatest amount of skill, the least amount of equipment, and the best attitude."

It seems that, despite the rising cost of climbing in the Himalaya and trying to meet the needs of the media and sponsors, mountaineers still hold alpine-style climbing with the highest regard. Michael Kennedy, former editor of *Climbing* magazine, is known for new alpine routes in Alaska and on Ama Dablam, and an alpine-style ascent of Thalay Sagar. Although he shares Twight's and others' concerns that fixed-rope, big-wall climbs are overly hyped by the media, and agrees that these ascents don't represent the ideal in alpine climbing, he says: "Part of that is a perception thing that doesn't reflect reality. There is still a lot of interest in fast and light climbing, it is just not getting as much attention. You do not hear about all the alpine style attempts except for maybe a little blurb in the *American Alpine Journal*."

And what does alpine climbing mean to him? "Pure alpine style—climbing at or near the limit of your ability as a team of two or solo, no fixed ropes, carrying just what you need—is still the ultimate in climbing. It's also the hardest to achieve. Everything has to work right if you're going after a hard alpine climb. When you start compromising—by going with a bigger team, fixing part of the route, or climbing in capsule style—you increase your chances of success and survival. That doesn't mean these experiences are worthless. But it's important to keep the ideal alive, to have something to strive for."

American alpinist Kitty Calhoun began climbing at the age of 18 on the crags of her native South Carolina. Soon afterward she turned her attention to the Himalaya, focusing on small teams and extremely committing objectives. She made two strong attempts on Thalay Sagar in the Garwhal, one of which was defeated by hunger and exhaustion after an eight-day storm that pinned the climbers on a portaledge on the face. She successfully climbed Dhaulagiri in alpine style and three years later led an expedition to the West Pillar of Makalu and summitted. She was the leader of an attempt to climb the North Ridge on Latok I in Pakistan, climbed big walls in Kyrgyzstan, and climbed a new route on the West Face of Middle Triple Peak in Alaska. In 1998, she attempted a new route on the West Face of Latok III.

Calhoun is a professional climber on the Patagonia team, and she was on the international jury at the Banff Mountain Film Festival in 1999.

THE MINIMUM OPTION

MICK FOWLER

For the past 25 years I have spent as many of my holidays as possible climbing and have enjoyed eight trips to the Himalaya. Being a man who worries about things like lost brain cells, fingers, and toes, I have steered clear of the 8,000-meter giants and concentrated on the sub-7,000-meter peaks. All of my Himalayan trips have been completed inside six weeks, and the highest mountain I have climbed is Spantik (23,059 feet) in the Pakistan Karakoram.

My climbs have always been mixed routes done in alpine style. I aim to climb in a rope of two with both climbers climbing every pitch on the route. Sacks are generally carried on our backs but are, of course, hauled if a pitch is just too difficult to lead wearing one. The sacks weigh about 55 pounds to start with, and the maximum time I aim to spend on the mountain is about ten days. I am proud that I have never carried bolts on any of my climbs. I have never placed one and never intend to do so.

When trying to predict the future, one starting point has to be considering the path that has led us to the place we have reached today. My career involves valuing stocks and shares; however, I never cease being amazed by how wrong even the most carefully thought-out assessment of future value can be. As a result, it's with some trepidation that I offer these thoughts on the likely future of Himalyan extreme climbing.

The Himalaya have been a very time-consuming and expensive place to visit. In the 1950s heyday of unclimbed 8,000-meter peaks, the cost was such that sponsorship was a virtual necessity. In this era the unclimbed 8,000-ers were obvious objectives that were also attractive to commercial sponsors, who saw benefit in their products being associated with conquering the highest mountains in the world.

In this environment it was hardly surprising that the easiest routes up the biggest mountains became the focus of Himalayan attention. It was also understandable that these ventures tended to try to maximize their chances of success by being large-scale affairs with a full array of camps, high-altitude porters, oxygen, and fixed rope. The lure of unclimbed 8,000-ers and free (sponsored) trips to areas that would otherwise be unaffordable effectively curtailed any more technical Himalayan aspirations climbers had as individuals.

The result was that Himalayan ethics got off to a bad start. Annapurna, the first 8,000-er to be climbed, fell in 1950 and by 1964, siege tactics had been used to overcome every one of the 14 peaks over 8,000 meters.

Thereafter political problems led to access difficulties, and by the time these eased in 1969, the emphasis had changed. With all the 8,000-ers now climbed, the focus of cutting-edge activity was aimed at using siege tactics to force more difficult new lines on the highest peaks.

Examples from 1970 alone include the Japanese ascent of Makalu's Southeast Ridge, an Austro-German ascent of the Rupal Face of Nanga Parbat, and the British ascent of the South Face of Annapurna. After 1975, when the obvious "last great challenge" of Everest's Southwest Face was climbed by Chris Bonington's British expedition, public interest in Himalayan climbs began to wane and sponsors became less interested. Something fundamental had to happen if the scene was to free itself from the burden of siege style. The changes were not long in coming.

First, the siege expedition era had seen rapid developments in clothing and light-weight technical equipment, but secondly—and most importantly—by the mid-1970s it was becoming increasingly cheap and easy to organize small-scale trips to the Himalaya. Airfares had dropped to affordable levels and mountain roads were being extended deeper into the high valleys. Within the space of a few years what had been almost an exclusively sponsored sport for the climbing elite was suddenly transformed into something that was accessible to many.

In 1976, Joe Tasker and Pete Boardman forced a re-appraisal of what was possible for a self-contained two-man team. Their ascent of the steep and technically demanding West Wall of Changabang (22,521 feet) employed techniques new to the Himalaya and involved what was referred to as "capsule style" climbing. The climbers moved up the route in stages, fixing ropes from one bivouac site to another, and then clearing all the ropes behind them before repeating the process. On Changabang the absence of reasonable ledges was such that some of the bivouacs were in hammocks.

Tasker and Boardman's success showed that it was possible for a two-man team to achieve far

Heavily burdened climbers haul supplies on Trango Tower, northern Pakistan.

more than had previously been thought. The contrast between their style and that of a Japanese team, which climbed Changabang's Southwest Ridge just a few months earlier, was profound. The Japanese used full siege tactics with six climbers, 8,000 feet of fixed rope, 300 pitons, and 120 bolts. The two climbs were side by side. Ethical factors suddenly became a consideration.

The change in attitudes quickly took hold, and by the late 1970s "lightweight" and "alpine style" were new buzzwords. Even the 8,000-ers were dragged into this new way of thinking when, in 1975, Reinhold Messner and Peter Habeler climbed up and down the Northwest Face of Hidden Peak (Gasherbrum, 26,471 feet) in a remarkable three days.

By the late 1970s, those leading technical climbers, who previously would have spent their Himalayan days gridlocked in siege expeditions, were suddenly free to organize small-scale trips with their friends. Compared with the frequent drudgery of traditional siege climbs this was FUN!

By 1980 the number of teams operating in the Himalaya had increased substantially and—vitally important to any healthy climbing scene—competition had begun to develop for the best objectives.

Also, interest started to be shown in large-scale technical rock climbs. The British climbed the Trango Tower in 1976, but the American ascent of Uli Biaho in 1979 marked a real change in attitude to big Himalayan rock walls. Eschewing the easiest-looking line, the Americans, led by John Roskelley, used Yosemite-developed, big-wall techniques to tackle the 3,600-foot vertical and overhanging East Face. It took them 10 days and, with hardly any ledges on the route, portaledges were used to great effect. Henceforth it was clear that with the equipment and the commitment, even the smoothest Himalayan big walls were viable objectives.

The last 20 years have seen a logical progression to harder and harder objectives. In general the theme has very much been the idea of, as Stephen Venables put it in his excellent book *Himalaya Alpine-Style*, "doing more with less."

By the mid-1980s even technical routes on the 8,000-ers had started to succumb to alpine style assaults. Enric Lucas and Nil Bohigas's ascent of the South Face of Annapurna in 1984 and the 1985 Voytek Kurtyka/Robert Schauer route on the West Face of Gasherbrum IV stand out as particularly noteworthy early examples. Both involved self-contained, two-man teams tackling hugely committing objectives and trusting on nothing but their skill and judgment to see them through.

In the 1990s a further noteworthy development, which has prompted a steady flow of impressive and well-documented climbs, has been the appearance of professional, sponsored climbing teams. These are a new concept to the mountaineering world because team members are basically encouraged to climb spectacular objectives and draw attention to their sponsors. Himalayan achievements in this vein include big-wall lines on Latok II (1997) and Great Trango Tower (1999).

The Latok ascent saw big-wall techniques being used for the first time at over 23,000 feet, but the Trango route was remarkable in another way. Sponsored partially by an Internet company, the climb hauled computers up the route and the public was able to follow progress on the team's Website. There were even live question-and-answer sessions with members of the public, safely ensconced in front of their PCs, bombarding the storm-bound team with enlightening questions such as "How do you go to the toilet?" and "Is there less gravity at altitude?"

One thing is for certain. Cutting-edge mountaineering is no longer a matter of simply getting to the top by fair means or foul. Ethical considerations are increasingly rising to the fore. The style of ascent is becoming as important as the ascent itself. But what is acceptable in one climbing circle is ridiculed in another. We may be

moving together but we are not yet one global climbing community.

To consider where we go from here, I think it is necessary to break mountaineering down into the various different styles currently on the market and ask ourselves how each one might develop.

1. TRADITIONAL (NONTECHNICAL) SIEGE ROUTES

In today's climate an invitation to join an expedition trying to siege a major unclimbed Himalayan snow slope is unlikely to generate much enthusiasm. In fact, since Messner's solo of Everest in 1980 siege-style ascents of nontechnical routes seem to have contained a serious element of overkill. And now, to add to the problems for any remaining would-be enthusiasts, the environmental impact of large expeditions is coming under ever closer scrutiny.

In such circumstances I simply cannot see that such climbs will ever again play a role in pushing Himalayan frontiers.

2. TECHNICAL BIG MOUNTAIN SIEGES

Large-scale siege ascents of technical objectives are now largely frowned upon in the West, but there are still strong Eastern teams actively on the lookout for the "last great problems."

The Russian 1997 siege of the right-hand side of Makalu's West Face is a recent example of a successful ascent in this mold. But how do we view this style of ascent against previous lightweight attempts on this face and lightweight successes on objectives such as the West Face of Gasherbrum IV and the South Face of Annapurna?

This becomes a difficult and much discussed problem. Those who first travel a particular path are trendsetters who carry with them a heavy responsibility for the future health of the sport. With enough climbers, good weather, fixed ropes, bolts, portaledges, and haul bags, it is now possible to hammer just about any mountaineering objective into submission. But to do so devalues mountaineering and shows scant regard for the ability of future generations.

It seems inevitable to me that the next few years

will see further large-scale sieges of technical objectives. But as small groups of "alpine style" climbers stray more and more onto terrain that was once the exclusive preserve of big sieged expeditions, sieging appears more and more difficult to justify. And as we move increasingly toward being a global sport with universally acceptable standards, my guess is that in ten years time the pockets of resistance will have faded, and full-scale old-style sieges will be regarded as unacceptable by everyone.

"Small is beautiful" looks to be the way of the future.

3. SOLO ASCENTS

Himalayan soloists were long regarded as being in the dangerously eccentric category, but Messner's solo of Everest in 1980 changed all that and gave soloists a healthy cloak of respectability. Since then, aims and aspirations have moved on considerably, although major successes are notably thin on the ground.

Tomo Cesen's efforts on Jannu (1989) and Lhotse (1990) have been well publicized. Although they are now disbelieved by many people, his efforts certainly focused attention on soloing and the fame and glory awaiting anyone who could succeed on such wild objectives. Tomaz Humar's 1999 ascent of the South Face of Dhaulagiri (26,810 feet) probably represents the pinnacle of soloing achievement so far, but fatalities such as that of Slavko Sveticic on the West Face of Gasherbrum IV serve as potent reminders of the dangers that are involved.

For the future I would guess that we will see in the next few years proven ascents that duplicate what Cesen claimed. Beyond that, I think we can look forward to a steady stream of cutting-edge solos, but the loneliness and danger of solo climbing major Himalayan technical objectives are such that I can never really imagine that this activity will have mass appeal.

4. ALPINE-STYLE ENCHAINMENTS AND THE RECORD BREAKERS

Perhaps there is not a lot to say about enchainments (climbing lots of peaks on the same outing) or speed climbing, other than it seems certain that the human desire to surpass the achievements of previous generations will result in the growth of enchainments. Also, timed ascents will be featured more prominently.

Of more interest is contemplation of what else might take place under the "record-breaking" heading. The Scottish ice scene has already seen the first naked ascent (technical gear aside) of Elloitt's Downfall, a Grade V climb in Glencoe. Is this the way for the Himalaya? In winter? The mind boggles but I am sure that we can look forward to plenty of competition from all sorts of record breakers keen to get their names in the record books.

5. ALPINE STYLE

Now I am getting more serious. Under this heading I am thinking of mixed or pure ice routes. I am assuming that alpine style involves a small group of climbers (usually two) making progress in one self-contained unit. They are not connected to the ground by a chain of fixed ropes and, within reason, they can rely on nobody but themselves if something goes wrong.

To me, this pure style of climbing will ultimately become the only respected way of tackling new ice/mixed objectives in the Himalaya.

This area also has the potential for serious controversy. I simply cannot see the huge range of styles and ethics, currently encompassed by alpine style, sitting comfortably together for much longer. The problem is basically one of ego, and the need to be prepared to accept failure and thereby preserve challenges for the climbers who are more capable than ourselves. And we should bear in mind that history has shown that we continually underestimate the advances that the next generation will make.

At present, alpine-style Himalayan ascents can vary between the following:

(a) The Minimum Option, which
    consists of these items and activities:
        A two-man team.
        No fixed ropes.
        Climb done in one push.
        Minimal hauling.
        No bolts.

> ∿ [Alpine-style climbing] will ultimately become the only respected way of tackling new ice/mixed objectives in the Himalaya.

Both climbers climb all pitches.

(b) The Maximum Option, which
consists of these:
> Four or more climbers operating as one
> self-contained team.
> More equipment than the team can carry
> in one go.
> Fixed ropes between bivouacs. (They
> are pulled up and reused once the next
> bivouac has been established.)
> Climb can take many days.
> All equipment is carried in haul bags.
> Bolts are used.
> Only the leader climbs the pitches; the
> others jumar.

It is interesting that the climbing press used to make hardly any effort to distinguish between such contrasting approaches. But times are changing, and reporters and climbers alike are increasingly focusing on the exact style of the ascent.

This change of emphasis is an understandable progression. In the past the number of activists has been small and the number of objectives huge. To many people the exact style adopted mattered little. But now what you might call globalization of objectives is focusing climbers onto the same unclimbed faces, and we are beginning to see contrasting styles right next to each other. Take the British (1997) and Russian (1998) lines on the North Face of Changabang, for example. I can only foresee that the focus on style will sharpen even further in the years ahead.

There will, of course, be natural progressions—lightweight carbon fiber portaledges, for example—and I am sure that we can look forward to plenty of robust debate. But I will keep my fingers crossed and boldly predict that the trend of wanting to do more with less, combined with increasingly balanced and ethically aware reporting in the climbing press, will gradually sway frontline activists toward the minimum option.

What will be climbed? Well, what can the human body achieve? A minimum option ascent of the true West Face of Makalu, for example? The odds are against it at the moment, but I wouldn't rule it out forever.

6. BIG-WALL STYLE

This is an interesting one to predict. Perhaps even more so than with mixed climbing, it is often argued that big-wall techniques with portaledges, bolts, haul bags, and good weather enable just

THE
COLLECTORS

PAT MORROW

KRZYSZTOF WIELICKI

ED VIESTURS

PEAK BAGGING

PAT MORROW

I became a "collector" of peaks quite by accident. Until the early 1980s, all the mountain adventures I had been on were expeditions with solitary and self-sufficient goals: Each trip was dedicated to climbing one mountain, with the single summit being its own reward. By 1982, without any broader goal in mind, I had climbed the highest peaks in North and South America and I had summited Everest as a member of the first Canadian team.

Then, curiosity got the best of me. I had climbed to the summits of three continents and this naturally led me to wonder about the high points of the remaining four. On my walk out from Everest's south base camp, I realized I had already taken several steps on what could prove to be a very interesting journey, and I committed to completing what seemed to be a natural adventure: the first Seven Summits project. This project was the beginning of my career as a "collector," and, in the eyes of some people at least, was one of the sparks of the modern trend of "peak bagging."

When I set out to try to climb the highest peak on each continent in the early '80s, there was no precedent to follow. I had to find my own financial and logistical means to reach the Seven Summits, each in a very different geopolitical corner of the map, but this was, of course, one of the most important elements of the adventure for me. I realized that I was seeking the adventure and challenge of the project, and that the summits themselves were simply a vehicle through which to live those adventures. If I was collecting, I was collecting life experiences; the peaks simply became high-altitude stepping-stones.

The project came at the right time in my career as an adventure photographer, and it ultimately set the stage for my life's work: to see and document the world from high and savagely beautiful places. As my story on the Everest expedition went to press, James Lawrence, publisher of Canada's *Equinox* assured me that he would help me out with assignments to document the remaining four peaks. While the Seven Summits project was initially just a personal challenge, it was soon apparent that I was not the only one with the goal in mind. By the end of 1984, I realized I was inadvertently locked in what could be called a media race with two wealthy American businessmen.

Someone had shown me a story in a Fortune 500 magazine announcing that American business magnate Dick Bass and Hollywood CEO Frank Wells were also after the Seven Summits. All of a sudden the project looked like a David and Goliath showdown, with me, the dirt-bag Canadian "frostback" climber, up against the might of the U. S. dollar.

The major hurdle was reaching and climbing Antarctica's highest peak. When I put in a call to Frank Wells to see if I could piggyback on their flight to Mount Vinson Massif, he asked me curtly, "Do you have $250,000? No? Well that's what it'll cost you to launch your own flight." This set the tone for the duration of the project. Although a certain amount of competition among climbers is to be expected, my experience of camaraderie and *esprit de corps* in the climbing community was shattered.

Wells eventually backed out of the game because of family pressures, but Bass persisted, getting Everest on his fourth try. Bass's precedent of bringing mountain guides to lead him up the Seven was, ironically, a precursor to the professionally guided disasters on Everest in 1996. By demonstrating that a relative newcomer to the sport could buy his way to the top of Everest, and somehow survive a near disaster during his descent, Bass unwittingly inspired dozens of others with even less mountain experience.

The Seven Summits "Competition" involved tensions and pressures that surfaced in the form of public quibbles that have lasted to this day. One of the most obvious twists was Bass's inclusion of Australia's Mount Kosciusko on the highest points list. Kosciusko is little more than a ski hill, and because there are a dozen or more real climbers' objectives in the Australasian region—which includes Australia, New Zealand, and New Guinea—I chose the highest, Carstensz Pyramid, in Irian Jaya (western New Guinea), for my seventh summit from the outset. And so, we have been left with two versions of the Seven Summits, two differing historical claims, and two standards for parties interested in repeating the project. Now that many of the logistical problems have been solved, a number of other adventure seekers have followed in both Bass's and my footsteps, with parties using whichever definition of the project best suits their own needs. As of February 20, 2000, 52 climbers have completed the project choosing Carstensz as the seventh summit, while 45 have done Dick Bass's Kosciusko version.

Although the Seven Summits project has been criticized as the beginning of an apparent modern trend in climbing toward peak bagging and tick-lists, it's important to see that in reality the collecting of peaks has been around for virtually all of climbing's history. While the reasons for collecting the peaks may be different over the centuries, there is ample evidence of people heading into the mountains with tick-lists for much of civilized time.

The Chinese, for example, long ago recognized the cosmic connection of nine mountain peaks to a shamanic, Taoist, Buddhist, or Confucian heaven, and they lined up to ascend these mountains and receive some form of spiritual blessing. They are not high by mountaineers' standards, ranging from only 6,560 to 9,840 feet; however, the devout use a different yardstick by which to gauge their mountains and measure their own worship. Not only did commoners and priests alike climb the peaks, but as a significant precursor to today's dubious act of chipping holds, they carved thousands of steps into solid granite to help them reach their lofty goals.

In the rest of Asia, there are many other peaks of importance to the indigenous peoples, most notably the Tibetans. Mount Kailas (in Tibetan, Kangrinpoche—"Precious Snow Mountain") is generally regarded as the holiest of Asian mountains. This handsomely symmetrical 22,028-foot peak lying on the desolate western reaches of the Tibetan plateau is on every Buddhist, Bon, Hindu, and Jain pilgrim's tick-list. Tibetan Buddhists don't climb so much as circumambulate their holy peaks, and peasants and well-heeled alike ride, walk, or prostrate themselves for thousands of miles to the mountain's base. Once there, they do the *kora* around the base in an effort to bolster their karma. It takes a long day for a Tibetan, fueled by a bag full of *tsampa* and a head full of dharma, to hike the strenuous 34-mile-long trail, which includes a crossing of the nearly 18,500-foot-high Dolma Pass. It took me and my companions, loaded down with camping gear, three days.

To up the ante, those who initiate themselves by completing the outer kora 13 times are entitled to embark on the *nangkor*, or inner kora route, which involves encircling Nandi, the pyramidal peak that stands directly below Kailas's south face. It is said that those who make the kora of Kailas 108 times will be guaranteed entry into Nirvana.

Dozens of other peaks throughout the Himalaya have accumulated religious significance and have drawn climbers as a consequence.

Nearby, on the islands of Japan, there are hundreds of major sacred mountains; the minor ones remain uncounted. With the introduction of Buddhism from China in the sixth century A.D., the practice of climbing the sacred peaks all the way to their summits, and thereby communing directly with their resident gods, became popular. This practice embodied the Taoist path of seeking freedom and immortality in the highest and wildest reaches of the mountains. As a consequence of their deep reverence for sacred mountains, the Japanese have one of the oldest traditions of climbing—and of peak bagging—in the world.

Climbing has also played a significant role in the religions of the Western world. The earliest collectors of mountain experience in the West were religious zealots, who, despite the Western penchant for monotheism and prescription against animism, had been inspired to seek out the mountain gods and icons so present in Western and Near Eastern mythology. This involved pilgrimages to the summits of Mounts Olympus, Ararat, Sinai, Hermon, and many others from scripture and myth. In the East, a panoply of gods was said to live in several different mountains, thus encouraging the pilgrim to tick peaks on a list of godly abodes. In the West, God was not meant to "live" anywhere, and so, ascents by Christian/Islamic pilgrims were not felt to be journeys directly to God. Mountain pilgrimages in the West thus tended to seek out singular peaks with historical significance. There was also an extended period during the Middle Ages when mountains were taken out of the religious experience in the Christian West. The all-powerful

Pat Morrow rappelling on the summit ridge of Carstensz Pyramid, the most technical of the Seven Summits normal routes.

clergy warned their superstitious flocks to stay away from mountains they believed were inhabited by evil spirits, and this restrained European mountaineering for several centuries.

By the early 1800s, however, mountains came out from under the shadow of the Christian church and collectors came out of the woodwork. With the development of organized guiding in Europe heralding the beginning of the "Golden Age of Mountaineering" in the 1860s, wealthy clients were certainly aware of the "must-do" climbs of the Alps. Even if the names of these climbs weren't publicized as a list in the October 1866 issue of *Outside*, had there been one in those days, they were surely on the lips of every climber and spurred races and competitions not too different from mine with Dick Bass.

I'd like to argue then that finding patterns in the mountains (such as the Seven Summits, the 8,000-meter peaks, the Grandes Courses of the Alps), listing these patterns as personal or public goals, and striving to "tick" these experiences off a list, is a completely natural human tendency and is as old as climbing itself. As natural and historic as the practice might be, however, some modern variations on how the collecting game has been played have been drawing considerable criticism from both within and outside the climbing community. A look at some of these criticisms might be illuminating:

The accusation that is most often leveled at modern "peak baggers" is that their lists are sometimes nothing more than an artificial concatenation of insignificant objectives, and that the completion of lists has somehow risen to have higher value than individual objectives themselves. In the worst case, peak bagging seems to involve linking a series of easy scrambles that have no

> The collecting project that has loomed largest over the past 20 years, and hasn't diminished in reputation or import, is the ascent of all fourteen 8,000-meter peaks.

natural or valid relationship save for the fact they are on the peak bagger's list. While some of these lists are indeed natural and valid, more than a few these days seem to be fabricated collections with ulterior motives. Some critics have suggested that these types of lists are nothing more than ways of making a name for oneself or of securing funding for what are essentially personal vacations.

In the very worst case, "artificial" lists are sometimes seen to be the brainchildren of peak baggers with limited talent, who are condemned by climbers for apparently seeking the easiest (and least-justified) route to fame. Most notorious in this group—at least among mainstream climbers—are those who appear to make the tick-list more important than the climbing itself, and thus give themselves permission to act in ways that orthodox climbers might consider unsporting, unethical, or disrespectful of the sport itself. This includes such things as being guided up the peaks (without developed talent); reworking the list to make it more personally possible (the Kosciusko phenomenon); using questionable methods (using oxygen on peaks that have been climbed regularly without, or using mechanized access); engaging in blatant self-promotion (especially in forums where uninformed listeners lionize

the promoter); and having no apparent long-term interest in the sport after the peak has been bagged.

The problems that result from peak bagging are not restricted only to less-experienced or questionably motivated climbers. Even among "real" climbers, being driven by lists and by "firsts" can lead to behaviors that others feel are harmful to the sport, to the environment, or to the public interpretation of climbing. There are legendary stories about some appallingly bad behaviors by climbers who are intent on a goal, and this kind of behavior can be greatly amplified by a race that involves several years of effort. The years that I put into the Seven Summits project, for example, had me thinking in ways that were distinctly different from my usual personal approach to climbing.

In terms of environmental impacts, the very existence of lists is enough to generate or amplify people's interest in going to places they wouldn't ordinarily venture. Carstensz Pyramid, the true high point in Australasia, for example, would likely never be on any climber's project list if it weren't on the Seven Summits tour. Its inclusion on that list has meant that this environmentally and culturally fragile peak has seen multiple ascents. When the fact of a "race" is added to the mix—as when several climbers get close to completing a list at the same time — the extra pressure can sometimes impel otherwise environmentally respectful people to cast aside their normal practices in order to grab the prize.

I want to emphasize, however, that in no way is all modern "ticking" and "peak bagging" unhealthy, invalid, or unnatural. Instead, in many ways the renaissance of peak bagging might be seen as a remarkable reflection of the amount of healthy, challenge-oriented free time we have in our lives these days. The fact that there are a significant number of climbers seriously pursuing goals such as summiting all 8,000-meter peaks is a sign of the current level of talent in our sport just as much as it is a sign of the dangers of overcrowding in the great ranges.

It's also imperative to acknowledge that completion of any of the more "valid" tick-lists in a respectful and honest style would be a significant accomplishment in the lives of most climbers. Also, the completion of some of the "lighter-weight" lists (e.g., all the 4,000-meter peaks of the Alps) would be significant exercises in endurance and commitment even if they weren't the greatest technical climbing achievements.

Many of the people who have ticked all the objectives on one of the major lists may have climbed the peaks simply because they love climbing. As was the case for me on the Seven Summits project, some of the collectors have accidentally stumbled into a position where completing the list is the natural thing to do, even though they initially had no intent of embarking on such a project. Despite the prevailing stereotype of the bumbling, untalented, and often rich climber being dragged up easy ticks by guides, many persons who embark on these projects are talented and committed climbers who are simply the types of people who are driven by bigger goals.

With all this in mind, let's take a closer look at some of the collecting, good and bad, happening today. One sees a huge number of variations on the practice: Some people create (or follow) lists and set out to collect all the items on the list (e.g., the Seven Summits); some people want to tick off single, once-in-a-lifetime experiences (climb Kilimanjaro but never climb again); some people want to collect experiences in several different domains (climb Everest and ski to both Poles); some people want to collect firsts (first ascents of a peak, or first by a route); some people seek firsts distinguished according to some stylistic parameter (first oxygenless ascent) or personal parameter (first female ascent of Big Ben on Heard Island); some people want to set records (e.g., fastest ascent of El Capitan); and some people collect numbers (e.g., the most 5.14s by an American).

At the core of the process is the keeping of records or lists and some community consensus that such things matter. In the history of climbing there have always been individuals or communities who have eschewed records of activity or accomplishment, but there always seems to have been far more people who have been attracted by records.

Without a list to follow, a peak bagger would not know where to turn, but there is no shortage of material to guide projects. The available lists (in various formats, from guidebooks to Internet sites) engender just as much praise—and wrath, depending on your point of view—as the collectors themselves. The most famous of the tick books—Allen Steck and Steve Roper's *Fifty Classic Climbs of North America* (or "Fifty Crowded Climbs"); *Sivalaya*, Henri Baum's guide to the 8,000-meter peaks of Asia; *High Asia*, Jill Neate's guide to the 7,000-meter peaks; Willi Burkhardt's *The 4,000-meter Peaks of the Alps*—can be viewed either as invaluable resource and planning guides, or as Bibles of the Antichrists, responsible for desecrating the sacred tenets of exploration and discovery in climbing.

In the best of all worlds, the lists themselves would simply be neutral catalogues of peaks and history, but it's important to realize that this isn't always the case. Stylistic, personal, and political agendas often influence lists. This is especially obvious with a book such as *Fifty Classic Climbs*, with its personal and seemingly arcane selection of climbs, but agendas also influence records or lists that purport to be neutral. The keepers of the lists that motivate the collectors have a very powerful, and not necessarily objective, role in determining the nature of the climbing game.

And what of the content of the lists? It is interesting that, at least as far as the inner circles of the climbing world are concerned, the Seven Summits quest has been demoted to the status of a goal for more amateur climbers. Though the project requires some degree of skill, it seems that the climbing fraternity has decided that cash and connections are the more fundamental requirements of the project. As far as climbers are concerned, a far more interesting and worthy Seven Summits project still awaits completion—climbing the second highest peak on each continent. In almost all cases, from a climber's standpoint, the peaks are more difficult and dangerous, with a completely new set of access and logistical difficulties as well.

The collecting project that has loomed largest over the past 20 years, and hasn't diminished in reputation or import, is the ascent of all fourteen 8,000-meter peaks. Even if negotiated by their easiest routes and surmounted by outdated siege techniques that are still being used, most notably on Everest, all the peaks offer a true mountaineer's challenge because of their ultimate elevation. By the spring of 1999, more than 3,000 individual ascents had been made of the 8,000-meter peaks; of these, 1,052 ascents had been made by 764 men and 44 women on Everest alone. But only seven people have collected all 14 of them. The famous Tyrolean climber Reinhold Messner first grabbed the prize in 1986 and did so in remarkable style, climbing oxygenless and completing most of the peaks alpine style.

A tick of Everest alone was long considered the greatest tick of all, though some of the shine of the mountain has dimmed in the past decade. Everest as a lodestone has spawned a wide range of accomplishments, driven by motives that range from curiosity and exploration all the way through to national pride and an unabashed desire for fame. The "first" ascents of Everest didn't stop with Ed Hillary and Tenzing Norgay's historic accomplishment. Since then, we have seen the first married couple to summit together (Andrej and Marija Stremfelj of Slovenia); the first walk from the Bay of Bengal to the summit (the Australian Tim McArtney-Snape, who managed another accidental first when he estab-

lished a new route, White Limbo, on the North Face in leather telemark boots because his regular boots were lost in an avalanche); the oldest (Lev Sarkisov of Georgia at 60); the youngest (Shambu Tamang of Nepal at 16); the first father and son summiteers (Pete and Ed Hillary of New Zealand); and the first to ride a bike, unsupported, from Sweden (Göran Kropp). The list goes on, sometimes with criticisms about the extent to which "firsts" are construed to gain financial support: In the ever wry words of humorist Tami Knight, "Help fund the first One-Legged, Polo-Stick Summiteers!"

Perhaps the most impressive set of statistics surrounding the ascent of Everest comes from Ang Rita, the most famous Sherpa since Tenzing Norgay. Thus far, the Solu-Khumbu native has managed to scale Everest ten times (and climb several other of the 8,000-meter peaks multiple times as well). To fully appreciate the level of his accomplishment, it's important to note that he hauled oxygen-guzzling Western clients to the summit and back while carrying regular sherpa loads of 44 to 88 pounds without the use of oxygen.

Two up-and-coming young climbers, Apa Sherpa and Babu Chiri Sherpa, have recently recorded their tenth ascents, also as working sherpas. These kinds of numbers make the accomplishments of most proudly boasting peak baggers seem absurd by comparison.

The consequence of Everest being on the peak baggers' tick-list, has of course, been an inevitable demotion of the experience and some profound environmental and cultural impact.

Setting records is another form of collecting. As technical and training standards have risen dramatically in all forms of climbing, speed climbing has been a natural consequence. The Russians were the first masters of the game, running speed competitions on big peaks since the 1950s, but the speed bug has caught on around the world, including on the Himalayan giants. On Everest, for example, the remarkable Swiss climbers Erhard Loretan and Jean Troillet started the race in 1986 when they sprinted up the North Face in just over 40 hours; they carried only light sleeping bags and took no tent. Hans Kammerlander hammered the record on the north side in 1996 when he made the climb in 16 hours 45 minutes, and in 1998, Kaji Sherpa shot to the top from the Nepal side in a relatively scant 20 hours and 24 minutes, only to be bested in May of 2000 by Babu Chiri, who breezed it in 16 hours and 56 minutes.

Ticks of speed ascents have also been changing the face of big-wall climbing, especially in Yosemite, where unbelievable times on single and multiple walls are getting racked up regularly, and where records sometimes last less than a day in the heated atmosphere of competition. The climbers playing this game have essentially created an entirely new form of climbing.

It's important to realize that while some collectors have a very public face, attract much media attention, write books about their achievements, and perhaps open themselves to criticisms regarding the integrity of their projects, there are also many climbers who are peak baggers with perhaps cleaner hands.

These include talented individuals who are ultracommitted extreme alpinists, pushing standards while racking up a quiet list of remarkable accomplishments that few of the less-talented peak baggers are ever likely to consider repeating. Climbers such as Catherine Destivelle, Peter Croft, Voytek Kurtyka, and the late Anatoli Boukreev have each formed personal tick-lists that bear no resemblance to the other mountains or practices already described. Desperate routes on peaks such as Gasherbrum IV, Cerro Torre, the Moose's Tooth, and Baintha Brakkh are sought after by only a prescribed few. Those who attempt these climbs need to do so largely for themselves, because only a valid and rich personal motivation will bring success on these climbs.

The motives of these individuals are understood only by their rare peers in the climbing world.

And there is another kind of equally pure collector: This person is the mountain nomad who collects ascents of peaks, very often silently and joyfully, simply because he or she loves being in the mountains exploring. The wilderness possibilities of my native Canada have permitted the existence of many such nomads, even in this age of roads and airplanes. People like John Clarke, John Baldwin, David Williams, Markus Kellerhals, and John Martin each head into the mountains every year with a drive to explore that naturally, but not necessarily intentionally, creates remarkable tick-lists.

My personal heroes, the famous British climber-explorers Eric Shipton and Bill Tilman, bagged 26 peaks over 20,000 feet on the 1935 reconnaissance of Everest. At the time, that was as many mountains of that height as had been climbed in all of history. Shipton, Tilman, and four others—plus a keen 19-year-old porter then known simply as Tenzing Norgay Bhotia—were just out looking for adventure. They prided themselves on being able to organize a Himalayan expedition in half an hour and on the back of an envelope; now, we take months and use a spreadsheet. Perhaps it's important to remember some of the beauty of simplicity and validity of their approach when we begin to consider committing ourselves to complex, expensive, competitive, and loud collecting of peaks, deserts, Poles, and oceans.

The last word remains with the late American superalpinist Alex Lowe, who clarified the point of it all: "The best climber in the world is the one having the most fun."

For Pat Morrow, Canadian photographer, writer, climber, and videographer, being a collector meant traveling the globe in search of high adventure and the wisdom of mountain cultures. Following an ascent of Everest in 1982, he went on to complete the Seven Summits, recounted in his book Beyond Everest, Quest for the Seven Summits. *For this achievement, he received the Order of Canada, the highest honor given to a Canadian citizen. At the 1990 Banff Mountain Film Festival, he was honored with the Summit of Excellence Award for his work in documenting the mountain experience.*

Together with Baiba, his wife and partner of 15 years, Pat continues to spend at least half of every year on expeditions and forays to the great ranges of the world. Their latest book, Footsteps in the Clouds—Kangchenjunga a Century Later, *was published by Raincoast in September 1999.*

THE CROWN OF THE HIMALAYA

KRZYSZTOF WIELICKI

When I was five years old and I saw the mountains for the first time I did not think I'd eventually spend five years of my life in the Himalaya. And when my adventures with the high mountains began, I didn't imagine conquering the 14 highest peaks on Earth. I had no intention of collecting. Climbing the 8,000-meter peaks was a follow-up to the serious mountaineering activities of Polish teams in the 1980s, those "golden years" of Polish Himalayan achievement.

The "competition" for the first ascent of all the 8,000-meter peaks wasn't really an important thing within the climbing community. As soon as Messner (1986) and Kukuczka (1987) achieved what the media expected of them, the Himalayan climbing community forgot about that so-called competition; after Kukuczka's completion in 1987, there wasn't as much media focused on the Crown of the Himalaya. Conquering the highest peaks once again became rather a private matter for the group of alpinists still active in the Himalayan scene—a group that was motivated by the extremely hazardous life style rather than a way of life based on competition and a media career. That attraction to lifestyle was the motivation for the events of my own path to the 8,000-meter summits—a path that began with my first Himalayan experience.

In the spring of 1979, my target was Modi Peak (23,686 feet) in the Annapurna area—by a new route on the unclimbed west face. I was euphoric on the summit; a month later, however, my frost-bitten toes were partially amputated.

But this was not enough to stop me climbing in the Himalaya: Within three months I would begin my affair with the 8,000-meter peaks. I received an invitation from Andrzej Zawada of the Polish Alpine Club to join the Polish National Expedition in an attempt on Mount Everest. This was not bad for a 29-year-old fellow, practically a greenhorn among the experienced team with a very significant objective: the first winter ascent of the mountain.

After enormous efforts by the entire team, working in extreme winter conditions throughout all of January and half of February 1980, we reached the South Col (26,202 feet) via the standard route. Our first camp was a struggle for survival against a hurricane wind. We didn't stand much chance of reaching the top. Yet, three days later we were back at the South Col, acutely aware that our permit expired the next day. At dawn on February 17, with minus 43° F temperatures and decreasing winds, we began a final summit attempt, and at 2:30 p.m. we made it.

My winter experience on Everest led me to attempt other 8,000-meter giants in winter over subsequent years. The third highest peak in the world, Kanchenjunga (28,210 feet) waited till 1986 for a winter ascent. Our Polish expedition, including Jerzy Kukuczka and me, chose the South Face from the Yalung glacier—a long, easy route. Our first attempt in the dying days of 1985 was followed by snowfall and strong winds that forced us back to Base Camp. With improving weather we began again, and on January 10 four of us reached 25,264 feet. At 6:00 the next morning, at minus 40°F, Kukuczka and I left Camp IV, headed for the summit. Cold and shade forced us to take a break where I tried warming my feet for one and a half hours on an ice platform. We decided that the acute pain in my toes was a good sign, so we continued climbing. The summit section was quite complicated, but fortunately we found some pieces of old ropes, signs of previous expeditions, which helped us to maintain our direction. At 2:00 p.m., January 11, I reached a rock tower with only the sky above and a magnificent panorama of the Himalaya. Jurek Kukuczka reached it as well.

We had to descend quickly to reach the tents of Camp IV before nightfall. Andrzej Czok and Przemek Piasecki were supposed to be waiting there in preparation for the next summit attempt. To our surprise, the tents were empty. We heard on the radio that Andrzej had to be taken down to Camp III in critical condition with pulmonary edema. That seemed impossible; he was the toughest guy I had ever met. But later that evening in Camp III, he passed away. His memory will remain with me forever.

In mid-January 1987, we were flying to Delhi: Wanda Rutkiewicz, Jurek Kukuczka, Artur Hajzer, and me. Our target was Annapurna I (26,504 feet)—also never climbed in winter. Our arrival at Base Camp under the North Face of Annapurna I was very late, and we were alone. It was a strange expedition. I was climbing with Wanda, who unfortunately felt so sick we had to come down. In the meantime, Kukuczka and Hajzer were making a risky attempt from Camp III, and sometime in early February 1987 they summited Annapurna I. It was my first experience where the summit was reached by someone other than me. I accepted it humbly and maybe became more respectful of the mountains.

The following winter was not much of a success—this time on K2 (28,253 feet). Again, we had chosen an ambitious target: the first winter ascent.

The extent of our ambition is probably best shown by the fact that the mountain still awaits a winter summit. It was a big international expedition—too big—and my longest expedition, lasting four months. I spent 80 cold, windy days in Base Camp below the Southeast Face of K2. We reached 23,950 feet—and not a foot more.

A winter later, we were again in the heart of the Himalaya, this time below Mount Everest and Lhotse (27,941 feet). Andrzej Zawada, Leszek Cichy, and I were the guests of a Belgian expedition. Although the Belgian target was Mount Everest, we chose to try Lhotse, never before climbed in winter. December 29, in our tent at 19,500 feet, we discussed our plans. My partners did not feel well, so they left things up to me. The morning was quite pleasant, and I decided to go for the summit alone. I reached nearly 24,000 feet in good shape. There, in an abandoned and torn tent, I spent a night. I could not turn back: the day was the last of 1988 and I was only 4,265 feet from the summit. But time was passing, and my fear of the swiftly approaching dusk forced me to sprint; I reached the peak before noon on one of the best days of the winter. I was wearing a medical corset after an accident on Bhagirathi II, and the descent was a real horror due to pain in my vertebral column. But there it was: the first winter ascent of Lhotse, the first alone, and probably the first one in a corset!

Then it was time to try the fifth giant, Makalu (27,826 feet). We started in winter 1990-91 as a small, four-person team. It took us 30 days of fighting with the wind and snow to reach Makalu La at nearly 24,500 feet, but the wind proved too strong. I changed the objective and twice tried to reach the top, alone via the West Buttress. In the second attempt, I reached 23,300 feet, but after a night out I surrendered to the very strong wind and, with extreme difficulty, retreated. A winter ascent of Makalu is still waiting.

My first solo experience was in 1984. A taste for solo climbing comes after years of experience, hundreds of bivouacs, and many difficult situations. One has to become mature, physically and mentally, for the challenge of soloing the Himalayan giants. One must also know one's body's limitations and deficiencies, and that challenge drove me as much as the challenge of winter did.

In the summer of 1984, I found myself at Broad Peak (26,402 feet) in the Karakoram, with Jerzy Kukuczka and Voytek Kurtyka. While these friends were off traversing the three Broad Peak summits, I offered myself a different challenge: Could I climb an 8,000-meter peak, alone, in 24 hours? I decided to find out. On the 7th of July, I was only able to reach just below 24,000 feet. Bad visibility in an unknown environment forced me to follow my instinct and retreat.

A week later, I began again from K2 (the Godwin-Austen glacier) at 20 minutes past midnight. Above me was a clear sky, a bright moon, and frosty air. All I could hear was the sound of ice, falling from the ridge. I passed through Camps I, II, and III to the col between the Middle and Main Peaks, which I reached at 3:00 p.m. After a short rest, I continued with a hurting head, but I was concentrating on the dangerous ice cornices, wondering how far I was from the summit. Finally, I reached the top at 4:00 p.m. To reach the summit had taken me 15 and a half hours and now I had to get down before midnight. Going down was a wild race with time. I ran with a flashlight to reach the tent on the glacier. I looked at my watch. Yes! It was 10:30 p.m. I did it: 22 hours up and down. Only then did I comprehend how long the day had been. I was so tired I couldn't even enjoy my success.

For me, impossible had become possible. But I was not the first person to break unbreakable barriers: There were others, the great ones of alpinism, and I bow down deeply to their memory. My contribution was just a part of the development in this domain.

In spring 1990, I organized a small Polish-Belgian expedition to Dhaulagiri (26,810 feet) and had another chance at a solo ascent. After two weeks of climbing, we reached an elevation of 23,300 feet on the normal route. From there, on April 24, 1990, I reached the peak alone in very fine weather, returning to Base Camp the same evening. Ten days later I moved to the East Face of Dhaulagiri. A few days later, at midnight, equipped with two ice-axes, a short rope, a small gas burner, a thermos with tea, and a walkie-talkie, I began to climb a new route on the east wall. After 16 hours of climbing, passing a very difficult rock barrier at 25,755 feet, I reached a ridge. Snow was falling and I didn't have camping equipment so, in this completely unknown terrain, I traversed the Northeast Ridge. As night fell, I found an abandoned tent. I made some tea and poured it in two cups. Why two? I don't know. I think I just needed a partner. In situations of extreme stress we are looking for a partner, even if we are alone because of choice.

In the autumn of 1993, I had permits for two peaks in Tibet: Cho Oyu (26,867 feet) and Xixabangma (26,287 feet). The first one I climbed with an Italian, Marco Bianchi, on September 18 via the 1986 Polish route. But returning to Base Camp, I hadn't had enough, and I decided to try again to reach the summit via the regular route in one solo push. I got dressed, equipped, ready to go. Then my friend came to the tent, put his hand on my shoulder, and said, "What are you looking for? What do you want to prove? For us, you are the best." That was it. Enough! I changed my mind.

But what I did not try on Cho Oyu, I did on Xixabangma. A few days after Cho Oyu we moved to the south face of Xixabangma, which, thankfully, very few expeditions visit! It's a magnificent, clean alpine valley. My friends chose the Slovenian route, but I was interested in the west summit with its outstanding unclimbed pillar. I left Base Camp in the morning and reached the face at noon, but I could see that without a belay I would not be able to cross the hundreds of huge and deep crevasses to the pillar. So I decided to do a new route.

I began at midnight and by morning had reached the upper level of the couloir without any problems. Then—a big surprise—a 984-foot face in front of me. I was trapped. It took me five hours to reach the summit ridge at more than 25,250 feet, and the Main Peak was still a long way from there. Following the tracks of my colleagues, I reached the top at 5:30 p.m.

My only companion was my rucksack. Exhausted, without water, I could only descend 1,300 feet before falling asleep on the snow without a tent. The night was wonderful, with thunder and lightning screaming over my head. I was terribly thirsty, not even able to swallow. I was struggling between sleep and freezing feet while waiting for dawn. Following the Slovenian route, I finally reached the bottom.

The 1984 Polish expedition to Manaslu was very different from the solo climbs—three camps, hundreds of meters of fixed ropes, a difficult south face. After a month we reached a virgin pass at 21,650 feet where heavy snowfall trapped us for ten days. Because of severe avalanche danger, we changed our tactics. We made a quick assault in alpine style along the South Ridge and, accompanied by Aleksander Lwow, we reached the summit on October 21.

In the autumn of 1986, I returned to Makalu (27,826 feet), this time to attempt a climb by the normal route. Marcel Ruedi offered me a partnership. Even though I was not very acclimatized, I accepted the risk of the quick approach that Marcel proposed. On the evening of the fourth day we were just below the summit. I reached the summit first, and after a while on top I started to descend because of the very strong winds, passing Marcel on the summit ridge. I could not have imagined that Marcel would never return. I still feel bad about that today, even though I know I had no control over the events.

In the autumn of 1991, I reached Annapurna (26,504 feet) via the south face. We chose the difficult and dangerous British 1970 route. The weather was fine and so was the splendid international team. I was the leader of the expedition and it was my best one; almost everyone got to the summit.

Although I had already climbed ten of the 8,000-meter peaks by 1995, it really wasn't until that year that I thought about the "Crown of Himalaya" for the first time. That year I had permits for both Gasherbrum I (26,471 feet) and Gasherbrum II (26,360 feet). This was a real opportunity, with a team of very experienced climbers: Ed Viesturs, Rob Hall, Carlos Carsolio, Jacek Berbeka, and me. I wasn't looking for a new route or ambitious targets; I just wanted to be efficient. And I succeeded. First Ed and Carlos summited Gasherbrum II, and four days later I reached the summit in a solo push. After four days of rest, four of us decided to climb Gasherbrum I. We left camp after midnight and reached the Gasherbrum La (21,327 feet) at noon. The slopes were melting

so we spent a few hours cooking and preparing for the night assault. All night we followed the Japanese route, and in the morning, with splendid weather, we reached Gasherbrum I. It was the thirteenth 8,000-meter peak for Carlos Carsolio and twelfth for me. This was also one of my shortest expeditions, with only 17 days in Base Camp.

There was nothing left but to plan for 1996 and the two remaining peaks— K2 and Nanga Parbat—but easier said than done. I had already tried three times on K2: In September 1982, we were stopped at 26,600 feet on the virgin northwest ridge; in winter 1987-88 we tried again and reached only 23,950 feet; and in 1994, together with Carlos Buhler and Voytek Kurtyka, we finally surrendered at 22,300 feet on Voytek's dream "magic line." We tried again on that same trip by the Basque route on the Abruzzi Rib, and I turned back only 165 feet from the summit.

But my experience and respect for K2 was to bear some fruit in 1996. I organized two expeditions; one started at the beginning of June 1996 for K2 and the second at the beginning of July for Nanga Parbat from the Diamir Valley.

Our international K2 team had exceptionally difficult weather conditions and heavy snowfall, unusual for that time of a year. We were cut off from the rest of the world, alone and totally self-reliant. After five weeks we reached 25,750 feet, where we set up Camp IV. Finally, on August 10, Marco Bianchi, Christian Kuntner, and I forced our way through deep snow and reached the summit very late, at 8:30 p.m.

After a couple of photographs, we descended into darkness, afraid of the approaching night. We managed only just under 1,000 feet. We had no camping equipment; we simply had to survive that night. Each of us tried to find a place to shelter from the wind and falling ice. One ice screw belayed me on my platform below a serac. I knew I could not fall asleep because sleep might be eternal. It was not easy, but singing kept me alert enough to make it till dawn.

I called my friends and they all replied. Good. We decided to continue our descent. After three hours, still early in the morning, we reached the dreamed-of tents of Camp IV where our friends were awaiting us. Suddenly Marco could not move anymore; he needed a bottle of oxygen, which we didn't have! With great difficulty we took him to Camp II where some Russian friends had oxygen. Marco was saved and the next day we reached Base Camp. The 13th peak was conquered.

That day I had a talk with Poland, but the news from my country was not so good. My friends had already left Nanga Parbat—they were in Poland! No one was at Nanga Parbat; no one had climbed the mountain this season; it was already the end of August—late to begin an expedition. I said good-bye to my friends and was alone in the Chilas Inn Hotel. Then Manis the sirdar arrived. He knew I was fighting with my thoughts about this last mountain in the Crown of the Himalaya. He gave me a letter from Zawada trying to convince me to abandon the risky idea of solo climbing Nanga Parbat. Still, I was inclined rather to trust myself. Maybe that was one of those important moments that we have in life when we know, somehow, that we have to move on, regardless of challenge. There was no return.

I left for the Diamir Valley accompanied by four porters. If the weather worsened I would have a logical excuse to withdraw, but it was excellent. I took my two rucksacks full of equipment and food and left for the face. I had never been to Nanga Parbat before nor had I studied the maps of the mountain. I just knew I would follow the Kinshofer route—but where was it? Intuition and experience helped me to find the beginning of the route. In the evening I spotted an abandoned tent below a face.

I made tea and during the night began to climb to the Eagle's Nest. Vertical ice faces and a near-1,000-foot rock band led to the galleries with traces of old tents. I fixed my tent and did some cooking. I began to feel an acute pain in my jaw. It was an infection that in the last two days had developed into a large ball. After I read the pre-scription (one pill every six hours), I decided to take four at once. But the exhaustion from the previous night and the four pills were too much. For 24 hours I was in a kind of semicoma; I was on the edge of dream and reality. The following morning, however, I was okay and continued. Passing traces of past expeditions, I reached the edge of the snowfields below the summit at 23,600 feet. I noticed a rope disappearing below a serac, dug it out, and discovered an old broken tent. It provided some protection against the wind and the cold. Half-sitting, half-lying, I made warm drinks and filled my bottle. At 2:00 a.m. I was so nervous I couldn't wait any longer and I started the final push. The summit section was so huge that it practically formed another mountain itself. I kept losing my way, but all I knew was that I needed to go up. It was like a trance—I was afraid to look backward. Finally I saw the summit, which I reached quickly. I was the only person that year to climb Nanga Parbat. For the first time in my life, I felt the need to collect proof of my ascent. I took some small stones, pieces of ropes, a piton left perhaps by Austrians with the initials G. S.-1976. I still have it today.

I had to get down to share my joy; otherwise success is a sad event. I reached the Eagle's Nest, rested a little, abseiled with the help of many old ropes. Suddenly Manam appeared in front of me to welcome me with a series of reports from his Kalashnikov. He embraced me and said like a brother, "Well done." Manam informed me that he and his village watched me for four days through their telescopic lens.

In that small stone house at the foot of Nanga Parbat, far from my loved ones, by the light of a small candle I made tea. Had anything changed in my life? I knew only that I would be back in the mountains.

For more than two and a half decades, Polish mountaineer Krzysztof Wielicki formed part of the hard-core Himalayan climbing machine emanating out of Poland. His climbing partners routinely included other Himalayan legends like Wanda Rutkievicz, Jerzy Kukuczka, Aleksander Lwow, and Voytek Kurtyka. Wielicki was uncompromising in his style. He concentrated his Himalayan efforts on difficult routes, new routes, or first winter ascents. In 1997 he became the fifth person in the world to climb all fourteen 8,000-meter peaks—half of them solo and three as first winter ascents.

He was a jury member at the Banff Mountain Film Festival in 1997.

in everyone. To a great extent that's meant finding those other people who are interested in challenging and pushing themselves in the same way. It's important to be "in synch" with the other person. As an example, when you're climbing without oxygen, it's far more pragmatic to be climbing with a partner who's also going without gas, so that loads and speeds are similar. I did a number of later climbs with Rob Hall, and he was using oxygen when I wasn't. The positive aspects of climbing with him far outweighed the logistics of Rob using oxygen on an alpine-style ascent. He was a great guy, and I loved climbing with him so I was able to disregard the logistical problems and say, "I'll do whatever I can to keep this partnership going." But now I'm being more selective.

I think this insistence on finding the best partners has led to an interesting aspect of this kind of climbing—and one that probably fuels one of the frequently voiced criticisms, which is probably a misconception. The group of people who are interested in the kinds of climbing that I'm focusing on—the big peaks in small teams without oxygen—is fairly small, and that means that we have tended to climb primarily with one another. If you look at the list of my partners over the last few years—people like Wielicki, Carsolio, and Veikka Gustafsson—you'll see that most of these people have also been after the same goal. But to suggest that we've been thrown together for the sake of the goal without regard for the "partnership of the rope" that climbers are typically familiar with is nonsense. This 8,000-meter group is probably the most international and multifaceted gathering of climbers we've ever seen in the sport, but it certainly isn't haphazard, or a consolation choice; these are truly the best partners for the task at hand.

By the time I signed on for an ascent of Xixabangma in 1993, I had set the goal of climbing all the peaks in the group. This experience, even if on one of the easier of the great peaks, offered its unique lessons to the project. On this trip, I climbed with others in the team, but climbed alone on the summit day. Reaching the central summit of the peak at 26,287 feet, I saw that the connecting ridge to the main summit (several feet higher) was in very poor and dangerous condition. Again, my commitment to getting off these peaks proved to be more fundamental than taking such a risk for a minor distinction in elevation.

I think this highlights the personal nature of the project for me. I have never climbed these peaks (or any others for that matter) for anyone else, and that has greatly helped the entire journey; I've been the one setting the standards for the climbs; I'm the one who makes the decisions about what should be done, and on what schedule. I feel sure I would be able to remove one of the peaks from my list of the 8,000-ers if it didn't seem right to me or was too dangerous. Failing because of my inability or ill-preparedness is something that I couldn't be happy with—I'd have to return—but I could easily walk away from a mountain that convinced me the risks of climbing it were too high. The whole project has really just served as a carrot out there for me to strive toward; it's never been a matter of checking something off a list.

An interesting thing about the list of 8,000-meter peaks is, of course, its convenient arbitrariness. In America, where we don't use the metric system, the list demarcates those "14 peaks above 26,256 feet," and that of course sounds somewhat absurd. The convenience of the grouping is best illustrated when you consider that dropping the objective down to all peaks over 7,900 meters (25,920 feet) would mean 56 more peaks to climb—a plan impossible in most Himalayan careers.

Once I began to attempt additional peaks some practicalities of the project made it very difficult for me—as has been the case for most other people involved in a similar quest—to stay out of the public eye. When Herzog and his team first climbed Annapurna in 1950, Himalayan climbing was, of course, in its infancy and was relatively unknown. By the time Reinhold Messner completed the first "crown jewel" ascent of all the 8,000-ers 36 years later, climbing was far better known, in some ways more complex, and certainly more expensive. If there was any way that I could have pursued my goal without media attention, sponsorship, or guiding, I would have, but it just didn't seem possible. I never wrote a word personally about my climbs in the climbing press because, again, I felt it was a private matter when it came to the climbing itself. But I did need to support the project somehow, and that entailed attracting sponsors, speaking to the public, working with an Internet site, and guiding big peaks to get me into the Himalaya. I think the important thing was to ensure that I was not compromising the climbing itself; I had to be fundamentally clear with sponsors, for example, that they were sponsoring my process and they never had any influence over the practice or decisions on a climb. I have had to make some decisions that have permitted me to climb, but they have never affected the way I climb or why.

The most important thing through the subsequent climbs has been to attempt to refine the process. I look at each of the ascents as a significant learning experience—getting better at figuring out how, when, and where to go. One of the most important changes for me was the realization that pairing climbs together, using one climb as an acclimatization springboard for another, was a very helpful tactic—and one that also helped to facilitate a style of climbing that I saw as a personal improvement. Seven days after reaching the summit of Everest in 1994, for example, Rob Hall and I were able to use that acclimatization to climb Lhotse in three days. The following year, our ascent and acclimatization on Gasherbrum II allowed us to summit on G I in only 30 hours. The importance of these efforts for me has been the success I've felt in pushing myself to achieve greater results, along with the satisfaction in seeing the outcomes of continuous learning.

I have also been conscious, again, that one of the main reasons for seeing these rapid ascents as successful has been that they limit the amount of time that I'm exposing myself to objective hazards. Since I first began this project, I've gotten married and have had two children, and my returns home have become just as important as any other part of the journeys for me. If I've developed a mission statement over the course of this project, it's been "Without Oxygen, Without Incident." If others criticize me for being safety-minded, believing that climbing is supposed to be measured only by the degree of risk suffered, so be it. I feel that any climb that is done by the skin of one's teeth is not a success, and I believe that my task on this project is to figure out every time how to get up with less risk while never compromising the mountain's integrity. I have a conviction that everyone I've met who had their eyes on the same target has felt the same way, and probably has to if he or she intends to succeed. This kind of project takes an enormous amount of work and commitment; we climb these peaks because we love them, we love the places they take us, and we love the process of learning about ourselves along the way.

In just a few days, I'll be packing my bags and heading back to the Himalaya. If I succeed, Annapurna will be my thirteenth 8,000-meter peak, but that is only an incidental reason for climbing the mountain. Far more important than ticking off the penultimate summit on the list of 14 will be the experiences, lessons, challenges, and partnerships with the other climbers on the mountain that I'm sure I'm going to have again. If I don't make the summit, my disappointment will be exactly the same as the disappointment I'd feel failing on any single peak. And if I walk away without completing the 14, it won't change the power of the beauty of the expeditions that went before at all. They've all been complete adventures unto themselves. Every time I have climbed a mountain, I've gathered those experiences and memories and have made them part of me. We all do. Every mountain is a collection.

"One of the joys of climbing with Ed Viesturs is that you know you are in the presence of a superior being," said David Breashears, a powerful climber himself. Viesturs's long list of climbing achievements is evidence of this incredible high-altitude ability.

He has climbed Everest five times. Viesturs's fourth expedition to the world's highest peak was as the climbing leader of the successful 1996 Everest IMAX Expedition. And three out of five Everest ascents were achieved without supplementary oxygen. Additionally, he has summited 12 out of 14 of the world's 8,000-meter peaks (summitted central summit of Xixabangma).

Viesturs is a doctor of veterinary medicine and is the director of his own enterprise out of Seattle, Washington. He appeared as guest speaker at the Banff Mountain Film Festival in 1998.

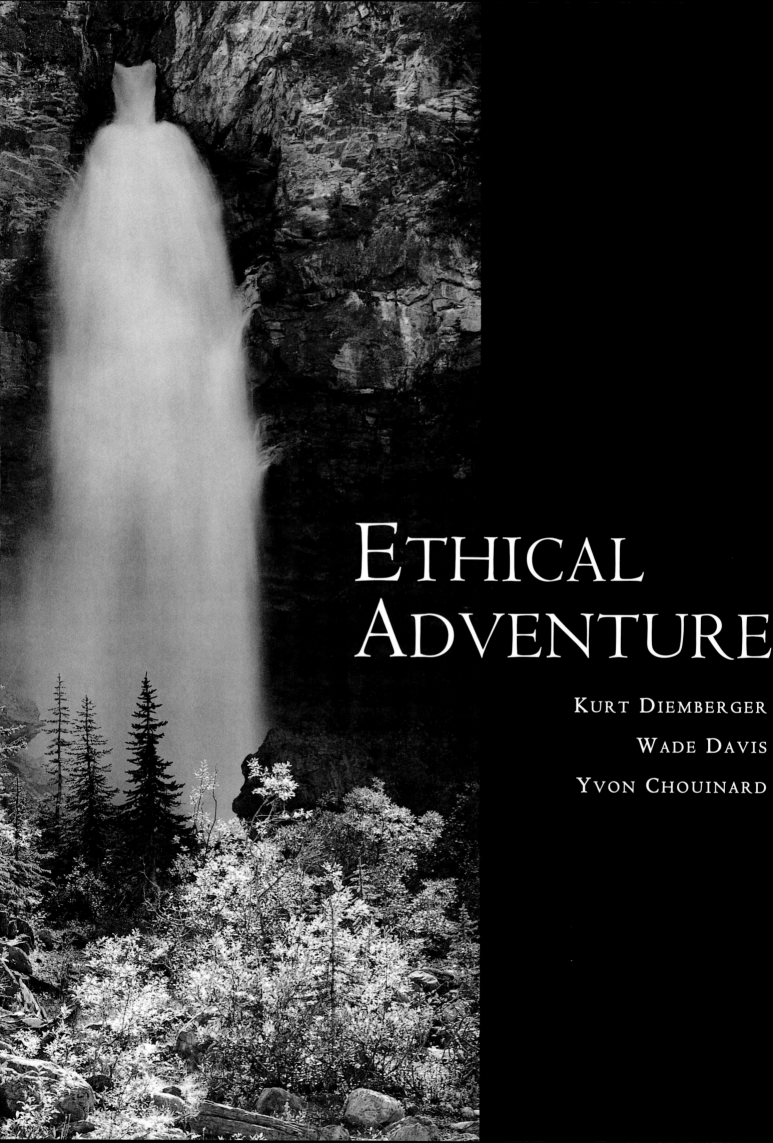

ETHICAL ADVENTURE

KURT DIEMBERGER

WADE DAVIS

YVON CHOUINARD

Into the Unknown:
A Shaksgam Odyssey

Kurt Diemberger

"**W**hat is there, behind the next corner?"

I want to know.

The everlasting quest of discovery is in our hearts from the very beginning. It forms our character and our life, and it is the root of "ethical adventure." One of the purest forms of this quest is exploration, and I'll offer my thoughts on ethical adventure through a weaving together of experiences during my journeys into the Shaksgam Wilderness, where I have been seven times so far. Was it a pilgrimage? Perhaps it was...

Standing on top of Gasherbrum II in 1979, I was spellbound by the view of an ocean of nameless peaks and by the deep furrow of a valley in front of me on the Chinese side of the Karakoram. Big glaciers and mountain desert appeared like ghostly processions of ice towers in the deep solitude. Looking down, I suddenly understood why Eric Shipton was fascinated by the Shaksgam and why Younghusband returned to this site of mystery. It was not only the thrill of discovery but also the place I was longing for, a nameless land of fulfillment. At that time, however, I had no hope of getting into the forbidden area at the southern frontier of Sinkiang, China. But now I had the wish in my heart and I would follow it.

There was also another factor in my wish: K2, a big mountain shaped like a crystal, is most beautiful from the China side, with the fantastic North Spur, never touched by man, facing the mysterious Shaksgam valley. Younghusband and Shipton were overwhelmed seeing the mountain from that side and, impressed by Shipton's description in his book *Blank on the Map*, I decided to go for the mountain from that side.

But when the Chinese authorities opened the area and allowed access to K2, the Americans were first in line. Then, the Japanese visited Beijing and brought home the permission for the first attempt from the north. During that tug of war for "the Mountain of Mountains" I was busy, too. While filming on Everest for the Italians, I found they shared my fascination for "the route of routes on the mountain of mountains"—the crystalline North Spur.

And perhaps it was destiny when my next Everest assignment involved Wang Fu Chou as our liaison officer. He was vice president of the Chinese Mountaineering Association. "Kurt," he said, "you have my promise: Climb whatever peak you choose." I had no doubts which one.

Spring 1982: A small caravan of six camels, led by two Uygur drivers riding their donkeys, accompanies Enzo De Menech (alias "Bubu") and our team through the canyons of the Surukwat River toward the heights of the Aghil Pass. The two Uygur camel drivers are real characters: one always praying, the other never, and both suspicious at first of the strangers. Within a few days, though, even the camels are part of this "family enterprise."

When the clouds open we look down into the strangest landscape we ever experienced: Wild, rugged, and still, the valley exudes a total peace that touches one's heart. The valley floor is made up of a hundred thousand round stones. Water is not visible during most of the year because it is moving underneath the pebbles or is stopped in the icy grip of the winter. But now the giant forces of the wild river have plowed the bed with a maze of curling, intertwined meanderings.

After several hours of descent through scree and boulder fields, we find a small green place—Durbin Jangal—with some bushes and a little spring where Younghusband lost his binoculars. "Durbin" is the local name for binoculars and "Jangal" is a kind of small oasis in the mountain desert. Here we run into problems. Although the two Uygurs are willing to continue our journey "downstream" toward K2, they refuse absolutely to move in the other direction: "Nobody," they say, "has ever gone there."

For a moment my dream of setting foot on the fascinating glacier I saw from the icy summit of Gasherbrum II seems to vanish. At long last the Uygurs, still refusing to move with their camels, offer us their two donkeys. And Sung, our Chinese interpreter, is willing to continue with me and Bubu, though none of us is sure how well the animals will play their role! Just two hours later, the river appears from the ground and must be forded. Pushing and pulling we finally drag the protesting animals to the other side. Not even Sung's "goodwill talks" are helpful: Uygur donkeys don't understand Chinese.

Bubu, Sung, and I move onward up the valley between nameless dolomite peaks, shining red and yellow walls. We are shivering in an icy storm and pass the night sheltered behind a rock. We are now about 13,780 feet above sea level and there is no sign of human presence; we are amid total wilderness. High on the Aghil saddle we had noticed the jagged line of white pinnacles of a glacier in the distance, perhaps 50 miles away.

In the morning, the donkeys have almost lost their voices. The bitter cold wind continues, and after hours of very slow progress our group decides to camp in a sheltered cirque and then continue without the animals. Big shields of fiber ice have grown overnight in the riverbed because the unusual wave of cold is so extreme. A transparent fog, a sort of thick haze, enwraps everything and, when hours later we finally reach the glacier, rows of tall icy figures emerge from the gray as if in a fairy tale. They make us feel like dwarfs. A magic spell emanates from them, but shrouds of freezing fog all around hide the big mountains. The fog only dissolves during the night, as we discover on returning to our sheltered cirque. A flash of an idea runs through my brain: Of course, start at night and be there at dawn! I wake up Sung, who is willing to come with me, and eventually we get a view of the ice-covered giants for a couple of minutes at first light! Almost transparent, the peaks of the enormous Gasherbrum wall seem to appear magically. Minutes after, Sung is affected by a neural circuit crisis and only sees black—a terrible situation, here at the end of the world. I manage to drag him to the river and try desperately to cure him with cold water. He can see again, but both of us remain terrified by this event.

Three days later, rounding a cliff, we have the view of views: K2 from its most superb side, as symmetrical as a huge quartz crystal. The question about how the Japanese may receive the foreign "guests" is hanging in the air; however, when leader Isao Shinkai sees our tiny group he is somewhat surprised, very polite. We then reach an elevated rocky point above the glacier, and with a big telephoto lens I can take all the important shots of the mountain for next year's ascent. Will it be a first? It is almost of no importance; this peak is so beautiful.

The Japanese were successful in a remarkable climb. Every step to the summit was new, from an unknown, unexplored side of the big mountain. Still, the Italians on our 1983 expedition will have their own go on the Mountain of Mountains—perhaps a more direct line can be formed through the final precipices below the summit. But it turns out that they have to follow the Japanese line—it is hard enough—and one of their summiteers even fell to his death. For Julie Tullis and me, the film team, it is a demanding task to capture what is happening up there on 16-mm. In a sort of adapted "alpine style" we climb with a single tunnel tent while the rest of the team follows the rigid pattern of a siege. We do it for the sake of living high—and with a small hope for the summit. I am impressed by how well the Italians work together as a team! It is a great experience.

Another human experience, only a few months ago, also comes to my mind. During my seventh visit to the Shaksgam in May 1999, the goal of which was an exploration of Hidden Peak (Gasherbrum, 26,471 feet high and still unclimbed from China), our expedition leader John Climaco, having climbed a nameless peak with another member of this Quokka.com Internet expedition, decided to dedicate that ascent to the legendary early explorer Ardito Desio, whom he believed to be dead. When I told John that he was wrong and good old Desio was still very alive in Rome at 102 years, he was overwhelmed and immediately asked the professor via satellite whether we could come to see him in Italy. When we got to Rome and entered his studio, the tough explorer was just correcting the proofs of the fourth edition of one of his geology books. He was extremely pleased about "his peak" and about a nice heavy pebble I had brought him from his Shaksgam. When we left, he waved, with a twinkle in his eyes: "See you again—perhaps in 30 years!" What a team for the beyond! I think this experience was a real ethical adventure, a link between explorers from 1929 to 1999 and even beyond.

But let us return to 1983 and our team on K2: While Julie and I are at 8,000 meters, a blizzard strikes and we are forced to retreat. Four climbers get to the top, some paying for it with frostbite but all returning alive. Julie and I have filmed seven miles of film and have taken many hours of sound on this expedition. We are "the highest film team in the world," committed to bringing others the experience of big mountains and their people. We are both working so well together; we have a complete understanding between us and, moreover, both our partners in life support us.

Still, as with any risky activity, there is the question of ethics, because nobody really has to climb mountains! If you fall to your death, besides other consequences, those who remain stay back in sorrow. On the other hand, how good a partner would you be if you were tied to Earth when you really need, and want, to go up? This is what Julie and I found: Life is a gift and you are meant to make something out of your being on Earth. Risks? You have to be careful, but nothing ventured, nothing won.

In June 1983, all the weather gods smile as our little team of three expedition members plus Julie and I enter the Gasherbrum Glacier to film, to explore, and to discover climbing possibilities on this never-attempted wall of giant peaks. We almost make it to the farthest of them, Broad Peak. We can see a possible route on that mountain, but the lower section cannot be seen. It probably rises out of a hidden valley that we burn with desire to enter, less for the route itself than for the wish of all explorers: to find what is behind the next corner. We lack just a day, but we must turn around. We promise to come back another year.

We return to K2 in 1984, this time from the Pakistan side, but we cannot forget the Shaksgam. Can we reach it? We are tempted to climb down into our valley as we stand on the snows of Windy Gap, but we have too much film work waiting for us on K2. Then the big mountain vanishes in storm clouds and our expedition goes home. Julie and I stay behind and see our Shaksgam again, this time from the top of Broad Peak. When will our Shaksgam journey come true? But there are two dreams in our hearts—the valley and K2—and we are under the spell of the big mountain. The winner was K2.

Two years later, on August 4, 1986, Julie and I hug on the top of the mountain that means so much to us. We are happier than words could ever tell. But during the descent, a blizzard imprisons us on the shoulder of the Abruzzi. K2 keeps Julie and four others. Forever.

After Julie's death I wanted to return to our world of discovery and go on with what we started. In June 1983, we had been only one day short of the hidden valley at the base of Broad Peak, which nobody had ever entered. We promised to come back, explore it, and perhaps discover the access to a route up the unclimbed East Face of Broad Peak. But the main lure was to enter the hidden place, that dream I carried with me all the time. Finally, there seemed to be a chance: Agostino Da Polenza—together with that remarkable Ardito Desio, then over 90 years old—set up a scientific expedition. An opportunity to film them gave me a chance to return to my Shaksgam in autumn 1988.

Every night the stars of Orion flicker just above the upper valley—my good-luck sign! I already understand that without climbing companions this time there is no way to enter the hidden valley below Broad Peak. So, does Orion tell me the right direction? Having finished the main job of filming the Italian scientists at work, I waste no time and leave with two Hunzas to try to reach the forbidding glacier world of the upper valley.

I remember an old book by Filippo de Filippi that Julie and I had studied in Paris. This explorer had discovered the beginning of the Shaksgam, but he had failed to enter the valley. Another explorer, Kenneth Mason, later successfully entered the upper valley with a small team but got halted in his exploration by a huge glacier with thousands of ice towers.

In 1983, we had discovered an old campsite of Desio's. Now I am going to follow in the explorer's footsteps of 1929. Struggling three days to find a passage through the fabulous ice towers of the Singhie glacier with my Hunzas, we finally have to give up when the "difficult glacier" (called so by Desio's Balti porters in 1929) honors its name. We retreat, fording the icy river during the first snowfalls of the near winter, then return over the Aghil Pass using our camels as snowplows. But the future is open; the ever changing moods of the moving ice will continue.

The hidden valley below Broad Peak was entered for the first time in autumn 1991, after I had revealed the long-cherished dream to Jordi Magriña and Oscar Cadiach from Catalunia. We explored the un-climbed East Face of the mountain up to about 21,300 feet in 1991, and in the spring of 1992, four of us reached the summit. On that trip I explored a nameless saddle, trying to find a traverse from the Northern Gasherbrum glacier to K2. Julie and I had hoped to see such a passage during the great summer of 1983. When this dream came true for me and two companions in another trip to the area in 1994, it

turned out to be pure alpine style for three weeks. All went well, but I started to feel the weight of a really heavy pack. After this enterprise I thought that a Sherpa might be good for the future. Friends at home said, "The globe is known now! At your age, you might look at any place comfortably via the Internet. Why go for the unknown?" Thinking of my beloved Shaksgam, I protested loudly. I was to go again.

In the spring of 1999, I was back in the Shaksgam. On May 13, 1999, Greg Child, Paula Quenemoen, and I stood on top of the same hill where, 70 years earlier, Ardito Desio and Ugo Balestreri erected their cairn. At our feet were still some black slates of the old explorers' cairn. We built them into a new one, full of wishful thinking, looking beyond the huge glacier with its shimmering forest of pinnacles. There, somewhere behind the pinnacles, was the end of the valley and the glacier world of the Karakoram Pass. Unfortunately we had almost run out of food and had to start down the valley the next day. But there is always another tomorrow.

How ethical is an adventure if you move within or between different ethics? Some years after my first trip into the Shaksgam, Russian mountaineers wanted to fly tourist groups beyond every difficulty into the heart of the mountain desert by helicopter. Would that be an ethical adventure? "Mountain Wilderness International" screamed and managed to forbid the sacrilege via the Chinese authorities. I think this action was right; it would have been bad to remove the "barrier of fatigue"—the only real protection of far, wild places.

Some might ask: Why should people drown in the Shaksgam River just to get to their beloved mountains? And the Uygurs might well protest that in their own country foreign helicopters are simply robbing them of their camel caravans' work! So, who is right? Which adventure is the "ethical" one? I would not want to be the judge, even if I am personally glad that the Shaksgam has no helicopter traffic so far. One thing is clear: Ethics can be very different for different people. Do we really have the right to place our ethics higher than the local people's ethics? How ethical is any experience in a place like the Shaksgam wilderness when the camels rip the leaves from the few bushes in the jangals? Ethics then come down to something as simple as the number of visitors, the number of camels carrying hay, and the length of stay in a jangal.

Ethics can be a moving, complicated floor: In the Durbin Jangal oasis in 1992 a hard discussion about garbage took place on return from our Broad Peak East Face expedition. The Uygur camel drivers had emptied the drums holding waste somewhere on the way. The drivers stuck to their opinion that we were abusing camel energy for nothing—carrying waste when we could simply dump it. The interpreter (a student) and I tried to explain to them the importance of clean countryside for future visitors, but the liaison officer insisted that the whole discussion was superfluous. Finally the Uygurs returned to pick up the waste, but then they buried the garbage in a hole in the ground, not—as we intended—in the military station dump a week later. So much for clean mountaineering ethics; we still have a long way to go.

Very rarely are the facts simple: If someone disregards obvious danger (for instance, acute avalanche danger) and goes into an adventure counting on eventually being rescued by others, his undertaking is clearly unethical—even more so if the rescuers might die. But there are ways in which this issue of hazard and risk can be more complicated: Is it, for example, unethical to climb with oxygen? Some say it is, and some others say it should be a personal freedom to decide style. One should certainly keep an eye on how pure the style of an ascent is, but perhaps also on the death-rate statistics for mountaineers with or without oxygen.

The most "ethical" path is rarely clear. Once I became an involuntary witness to a horrible custom: hunting eagles or other birds of prey with a net in the jangals. This is an adventure (or business) for some locals and seems to hurt nobody's feelings; hunting with the help of falcons is even known to the Westerner. Yet many cliffs in Germany are closed to climbers because of the falcons or rare plants on these rocks. There, climbing adventure is earmarked as illegal. Only in a few areas have the climbers reached a sensible compromise with the authorities, leaving the falcons, the plants, and the climbers their place. I think a certain breed of humans does need the rocks as much as the birds do, and that breed should have its rights!

There are places that are simply white patches on photos from space—still "blanks on the maps," luckily left for us. There are more "blanks" of all kinds, and not even today's scientists, using satellites to search for the unknown will be able to get into all of them. While measuring K2 with GPS in 1986, an expedition arrived at the conclusion that the mountain was higher than Everest—a result that saw two welcome "checking expeditions" created for me and my companions. Enigmas will always be with us. On a reconnaissance near the Mustagh Pass with geologists, we found beautiful fossils of an ancient ocean. The scientists had to confess: "We are not sure whether we are standing here in the Karakoram or rather in a part of the Pamirs, which has slid over to this place." The truth is elusive, even for those with the most modern equipment.

The view of K2 from the Shaksgam near Tek-Ri provided an overwhelming first view for Younghusband and for all those who came after him. This view reminded me of the unattainable that always remains and of the dreams that always live, making you go to succeed or fail.

My thoughts wander onward to ever white, uncrossed saddles and never entered cwms in this wild place that I am longing to reach. Will I succeed? I simply have to try: No airplane or satellite can ever give me that answer.

After more than 22 expeditions to the high peaks of inner Asia, Kurt Diemberger is the only person alive to have made first ascents of two 8,000-meter peaks: Broad Peak and Dhaulagiri. He has climbed Makalu, Everest, Gasherbrum II, and 27 years after his first ascent, he again reached the summit of Broad Peak. After filming expeditions to K2, Everest, and Nanga Parbat, Diemberger reached the summit of K2 with Julie Tullis in 1986.

With nineteen films and three books to his credit, Diemberger has received many awards for his creativity, including a shared Emmy for his camera work on the East Face of Everest. He has been a speaker and jury member several times in Banff.

ADVENTURE OF THE SPIRIT

WADE DAVIS

Some years ago I walked with several friends across the Cordillera Vilcabamba, the rugged knot of mountains in southern Peru that separates the Río Urubamba from the Río Apurimac, the river known to the Inca as the Lord Oracle. Our goal was to descend the Apurimac, headwaters of the Amazon, and conduct a botanical survey in a valley that changes by the day, an ecological transition that in but a week of river travel carries one from parched intermontane desert to lush tropical rain forest. As our mules, laden with white-water rafts and gear, worked their way slowly along the ancient trails, we had a chance to explore this last redoubt of the Inca, a landscape of holy shrines and lost dreams where Tupac Amarú waged war, and the spirit of the sun still ruled for 50 years after the Spanish conquest.

Late one afternoon, as we made camp in a high meadow just below the ice of a ridge we intended to scale in the morning, I noticed a tiny dark figure far below in the valley. Throughout the evening I watched with growing curiosity as this solitary individual slowly made his way up a route that had taken us much of the day to ascend. Darkness fell and I thought little more of the person, until I woke with the dawn to find an old man sitting quietly in the lee of a boulder, a bundle at his feet. He wore wool, homespun knee britches, knitted cap and poncho, and rubber sandals. His clothing was threadbare, and his face was weathered and deeply lined. A quid of coca bulged from his cheek.

My climbing companion came out of his tent to find me in gentle negotiation. Having spotted us on the mountain, the Quechua farmer had climbed several thousand feet for a chance to sell a few potatoes. My friend thought this highly eccentric, indeed comical, and with some glee later reported the encounter to the others in our party. In doing so, he totally missed the point. What was for us a wild landscape, a mountainous wilderness unknown and open to challenge, was for the old man a neighborhood, albeit an unusual one where condor outnumbered people, but a neighborhood nevertheless. He had strolled up that slope without thought or hesitation. We, with our nylon tents, redundant equipment, and impossibly heavy boots, were the ones less touched by the spirit of the place.

As travelers we are all prone to mistakes, misinterpretations of culture and behavior that are for the most part understandable and indeed benign. I once met a young Aymara woman on her way to market in a small Bolivian village. She had a basket full of eggs, and I offered to buy them all, hoping both to fill my belly and relieve her of a burden. A good deal for each of us, one would think. When she refused to sell more than half, it took some time for my dense brain to grasp the reason. If she had peddled them all, she would have had nothing left to sell in the market, and thus no reason to go to the town square. But going to market was the social event of the week, and to miss out in order to make a quick sale to a strange foreigner would not do. This, of course, helps explain why in Andean villages one often sees older women, in particular, seated stoically on the ground with only a handful of tubers or fruit, often in miserable condition, neatly piled before them on beautiful fabrics woven from wool. You cannot imagine who would buy such produce. But at least they have something to sell and a reason to be socially engaged.

Ethical adventure to my mind implies taking the time to learn enough about the lands through which we travel to ensure that the cultural blunders that we will inevitably commit do as little harm as possible—a Hippocratic oath, if you will, for the ignorant, and that generally means all of us, at least some of the time. Indeed, as a cultural anthropologist I believe quite strongly that anyone who seeks a direct experience of the other has an ethical obligation to be informed, a task made easy and wondrous by the vast amount of accessible information, readily available in the popular and academic literature.

Traveling along the spine of the Andean Cordillera, past the remnants of Peru's pre-Columbian temples and immense storehouses that once fed armies in their thousands, through valleys transformed by terraces, and past narrow tracks of cobblestones—all that remains of the 10,000 miles of roads that once bound the empire—it is difficult to imagine how so much could have been accomplished in less than a century. The Inca Empire stretched more than 3,000 miles, the largest ever forged on the American continent. Within its boundaries lived nearly all the people of the known world. There was no hunger. All matter was perceived as divine, the Earth itself the womb of creation.

When the Spanish first saw the monuments of the Inca, they could not believe them to be the work of men. Nothing created in the history of the Old World could compare. The Church declared the stonework, in particular, to be the product of demons, an assertion no more fantastic than many more recent attempts to explain the enigma of Inca masonry. A slew of popular writers have argued for an extraterrestrial origin, a suggestion not only silly but demeaning, implying as it does that the ancestors of the highland Indians were incapable of executing what was in fact their greatest technical achievement. Clearly, there was no magic technique. They needed only time, immense levies of workers, and an attitude toward stone that most Westerners find impossible to comprehend.

For the Runakuna, the people of the Andes, matter is fluid. Bones are not death but life crystallized, and thus they are potent sources of energy, like a stone charged by lightning or a plant brought into being by the sun. Water is vapor, a miasma of disease and mystery, but in its purest state it is ice, the shape of snowfields on the flanks of mountains, the glaciers that are the highest and most sacred destination of the pilgrims. When an Inca mason placed his hands upon rock, he did not feel cold granite; he sensed life, the power and resonance of the Earth within the stone. Its transformation into a perfect ashlar, or a block of polygonal masonry, was service to the Inca, and thus a gesture to the gods, and for such a task, time had no meaning. This attitude, once harnessed by an imperial system capable of recruiting thousands of workers, made almost anything possible.

If stones were dynamic, it was only because they were part of the land, of Pachamama. For the people of the Andes, the Earth is alive, and every wrinkle on the landscape, every hill and outcrop, each mountain and stream has a name and is imbued with ritual significance. The high peaks are addressed as Apu, meaning "Lord." Together the mountains are known as the Tayakuna, the Fathers, and some are so powerful that it can be dangerous even to look at them. Other sacred places, a cave or mountain pass, a waterfall where the rushing water speaks as an oracle, are honored as the Tirakuna. These are not spirits dwelling within landmarks. Rather the reverence is for the actual place itself.

A mountain is an ancestor, a protective being, and all those living within the shadow of a high peak share in its benevolence or wrath. The rivers are the open veins of the Earth, the Milky Way their heavenly counterpart. Rainbows are double-headed serpents that emerge from hallowed springs, arch across the sky, and bury themselves again in the Earth. Shooting stars are bolts of silver. Behind them lie all the heavens, including the dark patches of cosmic dust, the negative constellations that to the highland Indians are as meaningful as the clusters of stars forming animals in the sky. Lightning is concentrated light in its purest form. Places struck by lightning receive offerings of coca and are never forgotten; objects that have been hit become imbued with regenerative power. A person killed by lightning is buried on the spot and instantly becomes a Tirakuna. One who survives a lightning strike receives the gift of divination, the ability to read the future in the pattern of coca leaves tossed to the ground.

These notions of the sanctity of land were ancient in the Andes. Though the Spanish did everything in their power to crush the spirit of the people, they came in time to realize the impossibility of the task. Their priests could destroy the temples, tear asunder the sanctuaries, violate the offerings to the sun. But it was not a shrine that the Indians worshiped; it was the land itself, the rivers and waterfalls, the rocky outcrops and mountain peaks, the rainbows and stars. Every time a priest planted a cross on top of an ancient site, he merely confirmed in the eyes of the people the inherent sacredness of the place. In the wake of the conquest, when the last of the temples lay in ruins, the Earth endured, the one religious icon that even the Spanish could not destroy.

Mist sweeps over the ruins of the Inca sanctuary of Machu Picchu, Peru. Believed to be built around 1500, the site was never discovered by the Spanish Conquistadores.

Against such a backdrop, such a history of reverence, we move as travelers in the Andes. As climbers we have a special obligation, for the very achievement of our goals implies a violation of something sacred that for the Runakuna lies at the confluence of landscape and memory. A mountaineer who is intent on the summit of Salcantay or Ausangate must ask himself: Are these mountains truly sacred? Are they indeed Apus, powerful spirits that can direct the destiny of the living? If the answer is yes, why do we insist on treading upon their forbidden slopes? If the answer is no, or if we merely indulge the Andean convictions as something quaint but ultimately unimportant, irrelevant to our quest, then are we really, in essence, any different from the Spanish conquerors, who in many cases admired openly that which they were compelled to destroy?

In the early 1970s I lived for a time among the peoples of the Sierra Nevada de Santa Marta, the Ika and Kogi, descendants of the ancient Tairona civilization that flourished on the Caribbean plain of Colombia for five hundred years before the arrival of Europeans. Since the time of Columbus, who met them on his third voyage, these Indians have resisted invaders by retreating higher and higher into the inaccessible reaches of the Sierra Nevada, at 19,029 feet the highest coastal mountain range on Earth. On a bloodstained continent, they alone have never been conquered. Ruled to this day by a ritual priesthood, they consider themselves the Elder Brothers. We, who to their minds have ruined much of the world, are deemed the Younger Brothers.

In the settlement of Donachuí, on a river of the same name that drains the southern side of the mountains, I came upon an example of cultural insensitivity so egregious that the people had decided never again to allow the Younger Brothers into the upper reaches of their valley. A team of Japanese climbers, intent on reaching the summits of Bolívar and Colón, the two highest peaks, had passed through the village en route to the high snowfields. Seeking shelter, they had occupied a religious temple. For fuel they broke into pieces one of its doors. A nearby house, which they took to be abandoned, was used as a latrine. After two days they moved on, leaving in their wake a stunned community, reinforced in its conviction that all outsiders were barbarians.

> Anyone who seeks a direct experience of
> the other has an ethical obligation to be informed.

them all, "Why, oh why could not one of us Britishers have shared their fate."

Of Mallory's spiritual sense of the mountain itself, and the sincerity of his reverent intent, there can be no doubt. When the reconnaissance expedition of 1921 reached Shegar, the British were welcomed by Buddhist monks who had never seen a European. At the foot of the mountain monastery, on the road that linked Shegar to Tingri, the climbers met a prostrating pilgrim, a Mongolian 11 months out of Lhasa, moving toward Kathmandu one body length at a time. For the young Englishmen, fresh from the horrors of Flanders, it must have been a stunning affirmation of religious purpose.

They were totally unprepared for the extremes of altitude and weather, the cruel face of Everest in the springtime. Pathetically underdressed, they wore simple wool vests, flannel shirts, Shackleton smocks, gabardine knickers, soft elastic cashmere puttees, and—perhaps as headgear—fur-lined leather motorcycle helmets. They knew nothing of the death zone, the elevation above which oxygen deprivation reduces any climb to a pure and horrendous act of will. They had no idea that the peak of the mountain lay in the jet stream, where winds of 150 miles per hour drive ice crystals in dark plumes off the summit. They had oxygen to breathe but disdained its use, having no faith in a primitive apparatus that kept breaking down in the cold. At 27,000 feet, they read Shakespeare in the snow, in flimsy tents better suited for the mud and trenches of France.

Yet despite insurmountable odds, they came within hours of achieving the summit, guided one can only imagine by some inner compass of devotion to the task. George Mallory first saw Everest from the north as he climbed the Rongbuk glacier, having paid homage to the lama of the legendary Rongbuk monastery, a simple monk who found the passions of the English somewhat difficult to understand. "I was filled with great compassion," the lama later reflected, "that they underwent such suffering in unnecessary work."

But for Mallory and his comrades, all inured to death, the mountain was an exalted radiance, immanent, vast, incalculable. He described his first sighting: "We had mounted perhaps a thousand feet when we stopped to wait for what we had come to see. As the clouds rolled asunder before the heights, gradually, very gradually, we saw the great mountainsides and glaciers and ridges, now one fragment, now another, through the floating rifts, until, far higher in the sky than imagination dared to suggest, a prodigious white fang—an excrescence from the jaw of the world—the summit of Everest, appeared."

Though the lama was puzzled as to why one would tread upon sacred ground and disturb the spirit of the mountain, the British, in fact, approached the peak with a reverence that even Tibetans might find difficult to match. To placate the monks, Mallory and Howard-Bury, leader of the 1921 effort, described their expedition as a group of mountain worshipers embarked on a pilgrimage. Cryptic as they intended the message to be, it, in fact, perfectly encapsulated who they were, climbers willing to sacrifice all to reach the summit of the unknown. The word "sacrifice" means to make sacred, and when Mallory in his famous retort explained that the reason for climbing Everest was nothing more than the fact that it was there, he distilled the perfect notion of emptiness and pure purpose.

For Mallory the freedom of the heights always implied a deeper perception, the embrace of some mysterious and ultimate reality, rarely spoken about but never forgotten. Reflecting on his first ascent of Mont Blanc, he wrote: "Have we vanquished an enemy? None but ourselves. Have we gained success? That word means nothing here. Have we won a kingdom? No.... and yes. We have achieved an ultimate satisfaction...To struggle and to understand—never this last without the other; such is the law."

The quest of the righteous mountaineer is indeed as pure and inspired as that of any spiritual seeker, a sublime goal that ought never be denied. Mallory knew this as did Somervell, and indeed Noel Odell, the one witness, a brilliant climber who never doubted that they had reached the top of Mount Everest. Nor did he question the noble purpose that had taken them all hundreds of miles on foot from India and across Tibet just to reach the base of the mountain. Odell wrote of Mallory: "My final glimpse of one, whose personality was of that charming character that endeared him to all and whose natural gifts seemed to indicate such possibilities of both mind and body, was that he was 'going strong,' sharing with that other fine character who accompanied him such a vision of sublimity that it has been the lot of few mortals to behold; nay, few while beholding have become merged into such a scene of transcendence."

For the better part of a century Mallory would be lost to history, a mythical figure, the symbol of a nation's redemption, but in 1999 his alabaster corpse was found, face down, clinging to the side of the mountain. Eighty years before, in an ecstatic moment, Lytton Strachey had famously compared George Mallory's body to a sculpture carved by Praxiteles. In death he indeed made manifest the permanence of an Elgin marble, his face buried in ice and rock, his narrow waist sealed into the mountain.

The climbers who found him exhausted themselves in reverence and spent five hours at 26,700 feet prying sufficient rocks from the frozen ground to allow for, as the family had requested, a proper Christian burial. Conrad Anker, whose intuition and insight were responsible for the discovery, turned his back on the rough tomb and climbed for the summit, overcoming the notorious second step, and slowly made his way toward the peak. Close to his goal he paused, and in the impossibly thin air remembered the Buddhist admonition never to tread upon the top of a mountain. So he didn't. Reaching eye level with the summit of a mountain he had dreamed of climbing since childhood, he reached out his hand and gently tapped the top of the world. Then he came back down. Here was an act of ethical adventure.

Canadian ethnobotanist Wade Davis is the author of The Serpent and the Rainbow, *an international best-seller, which appeared in ten languages and was later released by Universal as a motion picture. He has written numerous anthropological books, including* One River *(1996) and* The Clouded Leopard *(1998), describing Davis's journeys from the rain forests of Borneo to the mountains of Tibet.*

A native of British Columbia, Davis has worked as a park ranger, forestry engineer, logger, and big-game hunting guide, and he has conducted ethnographic fieldwork among several indigenous societies of northern Canada. He has appeared at the Banff Mountain Film Festival and is on the Board of Governors for The Banff Centre. Throughout all of his travels in some of the most obscure places in the world, one thing remains constant with Wade Davis: He is truly passionate about cultural diversity. That basic premise underlies the way he travels, what he studies, how he thinks, and what he writes.

CLIMBER'S BILL OF RIGHTS

YVON CHOUINARD

Ethics concern values, morals, and the principles of right and wrong—not only the rules of conduct among ourselves. They also dictate how we treat the Earth for, after all, we are inseparable from Nature.

I believe that for climbing, there are some elements of style that help to define the rules of the game. I like to think we are free to do anything we want as long as we don't negatively impact our fellow humans and the Earth we live on. When I was learning to climb in the fifties, most climbing ethics had been established by the Western Europeans, who were out to bloody well conquer the mountains. In the Alps, pitons, slings, and iron railings were left in place to guide and aid others to follow. It was thought that a virgin rock wall was improved by the heavy hand and hammer of man.

The same Manifest Destiny principles had guided the pioneers in developing the New World. When Herzog and Lachenal stood at the top of Annapurna in 1950, the tricolor wasn't the only flag unfurled at the summit; for the first time in climbing history, a corporate flag—the Michelin Tire Company's—also dominated the peak.

But in America, our small group of climbers in Yosemite were following a different path. We were very influenced by the philosophies of John Muir, who advocated going into the wilderness but leaving no trace of having been there. We made our pitons of hard steel so they could repeatedly be used and removed. We considered it aid, or artificial climbing, if you rested or pulled up on a piton or sling.

We thought we had superior ethics until the early seventies, when there got to be so many of us placing and taking out pitons that the rock became scarred. You could look at this as unintentional hold-chipping, for these very piton holes and scars have made it possible to free climb some of the routes on El Capitan, but this impact on the rock encouraged a few of us to switch over to the runners and chock protection system of the British. It wasn't a universally quick conversion, however, because the average climber, accustomed to pounding in a 6-inch iron spike to the hilt with a 20-ounce hammer, wasn't easily persuaded to trust his life to a little piece of aluminum fingered into a crack.

I've found that in politics, business, and life in general, few people will choose to do the right thing unless it's to their advantage. The use of natural protection did not become popular until it was proved that you could climb more quickly, efficiently, and safely with chocks and cam devices. In Yosemite, it took some hammerless ascents of Half Dome and El Capitan to prove that almost every climb could be done "clean" and safely.

Soon after, with the same ethic in mind, some climbers attempted to de-piton routes in the Alps, like the Walker Spur, but democracy wouldn't allow it. The lowest common denominator prevailed, and within weeks they were pegged up again.

In the golden age of Yosemite climbing, when there were lots of virgin walls, we used to attempt a new big wall by first trying to correctly assess the difficulty and estimate the number of days required for the route. Based upon that, we would take just enough gear, food, and water to barely make it to the top. We took great pride in leading an artificial pitch and getting to the top with just enough pitons or chocks to set up a safe belay—and not one piece extra.

By contrast, the last time I climbed El Capitan I was with a couple of new-style big wall climbers. We took along a full rack of chocks, a full rack of pitons and bashies and hooks, a boom box, portaledges, and 150 carabiners to string it all together. It was not an experience I want to repeat. But that is pretty much the state of climbing protection ethics these days—around the world. There are chocks, pitons, bolts; we have it all and we use it all. There are routes in the Dolomites, done in the 1920s and earlier, that now have bolts placed every 10 or 12 feet—bolts drilled right next to perfectly good cracks.

The interesting question is whether we're talking about style or ethics here. I say it's pretty simple. Ethics are so you don't screw it up for the next guy, and style is so you don't delude yourself into thinking you're so hot. Here's all you need to know about climbing ethics:

The Climber's Bill of Rights—You have the right to climb anywhere, in any style you want, as long as you don't alter the medium or infringe on the next person's experience.

It's simple: If you use chalk, place a bolt, chip holds, leave fixed "pro," or dump your oxygen bottles and garbage on El Capitan Tower—it's all bad ethics. What's wrong with using chalk, you ask? Let's say someone goes and paints the words RIGHT and LEFT on every handhold of your favorite climb. I don't know about you, but I don't like to climb by numbers. When I do a

climb where all the handholds are marked in white chalk and the protection is all in place, I feel cheated.

The argument that some people sweat more than others has some validity. When I used to do big-wall climbs with Chuck Pratt, our hands would get black from the aluminum oxide of the carabiners—except for my palms, which were pink from the constant nervous sweat. It used to bug me that Chuck's palms stayed dry and black, until I rationalized that maybe he would suffer from Alzheimer's disease before I will. I think these days you can get an operation to take care of those pesky sweat glands anyway. Chalk isn't permanent you say? That's true; it washes off—but then it's simply replaced by the next group of climbers. And under overhangs it is permanent.

I don't care if Everest is climbed by an expedition of a hundred Rotary Club members all sucking O's from a hookah connected to a giant oxygen tank at Base Camp—as long as the mountain is not altered, and the style of the climb doesn't mar the other climbers' experience on the mountain. That means this: no leaving 30 ladders in place, no 10,000 feet of fixed ropes, no helicopters buzzing, no garbage everywhere. That's bad ethics and bad style.

The word "adventure"—like gourmet, sustainable, extreme, and quality—has become so overused and the meaning so diluted—that it is almost meaningless. According to Webster's, adventure has to contain the element of risk. Even a financial "venture" has—by definition—an element of risk.

I once had an argument with someone in the pages of *Outside* magazine. She maintained that family car camping was a great adventure for her because her family members were not serious outdoor people. I claim that adventure is not subjective. An activity either has a clear risk to life and limb—or it is not adventure. Like "sustainable development" and "gourmet hamburgers," "adventure travel" is an oxymoron. The only economic activity I can think of as being even remotely sustainable is organic agriculture.

When you sign up for an "adventure travel" trip, white-water rafting, and most guided climbs, the sales material guarantees there will be very little risk; therefore, the chances of having an adventure are slim. I've found that I had my greatest adventures when there was a problem. The goal of doing risky sports is to learn, to train, to get better at your craft so you can live life on the edge—because that is when your mind and body are most alive. But you never go over that edge, because then you're dead. This is a great lesson for life and society. Know your limits and live within your means.

Western man initially tends to measure his wealth by how much money or how many things he has accumulated. Then, as he reaches a certain age, he starts to define that measurement by how much free time he has left. This changes the way he approaches his adventures—and his life. Forget about the process, or Zen, of activities such as mountain climbing or fly-fishing; the process takes too much time. The Western man doesn't want to learn how to climb; he wants to get to the top. He doesn't want to learn all about the secret lives of aquatic creatures; he wants to catch fish.

Mountain guides, fishing guides, hunting guides, river guides—these occupations exist to help the client hit the bull's-eye without having to spend a lifetime in refining the skills of a chosen craft. Don't get me wrong. I've fished with guides; I've done some mountain guiding myself. But the best guides recognize their true role as teachers, not manservants.

Climbing or fishing or running a river with a guide can be a great educational experience, or it can be as brain-numbing as watching television. When you're watching television a certain part of your brain shuts down: the creative part, the part that imagines, the part that keeps you alert and alive. When you are being guided up

Yvon Chouinard ascends with jumars on Moose's Tooth, Alaska in 1972.

Everest, a similar thing happens. You aren't using your brain to route-find; you aren't looking for possible escape routes. And if your guide should become incapacitated, you would not know how to get down because you do not know how you got up there. Have you ever noticed that you can be driven several times to a place but, until you actually have to drive there yourself, you're lost? So learn from the teachers but, at some point, lose them.

The purpose of risking your neck in an adventure is to attain some sort of spiritual and personal growth. This will not happen if you are so fixated on the goal that you compromise the process away. You achieve out of any endeavor just what you put into it. If you want real adventure you have to leave open the opportunity for foul-ups. Leave the "Ten Essentials" at home; don't research and plan the endeavor to death.

About 20 years ago, or maybe it was 30, I went on an expedition to the Karakoram where we had the typical conga line of surly porters, bad weather, and personal conflicts. We climbed a few minor peaks. When it was time to leave, three of us decided to cut loose from the expedition and go out a different way, over some high passes near Masherbrum. As soon as we left camp it was like a breath of fresh air. For a week, we were completely on our own in unknown country. We fell in multiple crevasses, got lost, ran out of food, and had the time of our lives. It's the only part of the whole expedition that I can still vividly remember.

Although style is mostly defined in degrees, we need to establish an absolute cornerstone. Let's call it perfect style. In climbing, perfect style is a naked human soloing a new route on sight. Anything other than that is of lesser stylistic value:

~ I don't care if Everest is climbed

by an expedition of a hundred Rotary Club members

all sucking O's from a hookah connected to a giant

oxygen tank at Base Camp—as long as the mountain is

not altered, and the style of climb doesn't mar the

other climbers' experience on the mountain.

If you put on shoes—you get docked one point; extra sticky rubber—two points; previewing or reading a topo—another point; placing one piece of pro—another point; and so on ad infinitum. The farther you get away from Perfect Style, the less proud you should be of yourself.

As a sport matures it doesn't necessarily get better. Look at alpine skiing. In the 1936 Olympics, competitors' skis were painted to make sure the same pair was used in both the slalom and the downhill. Now the winner, riding some computer-refined pair of discipline-specific skis, has to be determined by an electronic timer, accurate to the millisecond.

Specialists are taking the soul out of sport. It's a great thing to run a marathon. You train a bit, maybe change your diet, give up smoking, and you knock it off in three hours. If you want to do it in two-plus hours, that's another story. You have to kiss off sex, your job, your friends, all the "nonessentials," and devote your entire life to the effort.

I say the last 10 percent of the way to perfection takes so much of your life that it isn't worth the effort. This overzealous attitude is what creates religious fanatics, body Nazis, and athletes who are exceedingly dull to converse with—unless you want to talk about their particular specialty or their bodies.

Specialization, when indulged in by true geniuses like Mozart, Babe Ruth, or Muhammed Ali, can create great art, which elevates mankind above the lowly beasts. But you and I can evolve more quickly by putting that energy into more than one direction.

As modern society goes lemming-like into virtual reality, there will always be a few contrarians with different priorities. The John Muirs, Walter Bonattis, Reinhold Messners, and Göran Kröpps are there to show us that we don't have to embrace all these phony extreme sport games. We don't have to destroy our sport, and the Earth, with more and more technology.

It's perhaps unrealistic to think we can go back to what climbing or skiing was like in the thirties or fifties, but we do need to constantly change the rules of the game to keep the sport evolving. When basketball players are all seven feet tall, raise the height of the basket. When the thrill is gone from alpine skiing, free up the heels and reinvent the telemark turn. Any activity, whether sport, business, or love, needs constant change, even revolution, to keep it from degenerating.

Western man, in his rush to blindly embrace all new technology, is missing a crucial stage in his development. We went from breath-hold free diving to the Aqua-Lung—missing the realization that learning to biofeedback your body until you can dive 60 feet and hold your breath four minutes is an evolution, both spiritually and physically.

The great climbs and adventures of our times were done in a style that rejected some of the technological paradigm. Kröpp's bicycle trip to Everest used high-tech gear but rejected the consumption of jet fuel, bottled oxygen, guides, and Sherpas. I just wish he would have left that cell phone at home. When Ed Gillette kayaked from California to Hawaii, he specifically requested that no rescue effort be mounted should he not reach his destination on time. He believed that to act otherwise was irresponsible on his part.

Guiding serves a useful purpose to society in that it introduces new people to the natural world—people who will then be more likely to become advocates for environmental protection. On the other hand, the negative result of guiding can be illustrated by the fact that, on any given summer day, there can be over a hundred people on the top of the Grand Teton, and about 80 percent of them were guided. It can take two or three years to be lucky enough to get a permit to float the Colorado River through the Grand Canyon, because the majority of the permits are reserved for guided motorized rafts.

All wilderness activities bring up interesting and complex ethical questions. Is it ethical, for example, for river guides in Tasmania to be lobbying for a road to be cut into the Franklin River wilderness so they can do one-day commercial trips? Should our national parks be open in the winter to snowmobilers because they vote and pay taxes, too?

Ecotourism—another oxymoron—can give indigenous people an economic motive to protect their wilderness, but it can also speed up the erosion of their culture and their natural resources. Already, one of every five people on Earth is hooked on *Baywatch*. Let's not be in such a rush to convert the rest of the world to our lifestyle of consumption.

Adventure capitalism, corporate sponsorships, eco-challenges, and the whole commercialization of outdoor sport can give the online adventurers and armchair mountaineers pleasure. But this movement also involves tobacco companies and other corporations not necessarily working in the best interests of the sports, or society in general. As was the case with the recent Great Trango Tower media climb, with its 137 porters, there will be significant adverse environmental impact when large-scale trips hit these fragile mountain areas.

We want ethical adventures? We want to stop messing up the Earth?

Many of the solutions to our complex environmental problems will not be achieved with increased complexity. Question every technology. Reject the unnecessary. Keep it simple. Leave room for serendipity. Keep it real and do no harm. We should seriously consider David Brower's advice: "...Turn around and take a forward step."

Yvon Chouinard is one of the most respected American climbers of this generation. He is respected not only for his climbing but also for his continued commitment to the environment. His climbing achievements include first ascents of North America Wall on El Capitan, Quarter Dome, the Chouinard-Herbert route on the North Face of Sentinel, and the North Face of Higher Cathedral.

His appetite for adventure is not confined to vertical rock, for he is equally at home in a kayak and on a surfboard. He is well known for his innovative technical advances in climbing equipment: He began by working on a small forge and selling equipment from the back of his car. He was the founder of Patagonia and created environmental stewardship goals for that company, which continue to set the standards for the entire outdoor industry. His words and his actions on playing "clean" and giving back to the environment are uncompromising.

Rock Climbing — The Future

Peter Croft

Lynn Hill

Leo Houlding

THE ENCHAINMENT PRINCIPLE

PETER CROFT

Although I think this is just another year, I feel it does have potential. After all, this *is* the millennium of *Star Trek*. It started off pretty ominously though: Newspapers said that computers would crash, causing chaos and financial ruin; tabloids said that earthquakes would rip round the planet, causing mountains to fall and huge tidal waves to rise against us; they said it was the end of the world and everything would change.

But come breakfast time on January 1, 2000, a lot of us were just holding an aching head in one hand and drinking coffee with the other. And after a global sigh of relief we looked around and wondered, "What now?" This, I think, is the significance of this New Year: Maybe we'll stop for awhile, think about our direction, and see things that were always there.

What I saw so clearly when I started climbing was adventure. Difficulty was only an ingredient. I never thought to wonder about grades, just as I never thought to wonder about what Tarzan might bench-press. I found the closer I moved to sport, the closer I felt to science—and the closer I moved to adventure, the closer I felt to genius.

If size matters—and I say it does—in a world where the biggest mountains and biggest faces have been climbed, where do we go and what do we do? Two possible directions present themselves, both so obvious that car-camping sightseers could point

them out, and often do. For these panoramic post-cards and glowing horizons show the way better than guidebooks. When we travel to the mountain regions of the world, the thing that leaves us awestruck is, more often than not, the whole picture: the collection of high faces that wall a deep valley or poke out of a glacier; the continuous knife-edge ridges that go from peak to peak and are so clearly etched at sunset or sunrise. The idea then, is to take in as much of them as possible in a single adventure, either in the form of a linkup (or enchainment) or a traverse, depending on the nature of the area. The main difference between the linkups and the traverses is the ease during linkups of getting food and water and—if need be—escaping between the climbs being linked. Traverses, on the other hand, have a greater degree of continuity, requiring a much higher level of commitment.

In Chris Bonington's book, *I Chose to Climb*, he recounts his ascent of the Walker Spur in the Alps. This was an early repeat and a very big deal. Chris and his partner Ian Clough did the climb very fast and, upon reaching the summit, didn't want to go down. Instead they decided to traverse the Rochefort Ridge, a spectacular knife-edge over many minor and not-so-minor summits. This was the book that got me into climbing and the story that made the impact. Although it would be years before I attempted anything similar, Bonington's account of that climb stayed with me, affecting many of my bigger choices, as well as infecting me with a cheeky inner voice that often asked, "Why stop now?"

That question and that attitude are perhaps best demonstrated by linkups and by speed climbing and taking walls, normally accomplished over a period of days, and completing them in a period of hours. For almost 40 years, with its legendary walls and good weather, Yosemite has been mecca for speed climbing. Not all of these speed climbs are interesting—or important. Often, they are just prized opportunities to get back to the deli early for bragging and beers. But there are fascinating ones that blow minds and change perceptions. The first one-day ascent of The Nose of El Capitan was one, and it led to the current theme of linkups. After all, if you can climb a big wall by lunchtime, what will you do before dinner? And what's for dessert?

This is, perhaps, the brightest future in places like Yosemite or the Bugaboos, where a lot of big routes are close enough together to make these one-day or single-push linkups feasible. But speed climbing by itself can be a bit of a dead end. It often focuses more on one-upmanship than on mind-expanding grand tours. In the same way that difficulty is only an ingredient of adventure, the speed record is only a by-product of speed climbing. In a realm defined by diversity, the stopwatch becomes ridiculous.

The importance of our ability to walk is not measured in miles per hour but in where it allows us to go. Similarly, the importance of speed climbing lies not in achieving speed records, but in how far it takes us. It is also important because it allows us the spontaneity that often accompanies moments of personal genius and brings us back to that heartfelt commitment to impulsive adventure we had as children.

Obviously, the attitudes and techniques used will transfer to the high mountains very well. Chouinard was right: The biggest future for speed-climbing is in the great ranges. As yet, however, only the first generation of his prophecy has come true. There have been isolated incidents, but this newer emphasis on speed (with its obvious benefits) has been largely absent in the high mountains. On a recent trip to a granite-walled valley in the Karakoram I found that the handful of big walls that had been climbed there had taken about ten to fourteen days. In Yosemite, each of these would have been day climbs. The future in places like this looks very bright.

But there is an even more magnificent potential to be found in the mountains, and it is clearly an extension of linkups. It is the concept of the "grand traverse," which is measured not in feet but in miles. If you want big, then this is it. At a time when many bemoan the fact that the biggest mountains and biggest faces have been done, we have climbs that are, for all intents and purposes, endless. Perhaps this is the reason for the relative inactivity in this area. You can never lay claim to the ultimate. Not even close.

The psyche necessary for these traverses is quite different than for other climbs. Often the end is just a point on the map, completely out of sight. And because of the size, and the fact that difficulties may be turned to one side of the crest or the other, they're next to impossible to scope in depth beforehand. Stopper cruxes where none were expected and heartbreak gaps are just part and parcel of this type of climbing. Instead of a structured game plan, what is needed is a kind of "take things as they come" attitude that expects the weird and is fueled by the unseen and the unknown.

Because of the cumulative effects of bivvying on a big traverse (more gear, food, and water), it's more important on these climbs than on others to try to go for a single push, through the night if need be. Unlike on walls where hauling, though possibly strenuous, is usually straightforward and conducive to long sieges, hauling on traverses is a nonstop nightmare of blistering pig wrestling. And because climbing is warmer than sitting, using the night for movement is necessary, preferably with a big moon. That's one of the greatest bonuses of single-push ascents—night climbing. It adds a whole other dimension, a fantastic lengthening of the day in a surreal atmosphere. As the days get longer I keep track of the moon like a Druid.

What are the intrinsic values of enchainments and traverses? Certainly one is the romantic appeal. That jagged skyline burning in a crimson sunset. Those sweeping panoramas you're granted when you visit the great mountain areas of the world. These are things that appeal to something very basic in us, not just climbers but as anyone who is moved by amazing places. Another bonus is the virtually endless potential. As far as the eye can see.

Climbing standards have risen so high and yet many of the most talented people still just fill in the lines between lines or go to Everest just because it's there. How many times have we heard "biggest" together with a wall or face or mountain? Even allowing for the usual exaggeration, the same can never be said of linkups and traverses—only the biggest "so far." On an evershrinking planet, here is an adventure resource that is practically limitless. And unlike space, this final frontier is available to anyone with the proper attitude adjustment—not just the hardcore, frothing-at-the-mouth type—but the weekend mountaineer, rock climber, or hiker. By looking at cliffs and summits as smaller parts of a continuous adventure, our scope broadens exponentially. Tone down the difficulty to a point where a cruising speed is possible for long periods of time and, with some practice, your future leads out to the horizon.

These basic ideas aren't new, of course. But mostly they've been viewed as oddities or exceptions to the rule that says that technical difficulty is where the real future lies. The truth is, multiple futures are out there. We don't have to mold ourselves to fit an overly defined sport. We can take our strengths, our ideas, and ourselves, and break away from the mainstream.

Today more and more people are drawn to so-called adventure sports. In our fear of the unknown—namely adventure—we change the definition, remove the unknown, and bravely call ourselves adventurers.

Are these our best hope for the future? The X Games, many of which make golf look sketchy, are making the inferred claim to be more extreme than, say, downhill skiing or gymnastics. I don't think so. Adventure racing, is the deformed offspring of triathlons, with contrived masochism and creativity-challenged participants. What about climbing on cargo nets, carrying sandbags across logs, and stuff like that? Is an obstacle course adventure?

Is this what the new millennium will call adventure? Does it matter that the media points more and more in this direction? Well, for those seeking inspiration, freedom from rules, or simply an outlet

for too much caffeine, I think it does. It's important that the communicators—the TV, the magazines, etc.—don't continue down this path simply because it's easy to report on.

Several "new" branches of climbing have appeared in the last couple of decades, each gathering the all-consuming intensity of a fad: sport climbing, competition climbing, and mixed climbing. Each has its adherents who practice it to the exclusion of all else. This is basically good because it allows the activity to reach a level of maturity that otherwise would have taken much longer. But once that level has been reached, most people gain perspective and realize that different types of climbing actually complement one another. For me, bouldering helps sport climbing, sport climbing helps speed climbing, and speed climbing helps big traverses.

Years ago, when I had my first taste of soloing, it was a revelation. Even though the climbs were very easy, it seemed like magic to be able to climb so much, so fast. It felt dizzyingly close to childhood dreams of flying. By cranking the volume way down on the difficulty, it felt like gravity took a vacation. There's a trick someone showed me as a kid. You stand in a doorway, raise your straight arms sideways up to the door frame, and then press as hard as you can for a minute or so. Then relax and step forward into the open room. Your arms, apparently freed from gravity, will float upward. This is the feeling of shifting from a difficulty-based activity to a movement-based one.

My first big linkup was in the Bugaboos in western Canada. It illustrated in living color what possibilities lay ahead. The plan was hatched in England while I was staring out of a pub window, watching the rain pour out of a thick black sky. Alone with beer and peanuts for dinner, I dreamed up my idea of heaven. Blue skies, white glaciers, and tall gray, granite towers. A month later there I was and it was there: the Bugaboos. Laid out in front of me was the circle of classic climbs I had come for: the Beckey-Chouinard on South Howser Tower, the West Face of Snowpatch, the McTech Arête on Crescent, and the Northeast Ridge on Bugaboo. At first hint of light, I left the hut with my friend Hamish Fraser, charging up the glacier in running shoes, and half trotted round to the backside of the Howser Towers. I can remember many burly approaches where I sweated like pork, but on this one the magic of a new idea made the hike seem like coasting.

We found the start and soloed up long hand cracks and corner systems on perfect rock. Slowing down near the top to look both ways at a dicey face traverse, I stopped to watch Hamish and was amazed to see the snowfields more than 1,600 feet below. It seemed too easy that, by changing attitudes, gravity was no longer the dominant force I was used to.

On the summit, we uncoiled the ropes we had brought for the descent. As we did this, I remember looking out at the surrounding peaks still glowing in morning sun, wanting to reach out and touch them. And after five rappels to the glacier, that's what I set out to do. Hamish took off for the hut and I went for the West Face of Snowpatch. I remember long corners, flaring cracks, and wide wet streaks leading up the middle of the face to an airy summit. I had taken only one rope for the rappels and needed two. So I combination down-climbed and rappelled to get back to the base.

I had momentum now and took off for the Bugaboo-Snowpatch Col and down from there to a flying long jump over the 'schrund and onto the McTech Arête on Crescent. This one was perfect splitters, Yosemite-style cracks for a couple hundred meters. Then onto the last route, the Northeast Ridge on Bugaboo.

Throughout the day I had the growing realization that I had found something fantastic, something important such as when I first discovered climbing. So, when I reached the top of Bugaboo, my last peak of the day, I felt I was looking into the future. Too far into the future, it turned out, because right away I got off route on the descent and had to scrape my way down the crux of the day—a licheny, overhanging finger crack. Soon though, I was down on the glacier, running toward the hut and turning in circles trying to take it all in.

I learned a few things that day. The first was the magic of the alpine start: getting up while others snored, many of whom would rather carry bivvy gear—and maybe use it—than lose a little sleep.

The second was going light. As I crisscrossed the glacier that day, I passed many people carrying two ice axes, crampons, and Himalayan packs and boots. With my much lighter load, my day seemed to expand exponentially.

Last and most important, what had appeared to be an ultimate pipe dream in a smoky English pub turned out to be eye-opening fun. Though nowhere near an ultimate, it was a good place to start.

I did my first big traverse along the Stuart Range in Washington State. The first peak on this ridge is Stuart itself, with its fantastic North Buttress over 1,950 feet long. The idea to climb this ultra-classic of the Cascades and then traverse the peaks to the east was inspired by the Bonington book I had read years before.

Earlier that summer I had found a couple of articles in some running magazines debating whether it was possible to train the body to better metabolize its own fat stores. The results were inconclusive, so I decided to find out for myself. For five days I carefully monitored my diet, eating between 500 and 700 calories a day. During this time I climbed at least 25 pitches a day, mostly 5.9-5.10. I found that after the first day or two, my energy fluctuated less and less. I had my answer.

In that summer of 1985 I drove down from Canada with some friends. We arrived in Leavenworth, Washington, around four in the morning, bivvied beside the road, and slept till the logging trucks started their morning rush hour about five. We climbed a little, but all I could think of was the big traverse the next day. That night I was so amped that I couldn't sleep till after midnight. I got up at one o'clock and started walking up the long logging road to the trailhead. Into my fanny pack I had squeezed climbing shoes, chalk bag, and a one-and-a-half-quart water bottle stuffed with a banana and water. My friends slept on, planning to climb one of the peaks later that day.

Several miles up the road, still in pitch-black darkness, some car headlights approached. I stood my ground, fighting an overwhelming urge to dive off the road. As the car slowed to a stop, I waited, half-panicky as the door opened. The dome light inside cracked on and I watched as a fat man in a red Hawaiian shirt reached beneath the newspapers beside him, pulled out a fat handgun, and stepped out of the car. My heart dropped like a stone. I had no time to run. This was how I would die.

Split seconds dragged out into twilight zone

minutes as the big gunman interrogated me before finally admitting he was an undercover policeman checking for break-ins at the trailhead. Overjoyed at my stay of execution, I explained my plan to the disbelieving cop. He looked me up and down and asked why I had no ice ax, no rope, no pack, and no friends. I waved all this away, pointing to my fanny pack. I don't think he really believed the hyperventilating freak with the leaves in his hair because his gun never wavered as he backed into his car and drove away.

Wired on adrenaline, I didn't calm down until sunup, terrorized through the night by squirrels, mice, and a massive porcupine. Then I spent the day traversing a half dozen peaks up on the skyline. After the horror of the night, climbing seemed so easy. I had to ration my water, though, because the lakes and streams weren't safe and, before the last peak, my bottle ran out completely. This left me hours on a parched death march, thirstily eyeing the stream I walked beside. Seventeen hours after starting, I wobbled back to the road.

I learned some valuable things about myself on this traverse. I ran out of water, but this happened when the climbing was getting less technical and was unpleasant rather than dangerous. Apart from two Fig Newtons my friends had left for me on one of the later peaks, and the banana I had stuffed in my water bottle, I had had no other food. This, as I had hoped, was no problem. And although I had slept only a couple of hours in the previous two nights, my lack of sleep seemingly had no effect. Excited by all this, I mentally stored it away for the future.

More than anything I learned that these traverses are not climbs. They're adventures in which almost anything can happen: nighttime close encounters with wild animals, bloodred sunrises, needle-sharp summits, knife-blade arêtes—even gunplay.

Because of the size of these climbs, the technical grade has little bearing on the actual difficulty. We are left with the Roman numerals I through VI to give an overall impression of the scale. This system is used in Yosemite and elsewhere and works alright in the mountains up to Grade IV, but at V and VI it becomes increasingly unwieldy.

Grade V traverses are harder than Grade V walls in Yosemite, and all Grade VI traverses are much bigger undertakings than, say, The Nose of El Capitan. Grade VI traverses hold the most unknowns, and they will become even bigger unknowns in the future unless an amended system is adopted. As longer and longer traverses are done, a closed system like this becomes increasingly useless, especially when we see two-mile traverses graded the same as twenty milers. The problem of grading, however, arises precisely because of the diversity we seek, so I suppose we have little cause for complaint.

Perhaps these climbs are a bit of a knee-jerk reaction to the oversanitized and sensationalized pseudo-adventures that are often glamorized today. But for those of us who find our knees jerking in this direction, it feels like cold, clean air, a hidden gem of an idea that's reserved especially for us. Is this the future? No. Is it a future? Yeah, I think so. It's kind of a parallel universe to the one we live in most of the time, with no billboards, no competition, no crowds. You invent your adventure and go where you want. This is the true freedom of the hills: Individuals can determine what climbing will be for them.

A native of British Columbia, Peter Croft has been climbing for 22 years in Canada, the United States, Europe, Asia, and Australia. One of the most distinguishing features of his climbing style is his commitment to soloing, with speed and technique providing him the safety margin required. Croft has an impressive list of first ascents and solo ascents beginning as early as 1982. His climbs include the first free ascent of University Wall, a Grade V 5.12 in Squamish, B.C.; the first solo ascent of The Rostrum, a 5.11 in Yosemite; the first one-day climb of El Capitan and Half Dome; the first traverse of the Waddington Range with Don Serl and Greg Foweraker; the first solo ascent of Astroman in Yosemite; the first free ascent of Moonlight Buttress, a Grade V 5.13 in Zion, Utah; the first solo ascent of the Minaret Traverse, Grade VI; and the first ascent of Sponsar Brakk, Pakistan.

Increasingly, Croft is taking his skills and experience into more remote places for bold, solo enchainments. An example of this evolution in his climbing is the first traverse of the Evolution Peaks (VI, 5.9) in the Sierra Nevada. Croft is clearly not a follower of trends, but one who makes his own way.

Journeys on the Rock

Lynn Hill

Over the past 25 years since I started climbing, I've seen dramatic changes in the way climbing has developed and transformed. In just three decades, nearly every facet of the mountain realm has been explored, been redefined, and become increasingly specialized in the incessant quest toward greater performance. Though I have explored various forms of climbing throughout the years, my primary interests and passions have been focused on free climbing.

Improvements in equipment, along with the expanding vision of climbers, led to advancements on all fronts, from powerful acrobatic maneuvers on 25-foot-high boulder problems to epic alpine adventures on the highest, most remote mountains on Earth. Yet despite the diverse changes that have taken place in the sport, there is still a common chord among all climbers regarding our spirit and passion for climbing. The perennial question— Why climb?—is clearly linked to our universal curiosities for learning, exploration, and adventure, as well as to the desire to adapt and play within the forces and forms of the natural world.

In looking back at the series of events shaping the development of climbing over the years, it's clear that the styles and attitudes of climbers were most significantly influenced by certain visionary individuals of each generation. I was a child of the sixties, born during a time when many people cried out for liberation from traditional social constructs and began to question authority. Instead of conforming to the old ways, people chose to create their own paths.

Climbers of this era were also pioneering their own paths. These were the golden years of rock climbing, when the possibilities for doing new routes were abundant. Climbers were an eccentric collection of nonconformists who chose to give up the comforts of the material world in favor of pursuing exciting adventures on the rock. The ideals and attitudes of this generation of climbers laid the foundation for the culture that I was introduced to in the seventies.

By the time I started to climb, free climbing had already diverged from its origins as practice for the mountains. To a large extent, the early development of rock climbing paralleled the technological improvements in climbing equipment. The introduction of nylon ropes and chromoly pitons during the fifties, removable protection devices during the sixties and mechanical camming devices during the seventies revolutionized free climbing throughout the world.

By the seventies, most of the major rock formations around the world had been climbed, and the goal of getting to the top of a mountain was no longer the most important measure of success; success was determined by how one got to the top. A "great route" included not only technical difficulty but also an element of boldness and commitment

assumed to be a traditionalist because I was part of the generation of traditional climbers. But since I had used hang-dogging techniques on my ascent of Vandals, I felt between sides. When it was my turn to speak, Jim McCarthy, the moderator of the debate, grilled me about my use of hang-dogging techniques on the first ascent of Vandals. A lawyer by profession, Jim made me feel as if I was being tried in court. I was guilty of hang-dogging, but I didn't feel guilty. Ironically, thanks to the American Alpine Club, of which Jim McCarthy was the president, I was invited to explore the world of sport climbing in France later that year.

Observing the nature of the rock (on these famous French crags) and the advantage of "rap-bolted" protection, it was easy to understand why the Europeans had been able to make such rapid progress in sport climbing.

While climbing in the Verdon Gorge in southern France, I happened to meet one of the organizers of the first Italian free climbing competition. He invited me to compete at the second annual Sport Roccia in 1986, and this is how I was introduced to the world of competition in Europe. Although the first competitions were held amid a great deal of controversy and disorganization, it wasn't long before competitions took root in Europe and later throughout the world.

The introduction of competition and artificial climbing walls marked the beginning of a whole new subsport within climbing. Within a few years, climbing walls were installed in public schools, local clubs, outdoor parks, and private homes throughout the world. A whole new generation of plastic climbers was born and, as the media and sponsors became involved in competitions, politics and professionalism entered the sport. I became a professional climber in 1988 when I received my first sponsorship contract from Chouinard Equipment. Soon I found myself in the role of a spokesperson: I did slide shows across the country, and participated in various photo shoots, gave interviews, and was involved in TV, radio, and film productions.

By the end of the eighties, the first international climbing competition was held in America, and it looked as though climbing was on the road to becoming an Olympic sport. While much media attention was focused on the game of competition,

progress on the rock continued to flourish. In 1988, Todd Skinner and Paul Piana did the first "team" free ascent of the Salathé Wall on El Capitan; Peter Croft free soloed Astro Man; Wolfgang Güllich became the first person in the world to do a 5.14b (8c) called Wall Street; and Isabelle Pattisier became the first woman to climb a 5.13d (8b) called Sortilege.

By 1990, the first official World Cup competition circuit was sanctioned by the UIAA. While competition climbing evolved toward an indoor, artificial environment, many climbers were able to make rock climbing a full time profession. During this period, European climbers took a clear lead in pushing the free climbing standards to a higher level. In the early nineties, Wolfgang Güllich did the first 9a (5.14c) in the world; the young Swiss climber Elie Chevieux did the first on-sight ascent of an 8b; and several other European climbers, such as Beat Kammerlander, began to push the standards of difficulty on bold free climbs on the big limestone walls of the Alps. In America, progress on the rock took a different direction. Using a combination of free climbing and aid climbing techniques, Peter Croft and Hans Florine did an impressive speed ascent of The Nose in 4 hours and 22 minutes!

I continued the competition game while pursuing a few of my own goals on the rock. In 1990, during a break between competitions in France, I did a climb called Masse Critique and became the first woman to climb a 5.14a (8b+). A few years later while climbing in Germany, I became the first woman to make an on-sight ascent of a 5.13b (8a).

As competition evolved and this way of life became more consuming, I began to feel as if I was losing a sense of freedom and spirit toward climbing. In most highly competitive sports, the price of victory or success means conforming to a rather restricted experience in life. I was a rock climber and I began to feel increasingly out of place in this arena of indoor climbing competitions. Though my early experiences in competition were beneficial to my personal development, after six years on the competition circuit, I began to feel as though training for competitions defined my entire purpose as a climber, so I decided that 1992 would be my last year of competition on the World Cup circuit.

In the aftermath of my competition career what

I wanted most of all was the freedom to pursue rock climbing again in the beautiful natural environment. One challenge that had long been lingering in the back of my mind came to surface: to free climb The Nose. Numerous climbers had tried to free the route over the previous decade, but none had been successful. The magnificent beauty and historic significance of the line—as well as my own efforts to free it, then later free it in a day—made this ascent the most meaningful achievement of my entire climbing career.

During the mid-nineties, free climbing big walls in Yosemite became a popular objective. In 1996 the Huber brothers repeated an all-free ascent of the Salathé, followed by a nearly perfect, on-sight ascent of the route by Yuji Hirayama a few years later. In 1998, the Huber brothers freed all but one section of El Niño on El Capitan, but the most impressive ascent of this route was done by the young English climber Leo Houlding, who did a nearly on-sight ascent. Taking this free climbing style to an extreme, Todd Skinner and friends spent more than 60 days free climbing a route on Trango Tower in Pakistan at over 22,000 feet.

In the late nineties, the image of climbing entered mainstream culture through various forms of media. The 1996 Everest tragedy resulted in widespread international press and produced a best seller—Jon Krakauer's book *Into Thin Air*. There have been films and numerous TV commercials using climbing in some form or another. Over the past five years, I've been involved in numerous climbing and filming trips to places such as Kyrgyzstan, Vietnam, Morocco, Thailand, Scotland, Australia, and Madagascar.

The proliferation of Internet technology has had an enormous impact on our rapidly changing world culture. Today we can follow expeditions via live satellite communication to places such as Trango Tower or even to the top of Mount Everest.

Despite the changes in technology and style and the imminent issues that we face today, the underlying spirit of climbing continues to prevail. Nearly every time I read about the current climbing scene, I learn about impressive ascents on the rock: Yuji Hirayama recently made the first on-sight ascent of an 8c (5.14b)! Katie Brown just did her first 5.14a and she flashed it on her first try! Spanish climber Josune Bereciartu recently became the first woman to climb an 8c (5.14b). The 22-year-old German Andreas Jörg made rapid ascents of two of the most difficult free climbs in the Alps—Silbergeier (5.14a) and The End of Silence (5.14a).

The new millennium will continue to see increasingly better performances in all aspects of climbing. There will be more specialization and refinement in the realm of competition, free climbing, bouldering, free climbing on big walls, and free climbing on alpine walls in the mountains. Traditional routes will be repeated faster and in better style: The challenges are infinite.

I would like to continue my journeys on the rock in beautiful places around the world. I enjoy all forms of free climbing, from bouldering to sport routes to traditional routes to long free climbs on big walls in remote places. What I love most about climbing is the beauty and diversity of the environment and the different rock types, climbing styles, and the people with whom I share these experiences. No matter how things evolve in the future, one element that seems to remain constant is my desire to continue climbing, exploring and seeking new heights.

"We shall not cease from exploration. And the end of all our exploring will be to arrive where we started and know the place for the first time."
— T. S. Eliot

Lynn Hill is one of the best rock climbers in the world. As a competitive climber, she has won more than 30 international competitions. She has climbed some of the hardest routes in the world.

Her boldest achievements, however, have been completed on The Nose on El Capitan—Yosemite's most famous aid route. In 1992 she climbed it in just over eight hours. The following year, she returned to make the first free ascent. A year later, she topped that feat with the first one-day free ascent of The Nose, leading every one of the 34 pitches in 23 hours. This will long stand among the world's great rock-climbing accomplishments.

She was a guest speaker at the Banff Mountain Film Festival and returned to be on the film jury. She produced a film on her free climb of The Nose and is currently writing her autobiography.

JOURNEY TO A
CALMER STATE OF MIND

LEO HOULDING

Once considered a subset of mountaineering, rock climbing has now become so diverse that facets of it have become sports in their own right: bouldering, indoor climbing, sport climbing, traditional climbing, and big walling. They are all very different activities.

Today it seems that the safer aspects of climbing have become the most popular. Bolts and indoor walls have enabled us to reach up into the grades of the "unthinkables" and to share the wonders of climbing with a broader spectrum of people. In doing so, however, we have sanitized and made safe most of a sport once renowned for its dangerous and fulfilling risk-taking.

To me, climbing is about adventure, and risk plays a large role in adventure. Bolts have removed risk and, therefore adventure from climbing. But there are still remote corners of the globe where mountains and cliffs lie virtually untouched; to find the spirit of adventure, I have focused principally on traditional, or "trad", and particularly bold rock climbing.

Why people climb dangerous routes is an incredibly difficult question, but I'd like to try to answer it.

First I must try to explain why I feel that climbing poorly protected routes differs from soloing. Soloing is the purest form of climbing: I love soloing, but the buzz it gives me is very different from that of climbing chop routes. Climbing toward my limit is what I enjoy most. When I'm doing this, my main concern is making the route I'm on as safe as possible. This enables me to focus on the climbing—not the possible consequences of a fall. Even on routes where a fall would still be fatal, knowing you've given yourself every chance makes it feel as if you're taking on a really great challenge—not making a challenge greater than it really is.

Outside Great Britain the only other stronghold of dangerous climbing I know of is the sandstone of the former East Germany and the Czech Republic. The communist regime that controlled these countries for so long prohibited people from leaving the country. Climbers from these countries realized that they would only be allowed to climb the same rock. This fueled a great respect for that rock and climbers rose to the challenges that the crags offered. They climbed the routes in adventurous style, adhering to strict, clean ethics; that is, of ground up, with the minimum of bolts and knotted slings for runners and no chalk. They created difficult and dangerous routes and left any too-great challenges for the next generation to attempt—using the same tactics.

Had they opted for a safer approach—more bolts and metal protection—the soft sandstone cliffs would have been ruined forever. They would have left no great challenges for the future generations to climb.

Fortunately, the climbers who came before us in Great Britain respected our rock the same way that climbers from behind the Iron Curtain respected theirs. The result is that we still have futuristic lines left undisturbed, just waiting to be climbed.

It would appear that countries with an abundance of rock do not value their rock as much as countries with a limited supply. Carpet-bolting and chipping are widespread, even though we have all realized that chipping will destroy the future of rock climbing.

The risk-taking involved in traditional climbing is a difficult thing for most people to imagine: Climbing routes in a style that is so dangerous, a fall could easily end one's climbing life—or life. Motivation is born solely through the respect we hold for the rock on which we climb.

I know of nobody who partakes in this form of climbing often, or even regularly. It is a game with very high stakes but huge rewards. However controlled an ascent is, an element of chance is always present. To play the game too often is to stack the odds against you.

Climbing cutting-edge, bold routes differs from the experience climbers of a lower standard get on easier bold routes. It is not ignorance or inexperience that brings us into these hideously dangerous situations. Fully aware of all the possible consequences of our actions, we choose to undergo these experiences.

It's difficult to explain what it is one gets out of such an ordeal. Desire far outweighs reward. It's not about adrenaline, ego, or bravado. It's something much deeper than that. It's like a kind of meditation: a journey to a calmer state of mind.

On the day I finally complete a serious project, I always appreciate the view on the walk out so much more than on the walk in. On the walk in there is one thing on my mind: Is it the right day? All I can think about are the moves on the route. On the walk out, however, when the route is finally complete, an overwhelming sense of calm commands all thought. Just being alive feels great. You feel elated. Every experience is a positive one. You appreciate the view for how beautiful it really is.

What is the future of this extreme and elite aspect of rock climbing? Standards will inevitably continue to rise. The tremendous difficulty of sports climbing will continue seeping into the world of the shockingly protected route. Although Great Britain's supply is limited, there are still lines of an inconceivable

difficulty waiting for somebody with the necessary skill and vision to climb them.

As for on-sighting "chop" routes, this is a game of patience and confidence. All the factors involved in headpointing play a role, but not knowing what the next hold is like, or how to do the next move, adds a whole extra dimension to the game.

The hardest confirmed trad routes around warrant the grade of E9. The hardest on-sighted grade is E7. Although there are certainly many routes of greater difficulty that will one day be on-sighted, I think these will be the safer examples. Once you have committed yourself to a dangerous route such as these, you eventually do a move you cannot reverse. There is no rescue. All that will keep you alive is a calm and complete confidence in your own ability. You only get one chance.

It is for this reason I foresee the standards of on-sight trad climbing beginning to plateau in the next decade. If you're lucky enough to survive one fall, physical or mental restraints will surely prevent you from reaching the same standards again, and this is a game of few players.

In Great Britain, risk climbing is experiencing a reawakening. I know there are talented, keen trad climbers in Norway, Sweden, and parts of the U.S., but they are undoubtedly the minority. In the time that I intend to spend climbing I would like to see an international resurgence in the popularity of trad climbing. Some of us have forgotten that climbing is not just a physical and mental exercise; it is a spiritual one as well.

In October 1998 the opportunity came for me to take the knowledge I gained climbing the small yet fierce, bold, traditional routes and loose rock of Great Britain to a much grander canvas—that of El Capitan in Yosemite, California.

I'd never seen a big wall before. I'd read books, seen pictures, heard stories, and been to slide shows about them. I'd dreamed of what it must be like to spend a week living vertically. I tried to imagine climbing hard free pitches, one after another for days on end. I considered myself to be a reasonably good climber, but the first few weeks I spent in Yosemite were a truly humbling experience. The place filled me with fear and intimidation. I didn't rope up once, opting instead to boulder and try to get my head around the ridiculously big, hard routes that surrounded me.

The problem I had was not a physical one. I knew I was capable of climbing at the technical standard of the free routes on El Capitan. It was a psychological one: Having the confidence and self-belief necessary to climb at one's limit in such an alien environment on such a grand scale.

This cliff was a mountain and needed to be treated as one. The thought of being hit by a storm 2,000 feet up a route terrified me. The logistics involved in climbing such a huge cliff confused me, but gradually I began to see things differently. A simple change in perspective was all it took to turn this nightmarish wall into my dream crag.

After being so overwhelmed at the start, what my close friend and climbing partner Patch Hammond and I achieved in the latter part of our trip exceeded our greatest expectations.

We didn't spend six days aid climbing The Nose or get a big-wall veteran to take us up a trade route to show us the ropes, as most people would. Instead we jumped in at the deep end and taught ourselves to swim.

We spent five days and four nights making the second ascent of a free route the world-acclaimed Huber brothers had just established on the East Buttress of El Cap. We taught ourselves to haul, set up portaledges and sat out a vicious 24-hour storm halfway up. Apart from two minor falls, I climbed the 30-pitch, 5.13c free version of the El Niño on-sight.

To me this is proof that what enables us to reach our limits, and to push them forward, is how we interpret what we see. Looking at the route as a five-day vertical camping trip and taking it on, one move at a time, is what enabled me to do it. I broke it down to bite-size pieces. There is no point in worrying about the next 20 pitches if you can't do the next move!

In 1959 when Warren Harding stood in El Capitan meadow and looked west, the view he saw was exactly the same as the one Patch and I saw in 1998. But then, El Cap was an unclimbed cliff. It was the frontier of climbers' imaginations. He realized that it was not impossible to climb, as many believed, but he was voyaging into uncharted territory. His only guide was his vision.

He saw it a necessity to use siege tactics. He spent 45 days, spread over half a year, aid climbing what looked like the easiest route up the cliff. He fixed a 3,000-foot "lifeline" from the bottom to the top of what has become one of the most famous rock routes in the world: The Nose. He took the first step on the big-wall ladder.

In 1962 when Royal Robbins looked up at El Cap, he saw exactly the same thing as Harding. But he saw it in a completely different way. With Tom Frost, Yvon Chouinard, and Chuck Pratt, he showed the way forward by aid climbing the Salathé Wall in a single six-day push as a self-contained unit, and with no lifeline fixed to the ground. He saw what Harding had done and took the next step forward.

In 1975 Jim Bridwell stood in the same spot and looked at the same thing. He saw a cliff he could aid climb in a day.

In 1998 Todd Skinner saw a cliff that was possible to free climb, using similar siege tactics to Harding's aid ascent 30 years earlier.

In 1995 Lynn Hill saw a cliff she could free climb in a day.

Ultimately, in 1998 when Patch and I stood and looked at El Cap, we saw a cliff we could free climb on-sight via a difficult route, with no prior experience of big walling.

Progression lies in changing the way we look at our cliffs. What we are willing to climb and the style in which we are willing to climb it depend entirely on how we look at it. Perception and vision are our keys to evolution in rock climbing.

***

Leo Houlding started climbing with his father in the English Lake District when he was ten years old. His first notable achievement was nine months later, when he became the youngest person to free climb an exposed Scottish sea stack in the Orkney Isles known as The Old Man of Hoy. He won the 1994 Birmingham World Cup and the British Indoor Climbing Competitions in 1996. On a recent trip to Yosemite, he put up a new route on El Capitan called Alfa Romeo and rated it 5.13c/d.

Climbing magazine refers to him as "the one-man rave scene…. with a boom box and 'anything's possible' attitude." Leo Houlding is 19 years old.

EUROPEAN CLIMBING — THE FUTURE

ANDERL HECKMAIR

CATHERINE DESTIVELLE

RICCARDO CASSIN

CLIMBING IS AN EGOCENTRIC ACTIVITY

ANDERL HECKMAIR

I have spent most of my life in the mountains; my active climbing period was almost 70 years ago and since that time there have been many changes in the sport of climbing, but many things have also stayed the same.

I consider mountain climbing an absolutely egocentric activity; I could therefore never understand why one would want to set up rules for it. "In the mountains, freedom rules" is an old poacher's saying. Whether and how I use artificial means is my business. To climb in the cleanest and smoothest way possible—that was my desire. How others climb is their business, and nobody else has the right to interfere. Most people abide by rules because they want to be accepted. I was only truly content when I succeeded in completing a climb the way I had envisioned it. Naturally, there is satisfaction when a climb is acclaimed by the experts, but basically, this was not as important to me as the recognition by my friends.

I never thought that the first ascent of the North Face of the Eiger would cause such a sensation, and that people would still talk about it today. To me, that wall was simply a personal challenge and a mountaineering venture—like many before.

From the middle of the 19th century to its end—a period some refer to as the classic period of alpinism—the conquest, development, and study of the Alps was a priority. I always held a great deal of respect for the climbers of that epoch

and their achievements. Their difficulties were not just technical matters, because they first had to find the way to "their" mountain—there were neither paths nor huts—and then achieve a climb with simple, quite often unsuitable, equipment.

From 1900 to 1950, mountain climbing was referred to as modern alpinism—a time of many great climbers and many changes in climbing. One great mountaineer of the period, Paul Preuss (1886-1913), was an advocate for climbing without artificial means (pitons and carabiners). His alpine achievements are still acclaimed, as well as those of Hans Dülfer and Wilo Welzenbach.

With the ascents of the North Face of the Matterhorn, the North Face of the Eiger, and the Walker Spur of the Grandes Jorasses in the 1930s, modern alpinism came to an end in the Alps. These three north faces were referred to as "the last problems of the Alps," and once they were climbed, the first expeditions to the major peaks in the world began.

Like most German climbers, I had to stop my alpine activities during the Second World War. Access to other countries was restricted for German climbers; all the borders were closed. Just to reach the small portion of the Alps still open to us took a lot of ingenuity. There was no equipment to be bought; we used old stuff and sometimes withstood hunger. Sometimes our clothing was so torn that we were mistaken for bandits. But we were clever and it didn't take us long to figure out where, and how, we could cross the border without a passport or visa. That's why German climbers were to be found once again in the Wilden Kaiser, Hohen Tauern, and the Dolomites. The young Martin Schliessler sneaked across borders to Mont Blanc where he conquered the Peuterey Ridge together, yet in a competitive way, with Hermann Buhl, risking imprisonment.

Equipment and technique really hadn't changed much in this era. One climbed the same way as before the war. The only difference was Tricouni nails on climbing shoes—if you could afford them. Then, rubber soles were invented and ropes were made out of nylon instead of hemp, which meant an enormous increase in security.

Mountain climbing in the middle of the 20th century came to be referred to as contemporary alpinism. Thanks to the development of better alpine equipment, it was now possible to make ascents in the Alps and the big mountains around the world—which would have not been possible before. Ropes, bivouac equipment, clothing, and packsacks were now made out of artificial material; pitons and carabiners were made out of light metal, and that meant considerably less weight to carry on your back. In addition, the ropes, pitons, and carabiners were much stronger and hence offered more security. I bought my first nylon rope in Chamonix in 1951 for the ascent of the Walker Spur. This new equipment and clothing made it possible for alpinists to conquer the most difficult walls—the *direttissimas* (direct lines).

I believe the immense quantity of technology used (pitons, bolts, stirrups, bivouacs with supply lines from below, etc.) and the enormous amount of time and money spent on climbs of this period, were out of all proportion to the ascents. For me, these were not harmonious routes, and the experience of nature was definitely lacking. After the ascent of the West Face of the Petit Dru in 1952, Guido Magnone talked about the "turning point in alpinism." This ascent was done with artificial means. I didn't consider this kind of mountaineering "climbing" but "work." Typically enough, the extreme climbers of today talk about their achievements as "work."

Naturally, extreme alpinists were thirsty for first ascents. Since all the peaks in our Alps had already

been climbed by this time, climbers found new ways to conquer the walls and ridges. One method that became fashionable in the mid-fifties was solo ascents at the most difficult grade of that time. This phase was begun by Walter Bonatti, who in 1956 did the first solo ascent of the Southwest Spur of the Petit Dru, the so-called Bonatti Spur. But I was never one for solo ascents. When I am mountaineering, I like to have a partner who shares the experience and adventure with me.

Also in the 1950s, the famous walls, ridges, and spurs of the Alps were starting to be ascended in winter. Although the danger of rockfall is minor in the winter, I have never personally been fascinated by a winter ascent. I always planned my trips for the most pleasant, best climbing conditions. Nevertheless, I had to accept the fact that I was often caught in the very worst weather conditions.

In 1961 the first winter ascent of the North Face of the Eiger was made. This was the beginning of the winter ascents of the big walls in the Alps: 1962, the North Face of the Matterhorn; 1963, the Walker Spur; 1964, the North Dihedral of the Lalidererwall. But this was not enough. In 1965, Walter Bonatti succeeded in the first climb through the North Face Direct of the Matterhorn. In 1966 was the first ascent—and first winter ascent—of the North Face Direct of the Eiger (later called the Harlin Route). Many alpinists, including myself, disapproved of this winter ascent with its enormous amount of equipment and radio contact with supporters.

In the summer of 1968, Reinhold and Guenther Messner climbed the central pillar of the Southwest Face of the Heiligenkreuzkofel in the Dolomites—in truth the beginning of Grade VIII, even though it did not exist by common agreement at the time.

Up until that point, there were six grades (extended by + and −) to measure the difficulty level of climbing. As the technical abilities of the climbers improved, however, the UIAA extended that scale to seven and for artificial climbing added three grades (A1-A3). But soon even this scale was not enough. In 1989 the UIAA decided to open up the scale even further.

Today routes on the north face of the Eiger,

usually climbed at the tenth grade with artificial means, are free climbed in one go. In order to achieve this, the climbers must train and memorize the route, section by section. This involves many months worth of "work" (here, the word "work" is justified), and in my opinion it is similar to studying a foreign language—learning words by rote in order to speak the language.

In the meantime, our Alps became overdeveloped with roads, gondolas, and mountain inns, damaging the natural environment considerably. Various groups (environmentalists, Alpine associations, politicians, and tourism agencies) responded to this trend differently.

Near the end of 1970, the expression "redpoint climbing" appeared. And in 1977, the Germans Reinhard Karl and Helmut Kiene successfully completed a first ascent that justified a new difficulty level of VII. The two of them agreed to put up a new route on the Fleischbankpfeiler in the Wilden Kaiser, an area that has often introduced new grades of difficulty throughout the history of rock climbing. Karl and Kiene wanted to outdo the climb's actual grading of VII. In addition to climbing the route free (without use of protection), they were striving for a "clean" attempt. They wanted to use the new chocks available for belays and running belays on the most difficult rope lengths. They refused to use pitons, so that all future climbers would find the route in the same untouched manner.

I fully support this approach. During my most active climbing period (end of 1920s and the 1930s), I was often berated by other climbers because I "cleaned" the walls and only left those pitons absolutely necessary (e.g., for belays). Unfortunately, chocks were not known at that time.

With a handful of Hexentric chocks, brought home from their climbing trips to California, Karl and Kiene climbed the Fleischbank Spur on June 2, 1977, calling their first ascent Pumprisse, setting a new standard for free climbing. They could honestly grade Pumprisse a VII. Moreover, the climb was done in clean alpine style. A new dimension in rock climbing was accomplished; a new ethic impressively documented. Their comment was unambiguous: "...for sure the most difficult route in

the Wilden Kaiser, which has to be rated at least one grade higher than Fleischbank Spur or Schmuck-Chimney—Grade VII is totally justified." Everybody talked about the Pumprisse. Every "sixth-grade climber" was challenged to discover if he could also be a "seventh-grade climber."

A lot of young climbers, influenced by Messner's provocative publications (*The 7th Grade*, for example) wanted to prove themselves to the old guard. They free climbed formerly technical routes and opened up additional VII routes. Then it became official in 1978: The UIAA recognized Grade VII and opened up the grading scale. The new standard was defined thusly: "A difficulty level obtained by increased training and improved equipment. Even the best climbers need to adjust their training to the kind of rock, in order to master passages close to the fall limit. In addition to acrobatic climbing ability it is imperative to handle flawless belay techniques."

In the eighties and nineties, sport climbing branched out with more climbers specializing in specific directions. Many new free climbing routes classified as level VIII were opened up in the Dolomites and the Wetterstein.

Sport climbing is different from conquest climbing, where your goal is to climb the entire wall. In sport climbing you master high difficulty levels on short walls without reaching the top. As sport climbing grew, many young mountaineers went to climbing areas that had formerly been used only for training, or had been totally ignored, and there was an undreamed explosion of performance in many climbing areas around the world. In 1991, the German Wolfgang Güllich achieved Grade IX.

Nowadays it is hard for young mountaineers to accomplish anything sensational in the Alps, so they invent extraordinary ideas such as the solo ascent of the North Face of the Eiger in 4 hours 50 minutes in 1983. I would call this particular way of climbing a mountain "sport," but otherwise I don't consider mountain climbing a sport. There is no doubt about the importance of the achievement, but what is of primary significance is still the climbing experience.

Some climbers transposed the spirit of sport climbing onto alpine walls. They repeated old and partially technical routes free and opened up new paths to Grades X and XI. At the same time, the climbers were conquering the big walls in the so-called big-wall style.

Even bouldering, once used only as training for alpine climbing, was being developed into its own art form by bouldering specialists. At the end of the 1970s and the beginning of 1980, the German Wolfgang ("Flipper") Fietz was one of the best bouldering specialists in the world. He opened up new boulder routes in the Frankenjura, which even later on were rated IX and X.

In the mid-1980s, climbing competitions became fashionable. These were originally held on natural rock but today are organized on artificial climbing walls, mainly indoors. This made it possible for climbers to become very famous and even become professional, thanks to sponsors and other climbing-related profits.

At the end of the 1970s to the middle of the 1990s, all-round alpinists were seeking new challenges by combining a variety of noteworthy accomplishments. In these so-called enchainments, they combined great classic routes on difficult walls and tried, either solo or in winter, to climb them in the shortest possible time.

With the growing involvement of women in alpinism, female climbers also started to make their mark, either with equal male partners, with other women, or even solo. In 1986, the Italian Luisa Jovane climbed with her partner Heinz Mariacher the Tempi Modernissimi on Marmolada and Catherine Destivelle of France solo-climbed the Bonatti Spur on the Dru (1990), the North Face of the Eiger (1992), the Grandes Jorasses (1993), and the Matterhorn (1994) in winter.

Secured, fully equipped climbing routes, or *Klettersteige*, have been extremely popular for the past 20 years. Unfortunately, tourism has been far too lenient with the "fit-for-fun" generation. That's why you find more and more of these routes in the lower mountain regions.

Many hikers are quite happy to be able to reach the summit using klettersteige, even though they never actually touch the rock. But there are so many beautiful paths on the mountains, high enough and yet just below the rock regions, that I think hikers should use these trails instead.

Some mountain areas prefer low-impact tourism, while others are more aggressive in advertising all kinds of recreational activities. They install snow guns to produce man-made snow. They don't hesitate to clear-cut areas for more ski runs and inevitably attract many inexperienced people into higher elevations where you still need a lot of alpine knowledge and experience. Unfortunately, this often leads to serious accidents.

Many new outdoor sports are also trendy in the current period—like canyoning, waterfall ice climbing, and paragliding. This is positive in that a professional mountain guide has more opportunities to make a living. The Alps's great value for recreation and nature has long since turned into a political matter. For that reason, Reinhold Messner, as a European parliamentarian, wants to fight against the overdevelopment of these mountains.

Everything evolves constantly, and rightfully so. It does not cause problems in sport to "always go faster, farther, higher;" but alpinism has two souls: the tradition with ethic and romance; and the athletic achievement.

This split leads to unnecessary controversies between traditionalists and modern climbers. Mountain climbing is, first and foremost, an egocentric activity, which allows you to do what you want—provided you are doing no harm to people or nature. Today, however, the economy, the media, and mountaineers have discovered that you can also earn money through climbing. Therefore, we now have branches on "the tree of alpine playing," and they are artificial means, secured climbing routes, transportation by helicopter, sport climbing (alpine or indoors), waterfall climbing, hang gliding, paragliding, mountain biking, river rafting, snowboarding, etc. Many of these sports are not directly related to mountaineering because you cannot climb mountains with them. They are nevertheless related to the mountains and are done by mountain climbers.

You have to separate climbing, as a sport, from traditional alpinism. But you can't ignore the fact that the improved training for sport climbing has enabled people to accomplish more difficult routes on rock, ice, or combined terrain than they ever dreamed or thought possible.

The trend in traditional alpinism is to do more difficult routes, faster, in redpoint-climbing style, and to apply these possibilities in the mountains around the world. It is already obvious today that many routes are less frequently climbed, if they are climbed at all. These are the routes that today's mountain climbers consider too dangerous (subjectively or objectively) or too difficult. This is where the discussion over "pleasure climbing"—securing routes with glued bolts, etc.—the dispute over the value of adventure and danger become important.

People call the trend toward natural climbing something new, although earlier generations of mountaineers already climbed in that style. History repeats itself in many areas. When you have pushed the trend to the extreme you return to the beginning—but in a modern form (with better equipment, for example).

Sport climbing, which can be done outside the mountains, has to be put into its own category. Many people hike to lonely valleys, explore unknown mountain areas, climb as extreme mountaineers, or enjoy nature while paragliding. It is remarkable how much these people can tell about their experiences. I am convinced that those who do trendy sports also experience a kind of adventure, but in my opinion, their climbing is too much on an athletic side that stresses measurement and lacks idealism.

The idealistic view stresses the inner satisfaction of having unforgettable experiences. The fact that you hardly ever read "experience" reports on sport climbing proves to me that sport climbing is not part of mountaineering—though sport climbing on big alpine walls may prove to be an exception.

The future of climbing will depend a great deal on how we handle our environment. The European Union (EU) in Brussels now likes to limit free access. When I hear about this, I am happy to be old and I am sorry for the youth who will have to deal with these problems in the future. By declaring certain areas off-limits, one does preserve nature; however, man and nature belong together. It is going to be very difficult to find a compromise for both.

I envision four directions for the future. The biggest issue will be the conflict between both mountain climbing and masses of hikers with environmental protection, as we see it today.

I believe that today climbing is not just about the technical perfection of mountaineering. It is also about the all-encompassing manner in which mountaineering is done (in the winter, how fast, by women, how extreme, by what artificial means, how fair, etc.). One is obliged to look at a climb in its all-encompassing meaning. The magic of the technique of mountaineering is gone. It is important today, but much more important in the future, to see alpinism within the framework of the evolution of society. There is also the process of globalization. How nice it would be to see climbing as innocent and separate from the rest of the world, but I don't think this is realistically possible any longer. Everything is connected. This is the general trend, and I don't like it.

My personal desire still is to hike in the mountains—alone or with a friend or my wife—and to climb mountains suited for me according to my condition, age, and other circumstances, without having to ambitiously look for great difficulties. I would like to experience the nature of mountains, sleep in simple mountain huts, and talk to the people who live in the mountains. In brief, I want to experience the mountains as a human being and an admirer. This is more a romantic rather than achievement-oriented point of view, but for me, experiencing the mountains is of most importance.

Anderl Heckmair was born in 1906. He started extreme mountaineering in the late 1920s and early 1930s with bold ascents of Tre Cima di Lavaredo, the North Face of the Cima Grande, Civetta Northwest Face, and Sans Maor East Face.

But it was in 1938, when Heckmair led team members Ludwig Vorg, Heinrich Harrer, and Fritz Kasparek on the first ascent of the North Face of the Eiger that he entered mountaineering history books in a profound and reverberating way. In 1951, Heckmair accomplished a personal alpine achievement when, under dramatic conditions, he climbed the Walker Spur on the Grandes Jorasses.

He has written seven books and lectured in Banff in 1996.

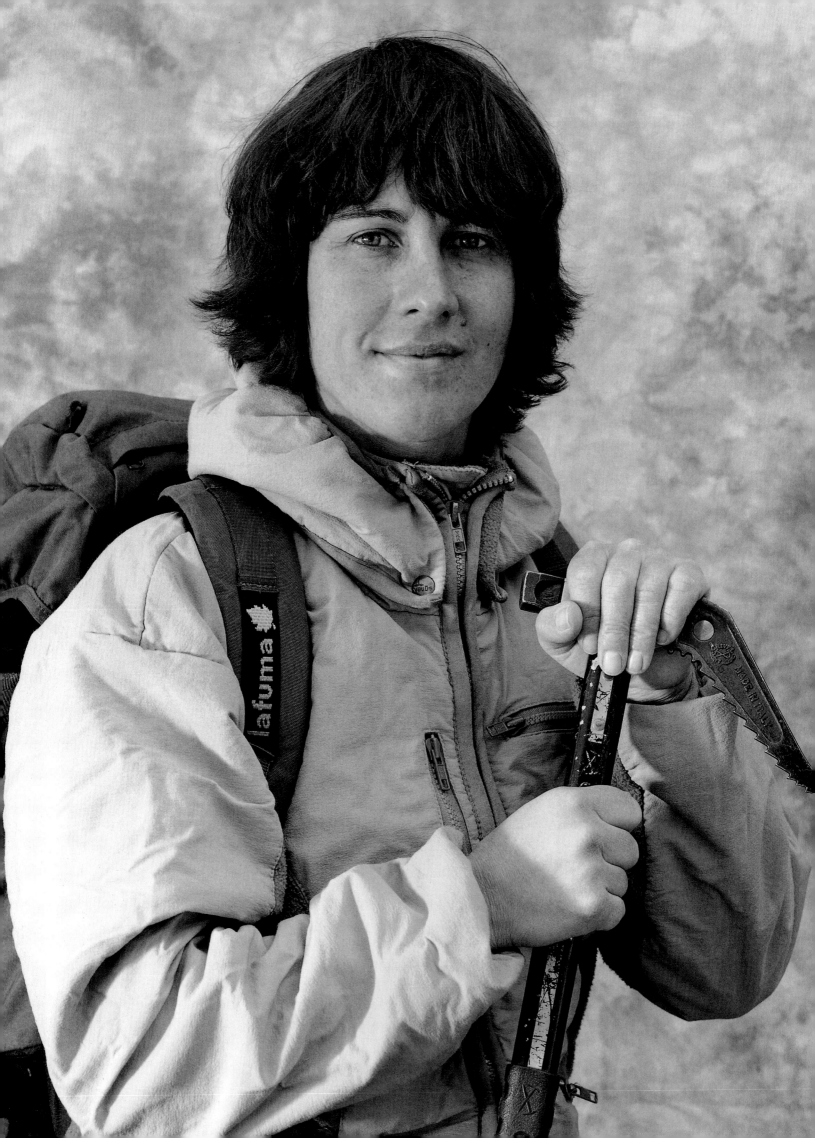

FULFILL THE DREAMS OF MY YOUTH

CATHERINE DESTIVELLE

1972-1980

My parents gave me my first pair of climbing shoes in 1972. They were "RDs," made entirely of leather. Because they were the most expensive shoes available, my parents had assumed they were the best. Actually, they weren't very good, but that didn't really matter because they were too big for me. I was 12 and had a size-36 foot (US 4 1/2), and the shoes were 38s; they weren't made any smaller. Until then, I had been climbing in old shoes passed down from my cousins, and they were so worn that their soles were as smooth as those of climbing shoes.

I was delighted with my RDs anyway, because they were designed by René Desmaison, the great alpinist who spent days at a time in winter on the big north faces. He was my idol; in winter, to the consternation of my teachers, I used to go to school wearing only a T-shirt in order to get used to the cold. That year, René Desmaison had just survived a terrible epic on the North Face of the Grandes Jorasses, during which his companion died of exhaustion right before his eyes. He had finally been rescued after surviving 342 hours on the mountain. It had been a gold mine for the press, with *Paris Match* leading the way. But René Desmaison was, above all, a great rock climber and a tremendous alpinist. He opened major new routes on north faces in the Alps. As Desmaison himself had done, I was cutting my teeth on the sandstone boulders of Fontainebleau near Paris. I loved climbing at Fontainebleau; it has the most beautiful boulders in the world!

As for climbing shoes, I would have preferred "PAs," the red and white canvas shoes designed by Pierre Alain, the veteran who had opened up the North Face of the Drus in 1935. All this was before my time, but I knew that Pierre Allain was a somebody; some of his routes at Fontainebleau, such as L'abattoir, La joker, and La boucherie, were still rated 6.

But in 1973 a shoemaker's initials—EB— began making their way around the world on people's feet. Edouard Bourdonnot made his EBs by hand. A few years later, when I was 15, thanks to Jean-Claude Droyer who like me had small feet, I was lucky enough to be given a specially made pair of size 37 EBs. I had grown a bit and was now beginning to explore bigger cliffs and real mountains.

Just before turning 13 I had attended a climbing course for youth, run by the Club Alpin in the Dauphiné mountains. I had found the climbs we were doing to be too easy. At that time there were very few women in the mountains, and they always climbed second. Climbing was a man's sport.

Fortunately, I soon met a group of strong Parisian climbers, older than me, with whom I went to all the places that mattered at the time:

Fontainebleau, the cliffs of the Saussois, the Vercors, and soon the Verdon, which became all the rage.

Crag climbing was very different then; people pulled freely on any available piton as they climbed, and what mattered was getting to the top of the route. Free climbing was not yet hugely popular in France, and Jean-Claude Droyer, who had imported free-climbing practices from Great Britain, was generally viewed either as a visionary or as an ayatollah, preventing people from kicking their way up the rock! I also went to the crags at Freyr on the Meuse River in Belgium. There, we played at free climbing, but that's not what we called it. We called it "yellow climbing;" the game was to climb without touching the pitons that were painted yellow. Once a climber was able to bypass a certain piton without using it as an aid point on a route, it was painted yellow, and that became a challenge for everybody. With each successful attempt, the beer flowed freely at the bar located above the cliff!

In the Verdon, long routes were the focus. Each outing was quite an undertaking; climbers walked in from the bottom, carrying packs, water, and headlamps for the tunnels. In the mid-seventies, things were done very differently from today.

When I first started crag climbing, I climbed with a piece of webbing wrapped around my waist. Later, I used a Desmaison harness with metal rings on it; I would always tie the rope around my waist in addition to tying into the harness, because no one really trusted the harness. At 17, I got my first real harness, made by Troll. That year, I climbed the north face of Ailefroide (the Devies-Gervasutti route), the Couzy-Desmaison route on Olan in the Oisans, and the American Direct on the Dru in the Mont Blanc massif in record time. I felt as if I had wings and I wanted to soar.

In the mountains I was still wearing knickers. My role models continued to be Desmaison and Pierre Alain, as well as Gaston Rébuffat—because of his books and photographs. I used to have fun sketching out his photos at school! Most alpinists were still wearing big climbing boots instead of climbing shoes and were more likely to use pitons than nuts. Nobody gave a darn about free climbing in the mountains, and winter ascents were still

highly unusual. But many things were changing in France during those years: Free climbing was becoming widespread, chalk was making its appearance (except at Fontainebleau, where resin, or "pof," prevails), and climbers were starting to use nuts and Friends—and to train off the rock.

1980-1985

From 1980 to 1985, I practically stopped climbing. I was working as a physiotherapist during the day and playing poker at night. But I was still keeping an eye on developments—just enough to feed the embers of my passion! In 1982, the first of several films featuring Patrick Edlinger had a big impact. The general public discovered climbing, and many alpinists became aware of free climbing and its very complex series of movements. The realization spread that things were changing; those changes, however, didn't always happen easily. What huge discussions there were to determine whether or not climbing grades should go beyond 6. Did the "limit of human possibility" then no longer exist? What a slap in the face for the old-timers! And what of the symbolic number 7—should it be used? I have to say that all these questions were a little beyond me. If you climb a harder section of rock, you have to call a spade a spade and grade it 7; that is, in any case, less ridiculous than using the Grades 6a, 6b, etc. all the way to 6g, as they do at Fontainebleau.

Buoux had become all the rage; there were lots of people in the Verdon. Christophe Profit was doing a speed ascent of the American Direct on the Drus and free climbing was being developed in the mountains. With this came climbing tights, the desire to climb light, the use of chalk, and the opening, by Michel Piola of Switzerland, of a string of magnificent routes on the Envers des Aiguilles de Chamonix massif. And bolts were showing up almost all over the place—on French crags, of course, but also in the mountains. Unfortunately, not everybody had Piola's good judgment regarding their use.

Women were also coming into their own: Martine Rolland of France became the first female guide. Nicole Niquille of Switzerland joined her a bit later; the Swiss, being more traditionalist, were also more hesitant!

One day in 1985 I get asked to be in a film because I climb fast; I will have to climb a 7b+ in the Verdon for the shoot. It's my chance to quit my job as a physiotherapist, which is becoming boringly repetitive, to collect my savings, and to leave for two months of training in the Verdon. I find a new life.

A project had been brewing in France and the rest of Europe for some time: climbing competitions. It was a very controversial topic. We had, of course, heard about the competitions in the Soviet Union—some climbers had even gone to check them out—but they seemed very exotic and far removed from our code of ethics. Nineteen climbers had signed a "manifesto" against competitions; I had also signed. And then, when the first competition took place at Bardonecchia in 1985, I felt like going—to check it out—like most of the other 19.

At Bardonecchia, there were difficulty, speed, and style competitions; I won all of them. It was a spectacular and convivial event, a celebration for the general public. This marked the beginning of an exciting period with many opportunities for climbers. Sponsors and the media were interested. Soon other manufacturers rivaled or exceeded the quality of EB and threw themselves into this new market—Boreal, One Sport, La Sportiva, etc. And they all wanted the best competitors on their rosters. What a windfall for climbers! Along with others, I was going to be able to make a living from climbing.

In France rock climbing had become an independent, full-fledged sport; people no longer rock climbed solely as preparation for the mountains. What quarrels broke out at the Fédération Française de la Montagne (French Mountain Federation) in order to change its name to the

Catherine Destivelle climbs the 865-foot Devil's Tower in northeastern Wyoming. More than 200 routes have been identified for scaling the tower's massive columns.

Fédération Française de la Montagne et de l'Escalade (French Mountain and Rock Climbing Federation). It turned into a big political game including threats of a split. But as with other debates, I was indifferent to them; I climbed and I trained.

Around 1987 the first climbing walls were built in France and very soon, especially after the failure of the Biot competition, indoor competitions prevailed. Crag-climbing standards had increased considerably, for both men and women.

In 1988, I became the first woman in France to redpoint an 8a+: Chouca at Buoux. The standard in competitions was around 7b for the men, 7a for the women.

In the Alps, there was an explosion in the numbers of solos and enchainments. Jean-Marc Boivin, Eric Escoffier, and Patrick Berhault were linking routes together with paraglider descents. Christophe Profit soloed the three big north faces in winter in 24 hours, and the entire Peuterey Ridge in one day— in winter. Going fast and light was the future of climbing in the Alps and soon, too, in the Himalaya.

The vocabulary of mountain climbing had changed. No longer was it a matter of "conquering," as it was in the time of Desmaison and his peers; it had become a "soft" activity.

My climbing career was going well: I was winning, I had good sponsors, and the media had taken a liking to me. There was a fine rivalry between Lynn Hill and me. I was starting to be known by the general public.

Competitions had evolved; as of 1987, only difficulty competitions remained. This made for an event that was slower, and more difficult for the general public to understand. As for me, I was getting fed up with training and not eating anything. I started wanting to be in the mountains once again, to be in wide-open spaces. I had been in the mountains from time to time on my travels. I had made a film in Mali, another in Thailand, and had been the subject of reports from the U.S. and Spain. This aspect of my career was also going well; the magazines loved these spectacular stories featuring the "star" of climbing. But I didn't do any climbing in the mountains because I was afraid my sport-climbing standard would suffer.

By 1990, the media's interest in competitions began to wane: they were too technical, too slow, always the same. I had won at Snowbird in 1989. In 1990, I didn't place first. It would be my last competition. I decided to return to the mountains.

1990-1994

My goals are simple: to fulfill the dreams of my youth, to climb the great mythical walls from the time of my role models, to see whether I can become a "real" alpinist. I want to do big faces, to climb in winter, to solo—to experience all that is the antithesis of a sterilized form of climbing. In 1990, I climb Trango Tower in Pakistan with Jeff Lowe and I solo the Bonatti Pillar on the Drus. In 1991, climbing alone, I spend 11 days putting up a new aid route on the west face of the Drus. Then, over three years, I realize three of my dreams: winter solos of the Eiger, the Grandes Jorasses, and the Matterhorn. One per year.

At times I was amazed by the reactions to my climbs, both in the general media and in the climbing world. In 1990, after doing the Bonatti Pillar, I was favorably compared to Walter Bonatti because he had taken several days to put up his route and I had taken just a few hours to repeat it.

Obviously there is absolutely no comparison, but when journalists find an "angle" to recount an event, everybody latches on to it and the story gets away from you, as does your public image. A lot of this may happen with the best of intentions; nevertheless, I thought those comments were unfair to Bonatti.

I was sure that taking several days to put up a big route was an outdated form of alpinism; soloing fast and light was, of course, the new trend. But spending days on a big-wall first ascent is an altogether different adventure, one that was unknown to me and that I felt the urge to fully experience. Since then, it seems that the "big journey up a face" has come back into vogue in France: Solos, repeats, and new multiday aid routes are attracting just as much attention as speed ascents and enchainments. Parties have also been accomplish-

> ∽ I was making a living from my climbs...
> but I never felt that I was betraying my passion,
> rather that I was contributing to the public's
> knowledge about the mountains.

ing long ridge traverses. Are we in the process of rediscovering some of the values of traditional alpinism that had been somewhat forgotten? Or else has the quest for speed already reached its limits in a context where competition remains informal, unspoken, and often denied? To go beyond these limits, will we have to bring out the stopwatches and hold competitions as in ski mountaineering?

While I was training for the Eiger in 1991, I ventured onto a frozen waterfall for the first time. I was really behind the times in the ice-climbing domain; frozen-waterfall climbing had emerged in France at least 12 years earlier. The forerunners were from the Pyrenees, climbing in the Gavarnie cirque. In the years following, Godefroy Perroux did a lot to make ice climbing known. The first ice gathering in the country took place in 1991. Today more and more women are making a name for themselves in ice climbing, whereas there are still few women climbing mountains.

My return to the mountains took the media somewhat by surprise; they saw me exclusively as a competitor and a crag climber. But they liked the fact that my story was taking a twist, and considered me the first woman alpinist. *Paris Match* magazine had long taken an interest in mountain climbing and liked to follow its "heroes" over several years; it covered all my climbs during that period. That was lucky for me, because when *Paris Match* goes for a story the rest of the press follows suit and the sponsors love it.

After my first ascent on the Drus, I had some unpleasant surprises from certain alpinists; was it jealousy, acrimony, or male chauvinism? I heard some real doozies: On the Bonatti Pillar, guides had checked the pitons for me; on my new route, I had been resupplied with water and a drill had been sent up to me; and so on. Some members of the Groupe de Haute Montagne (the elite of amateur alpinists in France) gave me a hard time about the use of helicopters by the photographers and cameramen, about the presence of the media, and about my relationships with sponsors—that is to say for being a professional climber. In essence, I was being accused of prostituting the mountains. This became the subject of a strongly worded declaration from within the Groupe de Haute Montagne that, fortunately, provoked a response from a prominent member of the organization reminding people that, in the end, I had still done an ascent worthy of interest. Of course I was making a living from my climbs and their spin-offs, but while doing so, I never felt that I was betraying my passion, rather that I was contributing to the public's knowledge about mountains. Coming as it did from a world that often feels misunderstood, I still think, even today, that this reproach is both paradoxical and insincere.

Sometimes I would console myself by remembering that Desmaison had been subjected to the same kind of controversy during his time. In my case there was also the fact that I was a woman. As far as sponsors and the media were concerned, this served me well, of course: the fragile young woman who faces huge risks in the mountains, that touched people. As far as my fellow alpinists were concerned, I would have much preferred that my gender not be taken into account. When I climb, I am an alpinist first, and not particularly a "female alpinist." I never felt concerned about issues such as "women in alpinism," nor did I see myself as a militant feminist, or ever want to participate in an all-female expedition. I never felt as if I had something to prove as a woman.

As a result, some of the reactions coming from the climbing world seemed strange or uncalled for. I was upset that people wanted to devalue my new route on the Drus. I would have preferred that it be valued for what it was: a difficult first ascent, a wall climb that was atypical for its time. If a guy had done it, I think there would have been less controversy. It was almost as if people were saying that since a woman had done it, it couldn't be very hard. That all calmed down after my ascent of the Eiger. The Eiger climb got a great deal of media attention even though it wasn't a first ascent; a winter solo had already been done several times by men, and I had found it far less difficult. But the Eiger inspires fear.

After these experiences, I knew I was capable of soloing any of the classic north faces in the Alps. This is why I chose to attempt the Bonatti route on the Matterhorn. The regular route didn't interest me because I was sure of succeeding on it; the Bonatti route represented the unknown, and strong alpinists had already failed miserably on it. This is also what made me turn to the Himalaya.

THE HIMALAYA

After my first visit to Nepal on a trekking trip in 1992, I developed some ambitious projects to do technical faces in alpine style with only one climbing partner. I wasn't interested in big expeditions. I have a lot of admiration for Loretan and Troillet, for their style and their speed. My first experience at altitude had been on Trango Tower; that had been followed by a trip to Latok in 1992. I performed well at altitude, but I found the objective dangers to be very significant. I realized that, at altitude, moving fast is not a choice but a necessity; otherwise, you don't survive.

opening one of the most majestic routes in the Alps: the famous dihedral on the gray and yellow face of Cima Su Alto overlooking Lake Alleghe. This dihedral, blocked by roofs and overhangs, had rebuffed many attempts—partly because the rock is very friable. Once they had climbed the dihedral, the way was paved for many free-climbing routes on rock faces without rest holds.

After the war, in 1952, the difficult face of Cima Scotoni in the Fanis group was climbed by Lacedelli, Ghedina, and Lorenzi. In 1956, Desmaison and Couzy climbed the sharp North Edge of Aiguille Noire de Peuterey, the most direct route on the West Face of the Noire. I can still remember the route put up on the Northwest Face of Pic d'Olan in 1957, one of the most difficult climbs in the Alps.

But it becomes increasingly difficult to analyze, without making mistakes, the most significant undertakings of the forties and fifties, which saw the growth of artificial climbing. This is particularly the case on the more difficult routes: First classified with one grade, they were now regraded, as the new climbers found pitons left by earlier climbers in the most demanding parts of the rock face. They were thus operating in conditions not originally found by the first climbers. The spread of artificial equipment in the Dolomites was faster than in the Western Alps, partly due to the nature of the rock, which facilitates the discovery of clefts where pitons can be placed.

We all interpret the mountains in our own way, relative to the objectives that we set for ourselves. I consider technical difficulty to be a healthy and necessary part of a rewarding mountain climb: I have always, therefore, used pitons, *étrier,* and ropes, mainly for safety reasons, because life is a priceless gift and undoubtedly comes before all the other factors that make up a climb.

Moreover, a rational use of technology, such as a logical piton placement at a key point where the rock face is practically impossible to climb, is in keeping with my idea of a climb.

Whatever your thoughts on the issue, there is little question that the shift in the style opened up a new wealth of climbs in the Alps during the period. The Pel e Os group of Monza included Walter Bonatti, one of the most well-known

climbers between 1949 and 1965. After many ascents of famous traditional routes throughout the Alps, in 1951 he set himself an arduous task: He would climb the East Face of the Grand Capucin, the first upper sixth grade opened in the Mont Blanc massif. He continued with a winter ascent of the Furggen Ridge on the Matterhorn. And in the early winter of 1953, he and Carlo Mauri climbed the North Face of Cima Ovest di Lavaredo.

In 1955, Bonatti opened an extraordinary route on the Southwest Pillar of the Dru. In 1957, he climbed the impressive Grand Pilier d'Angle on Mont Blanc. He climbed the East Face with Toni Gobbi, the North Face with Cosimo Zappelli in 1962, and finally, again with Zappelli, the Southeast Face in 1963. He did have another notable first on Mont Blanc in 1959 with Andrea Oggioni via the Pilier Rouge du Brouillard, and one year later, Bonatti climbed the Voie Major alone, while Carlo Mauri, of the Ragni group from Lecco, climbed the Pear, once again solo. In 1961, Bonatti lost his battle with the Central Pillar of Freney of Mont Blanc, where victory was won by two international roped teams including the Italian Ignazio Piussi, French climber René Desmaison, and British climbers Bonington and Whillans. But in 1963 Bonatti did the first winter climb of the Walker Spur on the North Face of the Grandes Jorasses and continued, in 1964, by opening an extremely difficult route on the North Face of Whymper Peak with Michael Vaucher.

In 1957 René Desmaison and Couzy did the first winter climb of Magnone's Route on the Petit Dru; Desmaison repeated it solo in 1963. The first winter ascent of the Central Pillar of Freney was achieved in February 1967 by Desmaison with Robert Flematti: It was one of the best examples of both technical and mental training and courage and one of the many difficult routes that Desmaison opened in the Alps.

These winter and solo approaches to difficult routes became increasingly popular, making this evolutionary period of mountain climbing very significant. It led to new directions, like those glimpsed in 1961 when Toni Hiebeler and friends climbed the North Face of the Eiger in winter.

I remember other winter climbs: Solleder on the Matterhorn in 1963 with Piussi, Redaelli, and Hiebeler; the route that I opened in 1937 with

Vittorio Ratti and Ginetto Esposito on the Northeast Face of the Badile, now climbed by three Swiss guides and three Italians in January of 1968. In the same winter, the South Face of the Torre Trieste fell to Piussi, who in the following year went on to do the first winter climb of the Guide's Route on Crozzon of the Brenta with Lanfranchi and Roberto Chiappa. This was one of the most important winter climbs in the Dolomites.

Meanwhile, the Rusconi brothers were notching up successes in the Retiche Alps. In 1970, they opened the most direct route on the Northeast Face of Badile—the Via del Fratello—continuing with the first ascent of the Northeast Face of Cengalo in 1972, and the first winter climb of the East Face of Badile with friends from Valmadrera, near Lecco. In the same year, this group conquered the Northwest Face of the Matterhorn and the famous Philipp-Flamm dihedral in 1973.

Soloing has always been the domain of very qualified climbers, but the climbers of the 1940s through the '60s were really something else: Hermann Buhl's first winter climb of Via Soldà on the Marmolada and d'Ambiez peak, the route he opened on Pala di San Martino using free climbing techniques, and Mauri and Bonatti's winter climb of my route on the West Face of Lavaredo.

Cesare Maestri, "the Spider of the Dolomites," accomplished many solo climbs on these mountains. He descended, with no artificial help, the difficult Guide's Route on the Brenta Face after having climbed it. He then moved toward artificial climbing in 1960 when he opened the vertical, most direct, route on the red face of Roda of Vael.

It is impossible to list all the climbs in the Alps during this period, or even the solo ones. In the 1960s, Reinhold Messner made many climbs and repeats of the most difficult routes on rock, ice, and mixed terrain—mostly in the Dolomites. He used a free climbing style that required severe ethical standards and a very strenuous training program. Just two examples are his ascents of the North Face of the Droites and the Philipp-Flamm dihedral of the Matterhorn.

The original ascent of this latter route was a special milestone in history in that it marked a return to the ethic of free climbing. In 1957, Walter Philipp of Vienna and Dieter Flamm conquered this beautiful, 2,950-foot dihedral on the Northwest Wall of the Matterhorn. This ascent reinforced the view that many new routes requiring considerable exertion and skill could still be opened. Both exertion and skill were characteristics of Enzo Cozzolino, an incredible climber from Trieste, whose name has been given to another great free route of the period, this time the climb on the right sector of the South Face of Scotoni.

Over the last two decades of the century, we have seen an increase in activity and a more flexible approach to climbing in the Alps, using different methods and approaches. The new generations following in the tracks of traditional climbing, free, and artificial climbing have always found a way to continue their way of seeing the mountains, achieve their goals, and experience satisfaction. Giorgio Bertone is one of the most enthusiastic climbers and guides of Monte Rosa. After climbing all the traditional known routes, he performed the first winter climb up the Sesia Gorge.

In the 1980s, we saw another development in the approach to mountain climbing: The young climbers, favoring free climbing and scorning the piton, concentrated on climbing, in the shortest time possible, those faces that their forerunners had taken entire days to scale. I remember when Boivin climbed The Linceul (Shroud) on the Grandes Jorasses in 2 hours 45 minutes—unroped, in perfect style—and the Via Bonatti-Zappelli to Pilier d'Angle enchainment in four hours. He moved from one mountain to another using a parapente and performed ever more original exploits, such as the ascent of the North Face of the Matterhorn, solo, in four hours—followed by parapente descent. This is one of the practices, used by new climbers, that respects the mountains in their intimate essence. Originality, the desire for new emotions, and the abundance of equipment are only the exterior facade of their love for the mountains.

The dangerous passion for icefalls has also returned in full. Frozen waterfalls are part of the new game, which involves their ascent using free climbing techniques. In Europe, the French are the most avid promoters of this experience. A prime example was François Damilano and Philippe

Pibarot's climb of the incredible 490-foot Massue Waterfall in the Haute Savoie in January of 1992.

I would also like to note the continuing activities in the Central Alps by Miotti, Maspes, and Merizzi, among others. Their climbs in the Dolomites were established with rigid attention to ethics and with a focus on extreme climbing. The Marmolada, the same wall that had seen the most traditional Dolomite climbing, was now attacked with modern free styles—getting away from the old artificial routes.

Just as our lives outside of climbing are changing and modernizing every day, so are our practices within climbing; Heinz Mariacher and Manolo are two of the best examples of this change. They select from and use everything they have learned and experienced in gyms and on smaller cliffs, and they apply those skills to the great faces of the mountains. They always use free-climbing ethics—a very rigid discipline that requires an almost professional level of training.

If I were young, I would also use this style because I believe it to be interesting, useful, and valuable as training for the big climbs. Those who practice this discipline acquire such a refined technique that they can maximize their physical endurance to include the use of the tiniest holds. They obtain results that were inconceivable only a few years ago.

The free-climbing ethic, applied in gyms and on crags, has been the launching pad for many young climbers committed to improving their style and stamina. While real, organized competitions are now common, competition in other forms has always existed in traditional mountain climbing. In my time, competitions raged for the ascents of routes like the West Face of Lavaredo, the Northeast Face of Piz Badile, and the North Face of the Grandes Jorasses. Young climbers who have opted for this sport because of its spirit of innovation, and who have been strengthened by competition, have performed incredible exploits on the great climbs of the Alps.

Some great achievements were seen in the 1980s: Manolo and Piero Valmassoi climbed the East Face of Sass Maor—a continuously difficult seventh grade—using seven pitons and just a few nuts. Heinz Mariacher and Luisa Jovane (one of the best female sport climbers in the world) opened an upper seventh grade route on the Marmolada of Ombretta. From 1981, high quality routes continued to be put up on the Marmolada: Two Czechs put up Via Attraverso il Pesce, not repeated until 1984. In 1986, Giordani climbed this face in winter with Cipriani and Lenatti and then soloed in August of the same year. Increasingly difficult routes continued to be established—such as Specchio di Sara, considered by Giordani to be a lower ninth grade. Generally speaking, the fear that the potential for new routes in the Dolomites was exhausted has been unfounded, despite a considerable number of routes that are disputed between the "purists" and the "artificialists."

In 1990, one of the most brilliant efforts was mounted on the Tre Cime of Lavaredo, where Slovenian Francek Knez mapped out several lines between the eighth and ninth grades. Similarly, Hainz Christoph of the Alto Adige region, one of the most qualified climbers of the '90s, opened an impressive route on the Pilastro of Punta Tissi on the Matterhorn in 1991.

The issue of style—and the eventual position of a route in history—is getting more and more complex as climbing changes. Routes, frequently squeezed between other lines, sometimes become simple corridors where the difference between rock climbing and mountain climbing becomes more and more unclear. The grade of the route is increasingly based on the lack of bolts or their very limited use. In 1993, the East Face of Torre Trieste fell with just three bolts and four anchors over its nearly 1,150-foot length. Obviously, climbing with the assistance of bolts and drills means that you can climb and descend anywhere, faster and with better guarantees of success, and you can create routes on the best faces with controlled levels of difficulty.

By the late 1980s and early 1990s, Michel Piola of Geneva and others performed spectacular climbs on the North Face of the Matterhorn, creating the most direct route to the Zmutt Arête, as well as establishing equally spectacular lines on the Central Pillar of Freney and the walls of Grand Capucin. The Swiss Daniel Anker opened three new routes and two winter ones on the North Wall of the Eiger, and Beat Kammerlander perfected the limestone routes on the border between Austria and

Switzerland, originally opened by Martin Schule.

Extreme climbing is more difficult on Mont Blanc due to the quality of its rock, but excursions by Manlio Motto of Piedmont and his partner Vogler were extensive over the last few years— especially in the Western Alps. He climbs extremely difficult rock routes with traditional protection but often uses a drill only so that others may repeat the climbs safely.

The discreet, sometimes decisive, use of bolts in the Valmasino and Val Bregaglia mountains has allowed route development at a high technical level, especially on those lines requiring considerable commitment, such as bivouacs and many hours on the rock face. This is of great importance from an exploratory viewpoint.

In the 1990s, Catherine Destivelle became well-known in the climbing world. After a childhood spent climbing, and after achieving success in the rock climbing competition in Bardonecchia, Destivelle returned to the large faces. In 1990 she climbed the Bonatti Pillar on the Dru in four hours, solo; in 1991, she opened a new route on the West Face of the Dru; in 1992 and 1993, she climbed both the Walker Spur and the North Face of the Eiger. She was followed by a helicopter and camcorders that provided close-ups of her climbing with elegance and confidence.

There was also the unforgettable Alison Hargreaves, who soloed the North Faces of the Grandes Jorasses, the Eiger, the Matterhorn, the Cima Grande of Lavaredo, and the Petit Dru, and the Northeast Face of Piz Badile in just a few weeks in 1993.

This modest summary of some of the climbs of the Alps from the Second World War until today offers opportunity for certain conclusions. Any comparison between mountain climbing of the past and today is out of place. Many decisions made in the past were based on intuition and trial and error,

because much had yet to be discovered. Today's climbing is built upon the experience of those years.

The accomplishments of today are also assisted by the progress made in clothing, equipment, and athletic training. Even though climbers are somewhat different—and accordingly, even though their objectives have changed, mountain climbing itself has not changed. The guiding forces remain: a passion for climbing, willpower, and the ability to conquer severe difficulties. I believe that at all times—as in the period when I was the most actively involved in mountain climbing—the most important thing is to feel real and deep satisfaction.

As long as the mountains exist, mountain climbing will never disappear. It is inevitable that we will continue with bolder undertakings, undoubtedly different in their exterior form and methods, but which do not change the spirit and soul of climbers. I must say that today, unlike in my time, the commercialization of climbing through sponsorships definitely makes certain ventures more spectacular, this is simply part of the world in which we live today. Direct television coverage by helicopters gives wider circulation of images and news that reaches people who do not have access to the mountains.

The future of mountain climbing is not in danger. The Alps, like all the mountains in the world, will always have something new to offer because we are the creators of our continuous interest in them. Inclined by nature to new conquests, we will always find new ways to express ourselves in harmony with the period in which we live. This inclination is accompanied by our search for experiences that are deep and unforgettable.

Who knows how many other technical and cultural devices will help—in this millennium—those people who love the mountains and who live their life in them to the fullest? I would like to be there, too.

Riccardo Cassin was born in northern Italy in 1909. After an early life as a blacksmith and a boxer, he discovered mountaineering. His legendary career has included about 2,500 climbs—in Italy, Switzerland, France, Austria, Spain, Yugoslavia, Scotland, the Caucasus, Alaska, Peru, Pakistan, Nepal, Japan, and Patagonia.

Over one hundred of these were first ascents, accomplished over a span of decades, from the Southwest Face of Cima Lavaredo Piccolissima in 1934 to the South Face of Mount McKinley in 1961 and the West Face of Jirishanca in 1965. At age 78, he repeated the Northeast Face of Piz Badile on the 50th anniversary of his first ascent.

Reinhold Messner has said of Cassin: "He's a milestone in the history of climbing."

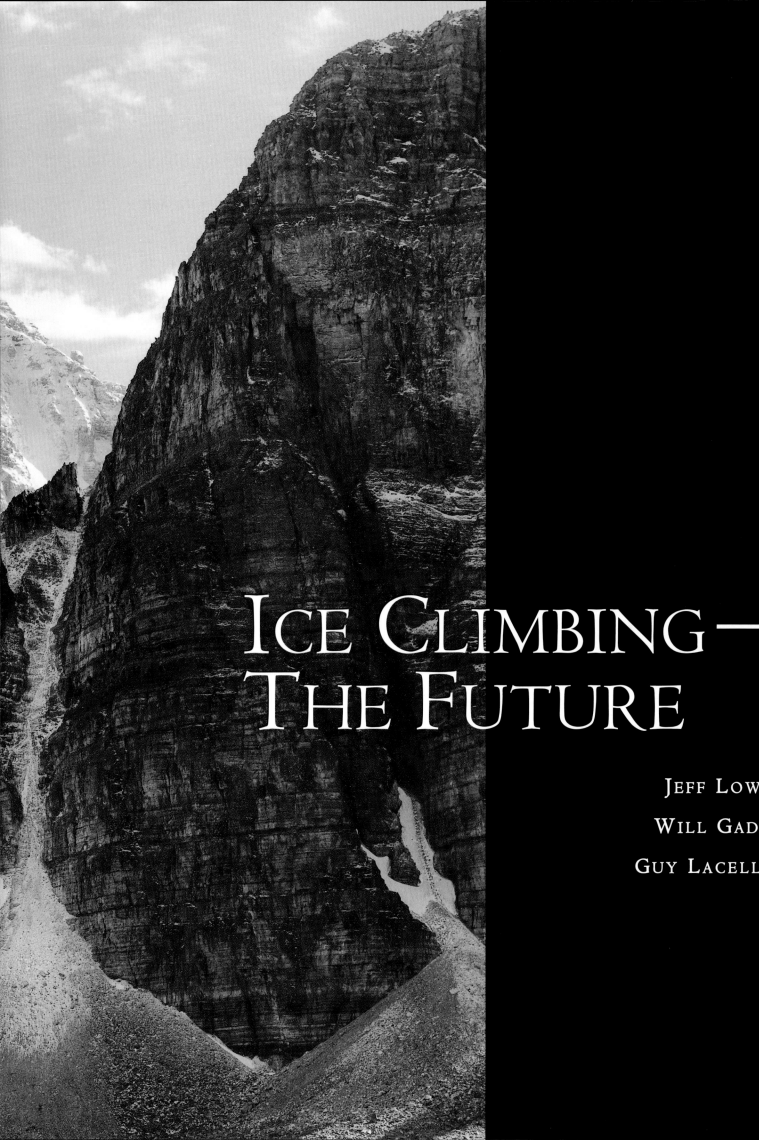

ICE CLIMBING —
THE FUTURE

JEFF LOWE

WILL GADD

GUY LACELLE

SOULS ON ICE

JEFF LOWE

Climbers who were introduced to the art of ascent through sport climbing on bolted crags might have difficulty understanding the appeal of ice climbing. T-shirts, shorts, and warm rock are as different from the frigid belays, heavy layers of clothing, warlike tools, and evanescent medium of the ice climber as the tropics are from Antarctica. In reality though, ice climbing is more deeply rooted than rock climbing in the history of ascent. Those who take pleasure in the frozen delights of the high peaks or winter waterfalls are directly linked to the adventurous spirit of the alpine pioneers who boldly traversed glaciers, snow, and ice to reach the summits.

We who are willing to endure stormbound wastelands on the approaches to castles of ice and fortresses of snow do so because, in such awesome conditions and wildly beautiful places, we discover things we never knew about ourselves. Our strengths and weaknesses are articulated with a cold clarity that is otherwise difficult to achieve. Our bodies and minds are positively stressed by the medium, which is at once fragile, harsh, and beautiful. A soul dancing on ice is like a dessert of baked Alaska: The contrast of flame and ice cream makes a tasty non sequitur.

In the early 1800s, English gentry holidayed in the Alps, hiring the local shepherds to guide them. Mutual interest led to improvements in equipment, the original three-pronged "crampon" giving way to

nailed boots and the alpenstock shortened and equipped with an adze to chop steps on steep icy slopes. There was no protection available except the rope and ice ax. Classic first ascents on snow and ice were made, and the sport of ice climbing was born.

During the latter half of the 19th century the Alps were all summited, usually by a great step-chopping guide such as Melchior Anderegg on the Brenva Spur of Mont Blanc or Christian Klucker on the North Face of the Lyskamm.

By the turn of the century, the Scottish Mountaineering Club began tackling difficult rock climbs glazed in coatings of ice and snow. To make the first ascent of Green Gully on Ben Nevis in 1906, Harold Raeburn wore nailed boots and cut steps. Eighteen years later Raeburn made the first winter ascent of Observatory Ridge. These difficult Scottish climbs were unsurpassed until the 1950s.

In 1908, British climber Oscar Eckenstein created a ten-point crampon and invented a "flat foot" climbing technique that reduced the need to cut steps. In 1924, Willo Welzenbach hammered in long, barbed ice pitons designed by Fritz Riegele to make the first ascent of the Northwest Face of the Gross Wiesbachhorn. Armand Charlet, a master of the new flatfoot technique, and his partner Camille Dévouassoux climbed the Nant Blanc Face of the Aiguille Verte in 1928. Ascents of the three most famous alpine north faces—the Matterhorn, the Grandes Jorasses, and the Eiger—capped the accomplishments of the early part of the 20th century. On the Eiger, the natural leader Anderl Heckmair used Laurent Grivel's 12-point crampons to front-point up the ice fields in a fraction of the time it would have taken to cut steps.

The 1955 six-day ascent of the North Face of Les Droites ushered in a new level of ice climbing difficulty. The route was much steeper than any previously attempted and involved hundreds of feet of thin, hard-to-protect ice over compact granite slabs. Near the end of the decade, climbs were made safer by the new Salewa tube screws, but crampons were still relatively unsophisticated. Though ice-ax shafts were now shorter and easier to handle on steep terrain, the picks were straight, requiring insecure "daggering" when front-pointing.

In Scotland, climbers such as Hamish MacInnes, Tom Patey, Chris Bonington, Jimmy Marshall, and Robin Smith were pushing the standards of mixed climbing on routes like Ravens Gully and the Orion Face Direct. These classic climbs—steeper and technically more difficult than their longer Alpine cousins—were accomplished with little protection, using ax and crampons, cunning and craft to their fullest in a uniquely eclectic Scottish blend of step-cutting, front-pointing, flatfooting, and mixed climbing.

In 1966 American Yvon Chouinard front-pointed the North Face of Les Courtes using the "ice dagger" technique with a straight-pick ax. The climb inspired him to experiment with curving and drooping the ax pick to make it stick and hook better in the ice. Chouinard's curved pick and Hamish MacInnes's concurrently developed Terrordactyl (an ax with a steeply angled pick) changed the sport of ice climbing for all time. Chouinard also developed rigid, adjustable crampons, which helped to alleviate the calf-muscle strain of front-pointing.

Using the new tools, the standards of the hardest alpine and Scottish climbs were equaled in New Hampshire with early-seventies waterfall ice climbs like John Bouchard's solo first ascent of the 600-foot Black Dike. But in Utah and Colorado, new free-climbing standards were being set on ice.

In 1971 my brother Greg Lowe utilized his own curved-pick tools on the first ascent of Malan's Peak Waterfall near our home in Ogden, Utah. Greg led the crux pitch—75 feet of vertical and overhanging ice—entirely free with almost no protection. Greg

introduced Mike Weis and me to frozen waterfalls in the winter of 1972, and in 1974 Mike and I completed the first ascent of Colorado's Bridalveil Falls using half a dozen of Greg's homemade chromoly tubes with tips beveled to the inside. These could be driven effectively into the extremely cold, brittle ice without causing it to shatter. The standard sixties-era Salewa tube screws and ice pitons commercially available at the time were essentially useless.

In the Canadian Rockies, Bugs McKeith, Rob Wood, George Homer, Tim Auger, John Laughlan, Laurie Skreslet, and other climbers were using MacInnes's Terrordactyls to make the first ascents of many great water ice climbs. Routes such as Bourgeau Left Hand, Takkakkaw Falls, Nemesis, the Weeping Wall, the Weeping Pillar, Polar Circus, and Slipstream are among the classic ice climbs of all time. Complicating the technical challenge was the northern Rockies' extreme winter cold, heavy snowfall, and avalanche hazard.

By the mid-seventies, climbers took their new tools and skills to difficult high-mountain routes around the world: Canada's Grand Central Couloir on Mount Kitchener by Mike Weis and myself; Jean-Marc Boivin and Patrick Gabarrou on the Super Couloir on Mont Blanc du Tacul; the Diamond Couloir on Mount Kenya by Chouinard and Mike Covington; and Kilimanjaro's Breech Wall by Reinhold Messner and Konrad Renzler. Frenchman Nicholas Jaeger made solo climbs in Peru on the South Face of Taulliraju and the South Face of the East Peak of Chacraraju that were as difficult technically as anything in the Alps. In 1979 I made the first ascent of the South Face of Ama Dablam in Nepal.

By the end of the decade, waterfall ice climbing was well established throughout North America, the Alps, Norway, and even Japan and Korea. During this time equipment had evolved greatly. Simple curved or angled picks gave way to reverse-curve, interchangeable picks with alloy shafts and specialized adzes. Footfang crampons and Snarg ice pitons appeared. The numbers of ice climbers swelled and climbs that were the ultimate at the beginning of the decade were now being cruised within the first few outings by avid aspirants.

In the 1980s Jean-Carlo Grassi and Renato Casarotto led the development of waterfall ice climbing in Italian Alpine valleys. In the Pyrenees,

Dominique Julien and Rainer Munsch were developing beautiful climbs in the Cirque de Gavarnie. In Norway, Hans Christian Doseth, Thomas Carlstrom, and Ulf Geir Hansen were leading the way on some of the longest, prettiest waterfall climbs in the world. Patrick Gabarrou, Jean-Marc Boivin, and Christophe Profit were pioneering such climbs as Cascade de Notre Dame and the Hypercouloir high on Mont Blanc. Dave Breashears and I climbed the Hungo Face of Kwangde in Nepal. Mixed climbing was taken to new heights in Scotland and Colorado by climbers such as Al Rouse, Rab Carrington, Duncan Ferguson, Mark Wilford, and Alex Lowe, and in the Canadian Rockies by Barry Blanchard and friends.

The winter of 1992 was a good one for water ice in France. François Damilano's climb of the incredible free-hanging pillar of Le Dame du Lac was only surpassed by Thierry Renault's climb of Le Lyre. Englishman Stevie Haston made another difficult route—Nuit Blanche near the Argentiére Glacier.

In that same year, climbing Blind Faith on the Tête du Gramusat with Renault got me thinking about the future of ice climbing. Although we had used several pitons for aid on the roof, I was curious about the possibility of free climbing with ax and crampons using nuts, pitons, and ice screws—for protection only.

Although the waterfalls in the Rigid Designator amphitheater in Vail, Colorado, had all been climbed, there was a free-hanging dagger of ice dangling ten feet out from a sketchy traverse near the top. With the Blind Faith roof under my belt, I was convinced it could be free climbed using a combination of rock and ice techniques and tools. "Dry tooling" out the roof, I fell off several times before figuring out how to make the moves—including figure fours—to allow high placements over the lip into good ice above. Photographs of this route (Octopussy) galvanized the climbing world into a new style of overhanging mixed climbing. Overnight, areas that had seemed climbed-out were suddenly bristling with exciting new challenges. By the end of the century, hundreds of the new-style climbs had been created around the world, led by Stevie Haston, Will Gadd, Kim Csizmazia, Robert Jasper, Raphael Slawinski, and others.

Ice climbing has even become a social activity. Ice festivals and competitions bring people together to share information, play with gear, climb a bit, and party a lot. People who train on sport mixed routes develop greater technical abilities that can be applied to the high mountains. The ultimate proof is Tomas Humar's 1999 seven-day solo ascent of the 14,000-foot-high South Face of Dhaulagiri.

I don't think it's a good idea for young climbers to emulate Humar's example on objectively dangerous faces. After all, shouldn't climbing enhance life rather than threaten it on each outing? There are other, safer ways to challenge tomorrow's climbers; two young tigers could free climb the North Buttress of Alaska's Mount Hunter, or in winter a tight team could tackle the vertical ice seams on the North Face of Latok I in Pakistan. These are reasonably safe objectives that will require all the strength, skill, experience, and commitment that climbers can muster.

I hope more ice parks will be created like the one in Ouray, Colorado. Clothing, equipment, technique, and climbing styles will continue to evolve in ways we can't foresee. But I'm convinced that adventure and challenge will remain the essence of the sport. I envy young climbers the crystalline experiences that lie before them.

Jeff Lowe has been a climber since his father took him up the Grand Teton in 1956 at the age of seven. With more than 500 first ascents to his credit, Jeff Lowe is a leading proponent in the movement toward light and fast climbs of the most technically difficult routes in the most remote mountain ranges on Earth.

In the late 1960s and early '70s he specialized in big-wall climbing, completing numerous early ascents of the Yosemite classics. He is also a renowned free climber, the author of hundreds of classic traditional rock climbs throughout the western U. S.

Lowe has written numerous magazine articles and is the author of three books: The Ice Experience *(1979);* Climbing *(1986), written in conjunction with Ron Fawcett, Paul Nunn, and Alan Rouse; and* Ice World *(1996). He was guest speaker at the Banff Mountain Film Festival in 1983.*

committing lines to stand with honor in the gaze of those who came before us. There are some alpine climbers who can redpoint 5.14, on-sight M8, and solo WI6. There are also alpine climbers who resort to aid on 5.11 or M7 climbing. Steph Davis and partners recently put up a hard new free route at 20,000 feet on Shipton Spire in Pakistan. That scores a 14 on the GAG scale. Another party put up a new aid line at the same time, but I think the aiding was at a far lower technical standard and without as much commitment. So I would rate that climb about a 10 on the GAG.

Traditional rock climbing is also experiencing a renaissance. Leo Houlding recently freed a massive new route on El Cap, with run-out 5.13 climbing, twenty pitches off the deck. That effort scores a 14 on my GAG scale and I think it points the way toward the future. Leo learned his skills sport climbing, as did Yuji Hirayama and Todd Skinner. Both have taken their movement skills and applied them to harder gear-protected routes. Yuji has on-sighted most of the Salathé as well as Sphinx Crack, a 5.13 in Colorado. Leo was a successful competitor, and he has moved onto the big walls with a vengeance. John Dunne's slate routes are also wickedly difficult and run-out. Partheon has hard 5.13 climbing way, way above the gear. If you want to climb that route then you had better be ready for it.

Everest gets a lowly 8 on the GAG for good reason: It is a low-angle pile of snow. Not surprisingly, it has been soloed often and fast. When Hillary first climbed Everest and Messner first soloed it without oxygen, their climbs had meaning in the mountain world. But Everest today is a dead end as far as new ground in mountaineering, if climbed by a standard route.

Climbing all the 8,000-meter peaks, while a noble goal in itself, is also fairly meaningless, as it does nothing to advance the state of climbing. Most modern ascents of 8,000-meter peaks are repeats of routes done up to 40 years ago, with a few notable exceptions. However, modern new routes on Changabang, Nanga Parbat, Logan, Denali, and in the mountains of Patagonia and Peru are hard and committing. They deserve the respect of the climbing community and the GAG chart reflects this.

The main purpose of this chart, other than having some good fun, is to examine where all the sub-

sets of climbing are in relation to each other. Ice climbing reached a relative impasse with Grade 7—which is often just Grade 5 with really bad gear. Aid climbing has also reached the point where a fall often means death. Both of these sports have reached their technical dead ends, and must be reincarnated to progress. Not surprisingly, many of the harder pure ice and aid lines are getting soloed very fast. No one wants to run it out farther on worse gear on hard climbing. But the moves are not that hard, so people are soloing them or doing linkups. The absolute technical level of aid and pure ice climbing is pretty much stagnant. Harder pure ice climbs do exist, but they are hard to find.

The hardest pure ice climbing I have ever done was on a serac in France. I would rate it "ice 8." Technically, it is worlds harder than any pure waterfall ice climb I've seen, but the gear is good. The other hard pure ice climbs I've seen are in competitions in Europe. They look like the bottom side of an iced flight of stairs—absolutely crazy moves that I've never seen the likes of in the wild. From a purely technical perspective, the hardest new ice climbs will probably be done on seracs, or on man-made ice. Rock climbers found it increasingly difficult to find harder rock climbs on natural rock and ended up chipping many of them (the mags won't show you this, but trust me, it's true). I think chipping on rock is weak, but farmed ice doesn't hurt anything. Ice farmers, start your hoses!

The top end of mixed climbing is currently at M10 or so. The only thing I've climbed that seemed M10 was Brennivin, a mixed climb in Iceland. After hard dry tooling across a 15-foot down-sloping roof and another 20 feet of very difficult footless dry tooling, the route climbs thin, overhanging ice with poor protection for another 100 feet. It receives a GAG of 13, because it is technically hard and has a very real commitment factor. However, the technical difficulty on that route is on the rock moves. Perhaps an ice climb is out there that could get the same technical grade, but I have yet to see it despite extensive searching.

There are much harder dry tooling routes that are possible, especially if they are done in summer when your body is warmer. But why not just go rock climbing? For me, a good mixed route has to combine both technical purity and commitment for a complete experience. I recently put up an M9 that is basically all on rock. The experience wasn't very satisfactory because I felt as if I was sport climbing again. I also put up a remote, multipitch alpine route with Sean Isaac that we rated 5+ R/X. If you fell on the thin ice pitch, you would die. I had a great experience with a good partner, but again I felt that in some ways it was a regression to an older form of climbing. Still, it was a beautiful line worth climbing and that is the heart of the game for me.

I am convinced that the future of ice climbing lies in putting all aspects of free climbing into one winter discipline. I have never enjoyed aid climbing. For me it lacks the purity of movement that defines good climbing. Besides, I always bruise the hell out of my knees. It also seems, to misquote another climber, to "reduce the mountains to a mechanical extravaganza." With ever evolving protection technology, there will probably come a point where you can just slap a patch of putty on the wall and clip it, making dicey aid placements obsolete. For me, the future is free, hard, committing, and cold.

Examples of this style of climbing include Dave Thomson, Kefira Allen, and Raphael Slawinski's recently established Rocket Man, a seven-pitch alpine mixed route at M7+ with Grade 6+R ice climbing. That effort also scores a 14 on the GAG and points the way toward more futuristic mixed routes.

They are out there—in the Himalaya, the Canadian Rockies, Peru, Alaska, and in other ranges—long, free, genuinely hard routes with a high degree of commitment. Those who can climb hard ice, then switch to hard free moves on rock, will eat up these routes. The routes will involve climbers capable of on-sighting 5.13, water ice 6+, and M9—all on natural gear. Climbers who can do all of these will redefine what is possible in the mountains—like no generation in the last 40 years. The climbers' gear bags will contain slippers, warm leather boots, and top-of-the-line ice tools. Those who are limited to one discipline are able to push that discipline upward in small increments. But the real leaps forward will come from those who can throw all the different forms of climbing into a blender and become stronger by drinking the resulting mixture. So train harder than you've ever trained on rock, ice, and mixed, and then go do them.

The only thing between us and these routes is our notion of what is possible. The limits of possibility were always proved to be eggshell thin by climbers who thought differently and had the guts to try. Jeff Lowe, Bugs McKeith, Bruce Hendricks, Leo Houlding, Ricardo Cassin, and many of the contributors to this book have all made climbing leaps of faith and created routes that defined their eras. If we are to live up to Jim Elzinga and John Lauchlan's efforts, then we must leap forward or our sport will stagnate. I believe we live in the true golden age of mixed climbing, as defined by the climber's ability to climb any type of terrain, no matter where or in what conditions.

And there will always be the call of a blue siren, screaming upward. Despite its relatively lower technical grade, Slipstream is no less of a route today than when Jim and John first climbed it. Classical routes will always be classics. The Dibona Arête on the Cima Grande di Lavaredo was first climbed in 1910. Today, it would receive a GAG of 3, but when Dibona made the ascent it was perhaps a 14. A modern climber, in sticky shoes and with a rope that will actually hold a fall, can make short work of it. I climbed it last year simply because, like a beautiful waterfall, it demands the respect of any climber. I often think that in our quest for harder and higher, ever more futuristic routes, we risk missing the joy of simply moving and being in the mountains.

Canadian-born Will Gadd is one of the top extreme sports athletes in the world. To climbers, he is known for radical ice routes and high-level competition results. Kayakers know him for pioneering new descents down wilderness rivers across North America, as well as for teaching and writing about paddling for magazines. In paragliding, he is best known for record-setting flights. But he also excels at rock climbing; mountaineering; telemark, downhill, and cross-country skiing; caving; and mountain biking.

He climbed his first waterfall at 12, established the world's hardest ice routes in '97 and '98, and won first place at every major ice competition in '98 and '99 (ESPN X Games, and the Courchevel Invitational, France).

CLOSE ENCOUNTER OF THE FROZEN KIND

GUY LACELLE

Winter has always been my favorite season. As a kid I loved big snowstorms and cold weather. When I hosed down my skating rink, I was fascinated watching the water freeze in perfect layers of ice. One winter in Quebec I slept in a tent for four months. As a dog musher in northern Ontario I found out that nothing could match the exhilaration of taking a team of canine friends into a snowstorm.

In 1979, my good friends Paul Laperrière and David Burger introduced me to ice climbing—a sport that would become a lifetime passion and bring all my winter skills together. Today, at age 44, nothing makes me feel more alive than taking my dogs and my ice tools out on a crisp winter day for yet another close encounter of the frozen kind. After more than a thousand ascents, I still get excited by another day on the ice.

My first ice climb was 20 years ago, on La Congelée, an 80-meter Grade 3 near Chute Montmorency just outside of Quebec City. My friend Pedro Tessier had a small ice hammer, which was approved by our instructor Paul Laperièrre. I had a hammer that looked very much the same, so I didn't bother showing it to Paul. It was only after the ascent that I found out my hammer with a blunt pick was the rock version of Pedro's ice hammer and was only designed to remove pitons. My second tool was a $17 Alpine ice ax.

The ice screws had only two teeth and required an incredible amount of strength and energy to put in. It was very cold that day and sometimes the ice screw would go halfway in and jam. We would have to remove the partially placed screw, put it inside our clothes to warm it up, and then try to remove the ice inside the narrow tube before placing it again. It's understandable that the sport wasn't very popular in those days. Climbing ability was only half of the game; the actual time spent climbing was minimal compared with the time spent placing gear and freezing at the belay station. It took us seven hours to finish the climb, and we descended in the dark, nearly frozen; it's no wonder I started soloing!

After a few years of climbing in eastern North America, I was hooked and was becoming more skilled. I wanted to test my abilities with bigger challenges. One of the things that excited me the most was a first ascent—exploring and discovering new ground. When I started climbing in the late seventies I thought at first that I had missed out on the great pioneer era. At the time, it seemed that the obvious great routes had been done—climbs like the Black Dike; Polar Circus; Nemesis—and that only minor, more remote climbs were left. I didn't realize the huge potential waiting; I learned that a psychological barrier was limiting me.

When I first came to the Canadian Rockies in the early eighties I thought the locals' level of climbing would be beyond my reach. I expected Grade 5 and 6 ice to be horrendous and the hard-core ice climbers to be superhuman athletes. For my first climb in the West I went to Professor Falls, a Grade 4 and one of my favorite climbs today. On the approach, I saw a big drip high on Rundle Wall: I thought *this* big drip was Professor Falls. I started thinking I should have chosen a Grade 3 for my first climb in the Canadian Rockies! As it turned out, the drip I was looking up at was the future—the line that would eventually become the Terminator (WI6+). I was quite relieved when I saw the real Professor Falls. It was beautiful, but not very hard. I soloed the climb and came down ecstatic. I was suddenly thinking again about the Weeping Wall, Polar Circus, Nemesis; maybe, just maybe, if I trained and climbed hard I could do these climbs. I realized the huge potential that was opening up for me. But it still didn't occur to me that there would be any significant first ascents left to do.

The day after I climbed Professor Falls, I paid the well-known Canmore climber, James Blench, a visit. I was looking for information on ice routes and possible climbing partners, but I didn't expect this climbing legend to have much time for an unknown with a strong French accent. To my surprise, he offered to climb with me later that week. I was delighted. I didn't even ask where we were going.

On the day of our trip, I was up and ready hours ahead of time. James picked me up and we drove up the Banff-Jasper Highway. Two hours later James stopped the car and pointed out this beautiful steep climb, relatively close to the road. "That looks great," I said. "What's the name of this climb?" "It doesn't have a name yet," was his response. "What? You're telling me this route hasn't been climbed yet?" I rushed out of the car and practically ran to the base of the route, worried someone else would beat us to it. James led the climb brilliantly. His technique was superb and more diversified than that of anyone I'd seen before. We gave it the name Oh Le Tabernac.

That day I realized the immense potential for new routes in the Canadian Rockies. Only years later would I understand I wouldn't be able to come close to climbing them all in my lifetime. My guess is it will be the same for generations to come.

The psychological change in climbing has certainly not been the only one in the last 20 years. Improvements in equipment have radically changed the sport and made it a more enjoyable, not so hard-core activity. In the last couple of years the clothing alone has seen great improvements, with four-way stretch material that keeps you warm and dry, even in wet conditions.

Hardware has changed dramatically as well. The ice tools are the most personal piece of equipment, and changes in them have revolutionized the sport and its popularity in a very short period of time. They are extensions of a climber's hand and will most likely see more changes and specialization for mixed climbing and for ice competitions. And now some of the ice screws are so easy to put in they don't much alter the flow of movement, and they are strong enough to inspire confidence.

The social face of climbing has also changed. With the booming interest in ice climbing many climbing sites are getting crowded. When we first started ice climbing, we would rarely see other people, and it used to be that objective dangers were the only dangers to worry about. Now, danger has many faces.

A few years ago I was on an ice-climbing trip in France to participate in the ice festival in L'Argentière La Bessée. It was a great occasion to meet ice climbers from all over Europe. Midway through the festival the organizers had to close the main climbing valley because of high avalanche danger. We ended up with a couple of hundred climbers sharing a dozen climbs. Add to this the diversity of languages, and you get the picture. I remember nervously watching a lead climber on a small ice pillar dodging the slipping crampons of a novice climber above him. He couldn't traverse to the other side of the pillar because a third party was climbing there! Below this second pitch, on the ledge between pitch one and two, a dozen climbers were waiting their turn. I wondered how many people would get hurt if the fragile pillar broke off. Meanwhile, back home in British Columbia, they were getting record cold weather on the coast and over 60 new ice routes were climbed! There's no place like home.

Even though a lot of climbers don't like to walk too far, the day might come when even remote valleys will be crowded. I worry about that, but for now, I enjoy the freedom I have and cherish moments of solitude in the mountains.

Some areas are farming ice to accommodate the growing numbers of climbers. The Ouray Ice Park in Colorado is probably the best example. Ten years ago there were only a dozen natural climbs in that canyon. Now, thanks to the hard work and ingenuity of some of the local folks who tapped the water from a large pipe running above the canyon, there are countless possibilities for pure ice and mixed routes. During the Ouray Ice Festival, everyone seemed to be able to find something to climb in a relatively safe manner.

Artificial towers are also becoming popular and will probably spread like artificial climbing walls. I would not be surprised if, in 20 years, most arenas have an ice structure in their facilities. This brings us to the ice competitions. I remember when the idea of rock climbing competition on artificial structures was disputed and controversial. Such structures are now widely accepted and most climbers enjoy an occasional visit to the local gym.

Modern ice climbing and ice competitions have evolved into a unique activity within the sport of climbing and are starting to get a lot of media attention, providing perhaps one of the biggest challenges for climbers of the future. For a young climber it might be easy to lose perspective and start performing for the media and for peer approval, instead of pursuing the sport for its own beauty. The media are interested in profitable performances; they don't care much about the person. During the 1997 Winter X Games, two great climbers and good friends of mine, Laurence Haston and Anne Smith, finished second and third respectively in the women's ice climbing difficulty and speed competition. Almost immediately they were television stars, with journalists and cameras all around them.

They were back again in '98 but had an off day for the difficulty event. Kim Csizmazia won and was the new star. I remember watching the journalists practically pushing Anne and Laurence out of the way to get to Kim for an interview. Anne looked at Laurence and said, "I guess we are not important to them anymore." Anne and Laurence, being mature, accomplished climbers, got over this quickly and moved on with their climbing careers, but I worried that some younger competitors, who have put all their energy into such events, might get

upset after a few poor performances and might even lose interest in ice climbing altogether.

For many years, it seemed that most of the women at climbing areas were unenthusiastically accompanying their boyfriends. Very few women seemed to truly enjoy themselves, and even fewer were interested in leading any of the harder lines. Things are changing. During the winter of 1998, I met up with some women friends of mine in the Ouray Ice Park. Sue Nott, Abby Watkins, and other very skilled women ice climbers were training in the canyon. They had set up all kinds of hard mixed problems in the M6-M7 range and were sharing routes back and forth. I stepped back for a while and watched the action. These talented women were flashing the routes with grace, their abilities very suited to these mixed problems. I also noticed the reactions of the male climbers in the canyon. They seemed astonished and a bit nervous. The women suggested they might be monopolizing the mixed routes and offered a ride on their ropes to anyone in the canyon. The guys quickly turned them down. Last year, Kim Csizmazia competed with us as an equal in the difficulty event at Pont Rouge Québec. She topped out the route and placed very well. But then, why wouldn't she?

What's ahead? In pure ice climbing the technical level of difficulty is approaching its limit. It is uncommon to find sustained overhanging ice in a natural setting, except for seracs and the inside of crevasses. Not many people enjoy climbing in and out of a crevasse for very long. Alex Lowe introduced climbing on icebergs during a trip to Antarctica, but I seriously doubt it will ever be popular. Neckier routes will continue to be done in the future, but very few climbers seem interested in pushing new standards on vertical verglas and vertical rotten ice. Most young climbers are interested in increasing the difficulty, not the danger.

To increase pure difficulty, ice climbers have to turn to mixed climbing. Just like in rock climbing, the possibilities for harder mixed routes are infinite. People such as Alex Lowe, Jeff Lowe, Will Gadd, Stevie Haston, Dave Thomson, Helgi Christiensen, Raphael Slawinski, Joe Josephson, Laurence Haston, Kim Csizmazia, Kefira Allen, and others have been setting the pace in that field. If young rock climbers with the potential of Chris Sharma and Katie Brown decide to invest their energy in mixed climbing, they should blow the standards through the roof.

For bigger challenges, there is potential for long mixed routes with very sustained difficulties. I expect that in the future the rock sections of these routes will become harder and longer, and the ice sections shorter and shorter.

A different style of climbing can also increase the challenge. A team of fast and efficient climbers can link many long routes in a day. An experienced climber might choose to climb alone. Soloing is not for everybody, and it's not for anyone all of the time but, if done for the right reasons, can be an incredibly satisfying experience. It can bring more focus and freedom to the climber. A big remote climb might be possible in one day. On a long route, the climber can enjoy hours of climbing without interruption of movement.

During the winter of 1997, the routes on Rundle Wall near Banff were in exceptional condition. It was a rare chance to link three outstanding routes. Ken Wylie and Keith Haberl were the first to climb Terminator, Sea of Vapours, and Troubled Dreams in a day. A couple of weeks later François Damilano and I wanted to repeat this feat. We started heading up the trail in the dark and were at the base of the climbs by first light. The temperature was minus 25°F. Other parties decided it was too cold, leaving us the whole place to ourselves. We moved quickly and stayed relatively warm. Using a hundred-meter rope (328 feet), we saved time and topped out on the last climb just before dark. For both of us it was an exceptional day of climbing, and the intensity of the experience reinforced our friendship and respect for each other.

Ever since I had heard of the three routes forming I had contemplated soloing them, but I had to make sure my motivation was genuine (for the pleasure and freedom it would give me). When would I get another chance to solo three routes of this size and this quality in one day? One morning I woke up with the right feeling and decided it was the day. I didn't put too much pressure on myself: I would go the base of the climbs and make the final decision then. Reaching the base by noon, I found only one other party on the wall. The con-

ditions were perfect and I was psyched. The next five hours of climbing were sublime. The flow of movement was only interrupted by the rappels. I felt safe and my enjoyment was almost overwhelming. I came down the trail with my dogs Sam and Jade with a peaceful feeling. Both of my trips on the Rundle Wall had enriched me and I was thankful to experience such adventures.

A climber can also find new challenges in simplicity. A few years ago I soloed Cascade Waterfall, a 1,000-foot Grade-3 ice climb near Banff, using only one ice tool. I had to put emphasis on balance and technique rather than strength. It was definitely one of the most pleasant days of climbing that I've had.

OK, let's get to it. What is it you want—really, really want? You want to know where is the best ice in the world—preferably unclimbed ice. I certainly don't pretend to know for sure, but I've been looking for it for a while now and I have a few tips. Just don't tell anyone else! Depending on where you live, the new routes might not be too far away. I've already mentioned the potential still available in the Canadian Rockies. You just need to be looking and using your imagination. There is great potential in northern British Columbia. In 1998 I did some first ascents with Marc Aubrey near Blue River. One of the climbs—La Vraie Nature De Bernadette—was a 1,300-foot Grade 6+ and was one of the top three first ascents of my career. Then, heli-skiing guides in the area told me that Bernadette was just a small piece of ice compared with the climbs inside the mountain range! There is also great potential in northern Quebec, but you have to hurry before André Laperrière climbs it all.

If you like to travel and you like big ice, check out Norway. There you can climb new routes for the rest of your life without ever having to leave the country. The potential for short- and medium-size ice and mixed routes in Iceland is phenomenal. Godefroy Perroux and Ezio Marlier are still finding great first ascents in France and Italy. Of course, the potential for big ice routes in the big mountains is infinite: Talk to Jeff Lowe. People say it is a small planet; it isn't from an ice climber's point of view.

The new challenging ice routes may lie in your own backyard. During the winter of 1994, I climbed at Pont Rouge, a very friendly climbing area near Quebec City renowned for its famous freestanding pillars. After two days of climbing, I had done most of the established routes and did not see much potential for new routes because I was focusing on pure ice. Later I heard of futuristic mixed climbs being done by the local young guns. In 1999 I revisited the area to see what I was missing. How could I have missed such potential? Thanks to the vision of climbers like Serge Angelucci, Jean-Phillippe Villemaire, Benoit Marion, and others, the cliffs were booming with fantastic mixed routes, mostly M6 to M8. I spent two more weeks; the climbing was fabulous and this time when I left, I could see plenty of potential routes for my next trip.

I started to think of all the areas I had been in the last 20 years and all the possibilities for mixed routes. I felt like life was too short and I would run out of time. I was envious of the young climbers with so many new adventures ahead of them. Then I thought, "What is wrong with you? You're not too old for this stuff!" I might not be able to climb everything, but it's going to be a hell of a party trying.

I'm not good at giving advice. I prefer that young people make their own way. But I did get some help along the way, and without that help I doubt I would still be around to share the future of ice climbing with you. I encourage upcoming climbers to be patient, to use good judgment, and to choose their climbing partners wisely.

One of the keys for survival is to have love and friendship in our lives. Family and friends should always come first. It has helped me to make the right decision on many occasions. It can also give you the additional will to survive in extreme situations. Many years ago, I was leading a particularly rotten and steep pitch on the upper Weeping Wall. It was in the early days when I thought I was invincible. I had never encountered such bad ice before. I ran out most of a rope length without putting in any protection. I started to get pumped and nervous with no good ice in sight. I decided to focus my remaining energy on digging through the surface ice to access better ice for protection. After digging a hole the size of a bathtub I realized I would never find any good ice for protection.

By now I was beyond being pumped. I couldn't even feel my hands on the ice tools. My arms where totally numb. I don't give up easily, but half an hour later I realized that a fall was imminent. I hung straight down from my tools. I figured it would shorten the fall by half a meter! I closed my eyes and took a deep breath. Then I saw the faces of my partner Marge and my mother Gilberte, the two people I loved the most. I thought there was no way in hell I was going to fall here and bring them such pain. I opened my eyes and the fear was totally gone. Somehow I found enough energy to traverse around the corner, find good ice for protection, and complete the climb. I promised myself not to get out of control like that again.

Ice climbing and the mentality of the people who practice it are perpetually changing, and that's what keeps it interesting. We shouldn't be afraid of these changes. Let's not get too serious about this. After all, climbing is only a game for people who can afford to play it. Climbing accomplishments are important to us but, in the big picture, they don't contribute significantly to mankind. What does matter is that climbers get enriched by their climbing adventures and carry the beauty of their experience into their everyday life. Just think of Alex Lowe—of all his outstanding qualities, his pure enjoyment of the moment was his greatest asset.

The unborn generations of climbers will surely redefine the ice climbing game. I have great faith in them. Let's hope we can inspire them and support them in their new adventures.

Guy Lacelle is widely regarded as one of the world's leading ice climbers, having established and repeated many of the most extreme ice climbs in the Canadian Rockies. He climbs almost exclusively solo and in remote locations that are difficult to access, his only companion being his faithful dog, Sam.

His first trip to the Rockies was in 1983, when he climbed Polar Circus, a fierce route near the Columbia Icefield. Typically, he spends 50 to 60 days climbing ice during the winter season. Guy's current base camp is in Prince George, British Columbia, but his climbing accomplishments span the globe.

His extraordinary level of commitment, combined with a refusal to indulge in self-promotion, has made Guy an unsung hero to the mountaineering community.

THE LAST
FRONTIERS

SIR CHRIS BONINGTON

TODD SKINNER

SILVO KARO

EXPLORATION, THE CORE OF CLIMBING

SIR CHRIS BONINGTON

Exploration is at the very core of this game of climbing that we all play. It started with exploration when our Victorian ancestors first ventured into the Alps in that golden age when so little had been climbed and just about every route was a first ascent; this desire to explore is still with us today, even though so many areas have been fully developed. The magic of exploration can be enjoyed on so many different levels. The rock climber on a 30-foot-high Gritstone crag in Britain, or among those miles of unclimbed rock walls and towers in the canyon lands of Utah, or indeed almost anywhere in the world, can touch a piece of rock that has never known human contact. On a grander scale there are still unclimbed peaks and untouched glaciers among the mountains of Asia, the Americas, and Antarctica.

There are, of course, other ingredients in the mix: the athletic satisfaction of having complete command over one's body, the thrill of risk, appreciation of the beauty of mountains, the comradeship of one's fellow climbers, and in most of us an element of ego gratification. The proportions vary in all of us and in our approach to our sport. Sport climbers, who never venture away from their line of bolts, regard the stimulus of risk as irrelevant in what is essentially an athletic challenge. In making new routes one can say that they are exploring, but

in this there is also a limitation: The very act of drilling for their protection, and through that process ignoring the natural features of the rock, is canceling out the very essence of exploration.

The vast majority of climbers show little interest in exploration anyway. They prefer to go where other people have been before, with the reassurance of knowing the grade of difficulty and having a description in a guidebook. This can even be said of the Himalaya, where the majority of expeditions tackle existing routes, many of which these days are guided ascents. Even experienced and talented mountaineers are being attracted by the siren call of peak bagging—collecting the fourteen 8,000-meter peaks—and opt, all too often, for the easiest, much climbed routes to ensure they achieve their objective.

But to me there is nothing more satisfying in mountaineering than the intellectual challenge combined with the romantic mystery of venturing where others have never been. It might be the challenge of picking out a route on a tiny rock face in the Lake District of England or it could be on a huge peak in the Himalaya. The principles are the same. You use your experience and skill to find a way to the top, fired by the knowledge that no one has ever been there before. This quality of exploration has contributed so much to the richness of mountain literature. It goes back to the earliest days of our sport, recorded in the annals of *The Alpine Journal*, from the first ascents of alpine peaks,

clouds each afternoon gave a piquant threat that never materialized. We were perhaps irresponsible. No one knew where we were or what we were attempting, and yet that very sense of absolute isolation and independence enriched the experience. We reached the summit ridge at the end of the fifth day and hacked out a tiny campsite from a knife-edge of snow that was a single long pitch from the top. We reached the perfect needle-like summit the following morning.

A moment of intense elation was dampened by the knowledge that we couldn't get back down the way we had come and by our ignorance of the way down the other side by which the East Peak had had its original ascent. Our descent commenced with a terrifying traverse of a steep avalanche-prone snow slope and remained gripping all the way down. We discovered later that this was a new route as well.

In the last few years I have had wonderful exploratory trips that confirmed this for me: There are any number of corners of the Earth that are still unknown, where you can even now find places that have never known the touch of man. Some of them are both close and accessible. In 1993 four of us flew into eastern Greenland in a twin-engine Otter, landing on a side glacier of the Frederiksborg Glacier in the Kangerlugsiak region just north of the Arctic Circle. No one had ever set foot on the glacier, and after the plane had left us the nearest human being was over 300 miles away. Yet we had flown on a scheduled flight from Glasgow, Scotland, to Reykjavik, Iceland, just 36 hours earlier. We pitched camp, had a short sleep, and set out for our initial climb, making the first ascent of Mejslen (7,612 feet) by a mixed route after 24 hours of exhilarating climbing.

The glacier basin was surrounded by jagged rock peaks that offered ascents of every standard. We felt an extraordinary sense of freedom from the rest of the world, of complete self-sufficiency. The Danish government insists on expeditions having an emergency beacon that, when activated, would send a signal that you hope will be picked up by a passing plane. The chances of it being spotted seem sufficiently nebulous not to intrude on one's sense of isolation. We climbed Mejslen as a foursome. The other three—Graham Little, Jim

Lowther, and Rob Ferguson—made another first ascent while I recovered from a bad head cold, and then we split into pairs. Graham Little and I went for a rock blade that we called the Ivory Tower after a pair of ivory gulls nesting high on its flanks. They had a haunting call as they wheeled and circled above us in the pale blue sky of the Arctic summer. Our best climb was up a magnificent needle of gneiss that reminded me of the Southwest Pillar of the Dru as seen from Chamonix. On it was one pitch that I was lucky enough to lead, up a steep groove that vanished into a blank rock wall. Small holds on a prow to the left led me on upward. With no cracks for protection I was getting more and more committed. I pulled up and over onto a little hidden gangway. No way could I have reversed the move and I was now a long way from my last runner. Thin delicate smears up the slab, a pull round the corner, rope dragging badly, and suddenly it steepened with off-balance moves in a dyke with bad rock at its base. With the rope almost run out, I reached a small ledge with some belays. I shouted and hollered and yelled in exhilaration. It was one of the best pitches I had ever led. By modern standards it was not that hard, but for me it was near my personal limit—I suppose around 5.10.

In a way that pitch encapsulated the joy of primary exploratory climbing with the thrill of climbing a truly superb stretch of rock, taking one's own ability to the limit. Alpine flowers clung to the back of grooves, some dwarf willow survived on a sheltered ledge, and a bee hovered lazily in the warm sun. These affirmations of life were all the more lovely in contrast to the sweep of brown and grey gneiss, of snow-clad glaciers and the deep blue shadows of the crevasses that made a counterpoint to the washed-out blue of the sky. The only reminder of civilization was the fading contrail of a high-flying jet carrying its cocooned passengers from Europe to the west coast of America.

And that was just the start. We were climbing in rock shoes, but two-thirds of the way up the natural line took us round to the northern side of the tower and we hit snow-covered slabs. I was glad that Graham got that particular pitch. The route took 24 hours up 2,300 feet of superb varied climbing to a fairy-tale rock summit. The pristine view of countless jagged peaks fading into the white dome of the Greenland Ice Cap was all the more lovely because of our heightened senses. This was just one of the rewards of this style of exploratory climbing.

I have spent the last three years expeditioning in an area of eastern Tibet that is certainly no wilderness. Farmers and nomads have grazed their yaks and sheep in the valleys and on the lower grass-clad slopes for thousands of years, but no climbers, and precious few foreigners, had ventured into this huge mountain region of the Nyengla Tengla Shan. I had first seen these mountains in 1982 on my way to the Northeast Ridge of Everest. I spent 14 years researching them and trying to get permission to go there before Charlie Clarke and I pulled it off and set out on a recce that gave me one of the best trips of my career—and it didn't include any real climbing. Our research told us that a peak we had seen to the far north, dominating everything around it, was Sepu Kangri, a mountain of 22,800 feet. This was what I wanted to climb, but first we needed to find a way to it.

With us we had a Tibetan guide who had never been to this part of Tibet, a driver, and a cook. It was an adventure into an exciting, colorful unknown, all the richer for the human and historic element, we saw rebuilt monasteries, villages high in the mountains, nomads in their dark brown yak hair tents, lifts hitched on ponies, winding valleys, high pastures, and eventually a holy mountain guarded by a complex array of natural fortifications—serried seracs, ice-veined rock walls, and tumbling ice falls.

We tried to climb Sepu Kangri in the spring of 1997 and the autumn of 1998 but on each occasion were beaten by the weather. Two members of the team, Victor Saunders and Scott Muir, came within 500 feet of the top, and yet our failure to summit seems unimportant when compared with the satisfaction of wandering through this wonderful area of unclimbed peaks and remote valleys, of getting to know a group of people from a very different culture, with different aspirations and values from ours.

You don't need to be a superclimber to experience this joy. Exploratory climbing need not be elitist; it is open to anyone who is prepared to leave the beaten track and who is no longer concerned with easily measured achievements. It is open to anyone prepared to spend time in research, a rewarding activity in itself, and then to embrace uncertainty, for this is at the core of exploration. There are still many places where we can taste the exotic fruits of the unknown. If you haven't tried them, do so, but I warn you, they can be very addictive. I believe this addiction is beneficial, however, and it is and always must be at the heart of our sport.

Born in 1934, Chris Bonington was educated at University College School, London, and the Royal Military Academy at Sandhurst. He spent two years at the Army Outward Bound School as a mountaineering instructor. During this period he started climbing in the Alps and rose to rapid prominence, completing the first British ascent of the Southwest Pillar of the Dru in 1958, the first ascent of the Central Pillar of Frêney on Mont Blanc in 1961, and the first British ascent of the North Wall of the Eiger in 1962.

Bonington is perhaps best known for his ambitious expeditions on new routes of the world's highest peaks. Some notable achievements are the South Face of Annapurna (the "last great problem" in the Himalaya), the Southwest Face of Everest, the Ogre, the West Summit of Shivling, the West Peak of Menlungtse, the West Ridge of Panch Chuli II, the Northeast Ridge of Ushba, as well as Mount Elbrus, Rangrik Rang, Drangnag-Ri, Mount Kongur, and Mount Vinson.

Since 1960, he has participated in expeditions to an amazing variety of remote places: the British-Indian-Nepalese Expedition to Annapurna II; Sangay in Ecuador; caribou hunting on Baffin Island; an exploratory expedition to Sepu Kangri in Tibet; and a sailing expedition to Greenland.

Chris Bonington has received many awards, including a knighthood in 1996. He has written more than 14 books and produced or collaborated on a number of films. His documentary The Everest Years *won Best Mountaineering Film at the 1988 Banff Mountain Film Festival, and he was guest speaker in 1989 and 1997.*

OBSCURED BY CLOUDS

TODD SKINNER

*"I am glad I shall never be young without wild country
to be young in. Of what avail are forty freedoms
without a blank spot on the map?"*
— ALDO LEOPOLD

December 1999. While flying over the Sahara at night on the way to Nairobi, I chanced to look out of the window. From the endless stretches of black in all directions, came the orange-yellow flare of a solitary campfire. While the smug businessmen slept, and the tourists wondered if they should dare to take off their 30-pocket vests, someone down below was crossing one of the most hostile stretches of terrain left in our ever safer world. I pressed against the window and realized that the campfire was pulling at my heart, a beacon harkening to a struggle that actually mattered. A slight error in route finding, a broken water container, a twisted ankle, or a waver in resolve, and that campfire would not be there the next night. The fire-tender below me was thousands of years too late to be the first to cross the Sahara, but shared the same frontier traits: to keep going, to be inspired more by the unknown than by the wellworn.

To set out on a journey knowing that all of the skill, experience, ability to improvise, imagination, thirst for knowledge, and animal strength you possess may not see you through, yet you go anyway—because there is also a chance they may see you through—that is the foundation of an adventurer.

We flew on and were eventually over one of the sprawling, underplanned, and poorly built cities springing up at the edges of all our last frontiers. I turned away from the window, no longer feeling a kinship with those on the ground. I couldn't help but notice that one of the businessmen had awakened and was staring hungrily down at the amassed glitter. The empty and trackless desert was void of potential for him, holding no opportunity for profit or commerce, while the city was full of possibilities. I was struck again, as I have been my whole life, by the different wiring evident in the human race, and the different set of values that each of us holds sacred.

December 1983. We were safely ensconced at Hueco Tanks, having a hell of a fine winter, when an unnamed acquaintance pulled out a photo of a beautiful white dome that looked like a 1,500-foot cardinal's hat. A few of us were mesmerized, as he knew we would be, and the hook was set when he mentioned that it was unclimbed. The wall was deep in the Sierra Madre of Mexico, two days downriver from a tiny town in the bottom of the legendary Copper Canyon. With no more knowledge than that, we packed ten ropes and a full wall rack and immediately started our journey. Two days and two nights later, we stood on the rim of the canyon, 5,000 feet above the village of Urique. The train moved on into the looming twilight, leaving us with our huge pile of gear. We spent all the next day in the back of a pickup, grinding down the switchbacks of an old mining road, the driver stopping repeatedly to cool the heated brakes with water and pray at the shrines located at every turn.

The vegetation changed steadily, from the mountain pines up on the rim, through a tropical transition until finally, the banana, coffee, and papaya zone of Urique itself met us at the end of the road. That night we arranged for burros to help haul our loads to the wall and then tried to sleep in the heat and humidity, visions of the white dome burning like a fever through our dreams.

We walked all of the next day through the gruesome heat, slept on a sandbar, and rose early to complete the last day of the longest approach any of us had ever encountered. All that day we strained to see around the corners of the canyon, impatient for the first glimpse of this fantastic and unknown wall. Could it possibly all be overhanging? Would there be clean, laser-cut cracks that deviated no more than six inches off plumb? One of us commented that it would probably be a geological anomaly, since the rock around us didn't appear to be able to produce a cliff over 50 feet high. This made the wall even more exotic, and as we pressed on through the heat of midday we spouted theories of rock type and origin far beyond our actual knowledge of geology.

As the afternoon wore on, we started asking the occasional local we passed how much farther it was to the Big White Rock. Our command of Spanish was pathetic, so we weren't surprised when they couldn't understand us. It was our unwavering belief in the endeavor at hand and the still, fresh image of the photograph seen less than a week earlier—not our feeble Spanish—that prevented us from understanding when the locals responded with, "What Big White Rock?"

As the shadows lengthened, the questions took on the tone of an Inquisition: "What do you mean,

there is no Big White Rock ahead? OK, maybe not white—tan. How far to the Big Tan Rock? Brown then, dammit! Gray! I don't care—how far to the Big Rock? I thought you said you'd spent your whole life here! How could you not have noticed this bloody huge cliff in your backyard?"

As total darkness finally forced a halt to our faltering quest, we unpacked the burros and silently chewed cold, three-day-old tortillas, struck dumb by the realization that there was no wall ahead. Oh, the wall existed all right—we had seen the photo—just not anywhere nearby. Out of the darkness there was a momentary pause in the gnawing of the moccasin-like tortillas, and a chilling comment came out of the sauna-like night, "Maybe he meant upriver from Urique." Responding with Biblical language, spitting, and mutterings about "paybacks," we eventually agreed this was the most probable reason why we were here—where our wall wasn't.

That we had to return to Urique was obvious, but our options from there held more complexities. We could be no faster on our return, so two more full days would be wasted. From Urique, should we go upriver for two more days to find the wall and then spend who knows how many days to climb it? Or should we get the hell back to Hueco where we knew the climbing would be good? We didn't have jobs, of course, or any other demands on our schedules, so it was purely a matter of what was most attractive to us.

As we marched back to the village, the discussion focused on the very foundation of our reasons to climb. The photo of the wall had been shown to over 20 climbers at the same time, and yet the three of us now walking along the canyon floor were the only ones who had leaped at the chance to climb it first. Some might have gone if we would have worked on persuading them for a week or so, but the majority said, "Hueco is a bird in the hand," and thought us mad for abandoning it so readily. Climbers have a much greater tendency towards exploration than a group of normal people, so I expected most to want to go. I have since marveled at being unable to find even three others out of the whole climbing population to join me on an exploratory trip with way more information than a photo—a reluctance to step off of the climbing map.

As an 11-year old cowboy on my earliest trips, I had started to look at the "backside" of peaks in the Wind River mountains, hoping to find undiscovered walls. That others had peeked around the corners looking for the same treasures, I could conveniently ignore. When I could drive, I began traveling to other Wyoming climbing areas, justifying the high cost of guidebooks by asking myself, "How else could I find out what hadn't been climbed yet without asking locals and prompting them to action?" Even then I was gaining an appreciation for the poker game that helpless addicts of first ascents eventually master. "Whoa!! Has anyone done that gorgeous overgrown slab that's running with nice, cool water? The one right next to that boring hand crack on the overhanging prow of that spire? Nothing done over there? Maybe I'll go have a look at it."

The expedition to Copper Canyon in darkest Mexico was like a stronger dose of the substance to which I had become addicted: pure, uncut exploration on a wall no climber had ever touched. The altered state that results is not easily shaken so, as we trudged back into Urique, our fates were already sealed; we were going upriver. We tried to justify the decision by rationalizing that, after all of the effort to that point, we might as well continue. The sad fact was, now that we had an option to leave, not one of us could break the spell the wall still held over us. We could go slower or faster, lighter or better provisioned, but we could not *not* go up that river. With fresh tortillas, a change of burros, and a shake of our heads, we left Urique and started toward the wall.

"Surely it will be so stunning as to be unequaled anywhere else on this planet, making all this pain worthwhile," I thought, putting into words the state of deception that all explorers fall into when the prize begins to prove elusive. The hard, cold facts (the explorers know them better and heed them less than anyone) are that the odds are increasingly stacked against great discoveries still being made. In medicine or computer science—sure—since those fields are still in their infancies, but not much is left to find in geography. On maps, "obscured by clouds" used to be the demarcation of areas on the maps that could not be seen during early aerial surveys. That label was as close as our generation will ever get to the "blanks on the map" that fueled the imagination of every other generation in history. The cartographers did not dare speculate on what they could not see, cursing the weather conditions that forced the publication of an imperfect product, a map only 98 percent complete. Those mapmakers truly believed they were helping mankind by bringing illumination to the last dim areas of geographic knowledge, never dreaming that some scanned the charts with a silent prayer for incompleteness.

In this age of satellites, infrared imagery, and handheld GPS devices, there really are no blanks left on the maps. There is, however, an astonishing quantity of unclimbed rock in corners both near and remote. To find the new climbing nearby, a climber needs only a desire to look over the next hill. A surprisingly small percentage of climbers will actually take a look, since most are happy to stay on the map. If new rock isn't found, most will go back to where they know the rock, and a much smaller percentage will look over the next hill. The percentage of those who keep looking over each subsequent hill gets smaller and smaller. And a very few have a need to look over the next hill—even when they have found what they were looking for: These are the lost and hopeless souls I count myself among. This character flaw was exactly what had brought me to the bottom of that Mexican canyon.

I fully realized that the addiction to the search was getting worse. Sitting around the campfire a full day upriver from Urique, it dawned on me that, if I had been living below the wall we were headed for, I would have abandoned it to go to Hueco Tanks if someone had shown me a photo of Hueco. I knew at that point that, even if this white wall turned out to be the best wall ever found, it would hold me just long enough to plan a trip to another, with the hopes it would be even better. The finding wasn't as important as the looking, and nothing was as irresistible as unseen rock.

The second day of upriver hiking perfectly illustrated the logic of being third, or tenth, or fiftieth to climb a formation. The tragedy wasn't that the wall was smaller than we had imagined, or that the rock was of lesser quality than we were dreaming, it was that it just wasn't there! Not one person at that end of the canyon had ever heard of a wall like we described. Fifteen days after we had left Hueco on our great climbing adventure, we stumbled back in, out of money and smelling of smoke and burros, proving the naysayers right by having never even uncoiled a rope. The gentleman who had shown us the photo and who hadn't had time to go with us had "gone north." He had, God's truth, gone to start selling shares in a gold mine he had located the summer before, called the "Pauper's Dream."

I could laugh a little more easily at what became known as the Phantom Wall expedition if it would have taught me a lesson. Instead, I began to look still farther afield, gathering a map collection of the entire world and fixating on the regions farthest from the mainstream of climbing. The harder the place was to look at, the more attractive it became to me. The search was about discovery, not climbing, so Europe ceased to exist in my landscape. Asia, Africa, and South America attracted most of my focus by virtue of having seen the fewest climbers, not necessarily by having better rock.

I made huge mistakes in judgment that resulted in myself and a variety of innocent partners suffering from thirst, hunger, physical danger, and, worst of all, a drought of climbing. We once stood on the shores of the Dead Sea, horrified at the blunder that had brought us there. We were flat broke and freezing in Europe, when we were told by an Israeli about long white cliffs at the lowest place on Earth. After weeks of picking oranges in Greece, we booked deck passage on a freighter to Tel Aviv. From there we moved with maximum speed overland toward the cliffs I had convinced myself were made of shining marble. The walls turned out to be basically made of crumbling salt. All of our momentum had put us in a region we couldn't afford to leave—one that had no climbing.

The famous football coach Bear Bryant said, "If you make a mistake, at least make it at a dead run." We had, which got it over with quickly and left us in possession of most of our orange-picking money. I found a Hebrew geology text with grainy photos of granite domes that the bookseller's translation suggested were in the Sinai. My partner joined a kibbutz in the Golan Heights, being much too smart to jump out of the frying pan again so soon. I hitched down to the Red Sea and found a Brit who had climbed, and two Australian girls who wanted to, and we headed into Egypt on an overcrowded bus. Just at sunset all four of us, the only non-Egyptians on the bus, were removed at a roadblock by soldiers with automatic rifles. Our passports were taken and we were put in a single-cell jail for the night. Two guys then swabbed the cell down with kerosene while smoking and gesturing lewdly to the Australians.

The next night, we were moved in the dark to another, more remote jail, and on the third night we were again herded by armed soldiers into the back of a truck and driven slowly out of town with all lights off. We had yet to find anyone who spoke English, nor had we seen our passports or the guy who had taken them. None of us liked the feel of this last move and, as we headed out into the desert on a dirt road, decided to bolt in four different directions when the truck stopped. About 45 minutes later, the truck took a left on an even smaller track and came to a halt. The Australian girls were crying; the Brit was strung as tight as a bow, ready to give it the Linford Christie when he hit the ground. When I stepped out of that truck ready to burst, zigzagging out into the desert night, I abstractly wondered if it would be considered a climbing-related death if I was gunned down, since climbing had brought me to this sorry patch of desert. As my foot touched down, I looked up to decide which direction to go, only to see the others getting their passports back and the soldiers jumping back into the truck and heading off in the same direction. "Bye-bye," one yelled back, the first and last English we were to hear, and as close to an explanation we would get for our detainment.

We made it back to Israel on the back of a water truck, and within a few days I persuaded two tough Canadians and a woman from Oregon to try again to get to the granite pictured in the book. There was no sign of our fateful roadblock of the week before, so we were soon winding through Joshua tree-like domes up to a thousand feet high. I would be unable to describe where the climbs were, so it wasn't about getting our names in a guidebook or becoming famous for giving the world a new climbing area. The winter was spent looking in the next canyon, around the next corner, and on the backside of each formation: the intent was to find and marvel at new rock, not to map it.

It might seem that I'm trying to dissuade others

from looking for new rock, but not all of my exploration efforts have been semidisasters. Two full winters were spent on the awesome limestone of China, Vietnam, and Thailand with a hard-core group calling ourselves the White Rock Safarians. We saw an incredible amount of great rock in a karst zone about the size of the continental United States. We saw nothing compared to what there is left to find. Asia will probably have more limestone climbing than the U.S. and Europe combined, from bouldering up to Grade 6 walls, all waiting for the touch of an intrepid hand. I haven't mentioned the granite and quartzite there because, although I know about it, I haven't seen it with my own eyes, so I'm holding those cards tight against my chest.

Then there is Africa. The entire continent is spangled with quartzite crags, from the best bouldering I've ever seen to fantastic, overhanging towers and walls. Like Asia, the problem is where to stop exploring, not where to start. It is oddly depressing to stand on top of a 75-mile-long cliff and see another in the distance. Why keep looking after having found 200 lifetimes of rock already? For that matter, I now understand that some of the cliffs I walked in Wyoming ten years ago are as good or better than any I've seen since—and I could have just stayed home. I'll climb on them, of course, but at night I'll pull out photos of walls in Greenland, towers in Bolivia, or boulders in Mali. I'll scan maps of Antarctica and Baffin, Ethiopia and Argentina. This climbing I need—like food, at regular intervals. The search for new places to climb is like oxygen—a continuous supply, mandatory to my life. And so I've accumulated hundreds and hundreds of volumes, charts, individual photos,

geology books, and aerial surveys that I am continually poring over, finding more rock than I can possibly go look at, much less climb on.

In 20 years of searching, I have uncovered wondrous gems unknown to the prying eyes of even the most dauntless climbing nomads, and I have also missed obvious prizes, usually because I was too immersed in looking in obscure places. I have never met another climber who knows more about the world's climbing potential than myself, or who has ferreted out more photos of strange cliffs and towers in unknown corners and forgotten canyons. But in all my searching, I have never again encountered a photo or description of the white wall that was the catalyst for the Sierra Madre fiasco. I have scrutinized geology maps of the region around Urique, and it is possible that the wall could still be there. I've thought a hundred times about the climber with the photo of the wall, and it's just possible we were dealing with a grand master poker player—maybe even of the Fred Beckey level. Perhaps the residents of that canyon were paid good wages to answer as they did. Maybe the wall was just out of sight all the time, and that man now lives in Urique, confident that we'll never be back. Well, one day I'll probably stand again in the dusty streets of Urique, looking up and down the canyon, pondering the great cosmic mysteries that rule my fate. Will any discovery ever be fantastic enough to kill the desire to keep looking? How will I find partners to climb in Iraq, North Korea, or England? Will I ever find an Overhanging Mile? Could there, just maybe, be a mother lode of gold in the Pauper's Dream?

Todd Skinner is one of the most diversely accomplished rock climbers of his generation. His achievements have been documented in film and magazines in eight languages. He has made more than 300 first ascents in 26 countries around the world and has established new climbs at the highest level of difficulty. He relishes the challenge of all aspects of rock climbing, from bouldering to Himalayan peaks, but most of all dreams about free climbing big walls in remote corners of the globe.

Todd's climbing highlights include the first free ascent of the Salathé Wall on El Capitan in Yosemite National Park; the first free ascent of the North Face of Mount Hooker in the Wind River Range; the first free ascent of the Proboscis Wall in the Cirque of the Unclimbables in the Yukon Territories, and the first free ascent of the East Face of Trango Tower in Pakistan's Karakoram Himalaya (the first Grade 7 free climb in the world).

Todd has been at the forefront of the development of free climbing in the United States for the last 20 years and believes the future of the sport lies in free climbing on bigger walls in remote corners of the world.

PATAGONIA: TERRA MYSTICA

SILVO KARO

I can still recall that day in 1982 when Janez Jegli and I first laid eyes on the East Face of Fitz Roy. We had gone to buy our first climbing shoes in the Italian town of Tarvisio, just over the border from Slovenia. The sales assistant threw in a free poster of Fitz Roy and we stared spellbound at the picture of this wonderful mountain. We rushed home as fast as our old Fiat 500 could take us, stopping on the way to plan our new route to the summit. By the time we got home the poster was all crumpled, but Fitz Roy was in our heads. We talked to Franc Knez, somewhat of a guru among Slovenian mountaineers, about the idea of climbing Fitz Roy and he was very enthusiastic. And so, we became a climbing team. Later, people would call us the three musketeers.

I had never read much about the mountains of Patagonia. My impression had been that they weren't really the best mountains to climb. And besides, if you read too much about a mountain you're heading off to climb, you start to get scared. Nowadays almost all the intrepid ascents have been described in various books and articles. We read about great dramas, fearsome storms, superhuman efforts, struggles to survive, and, of course, many fatalities. After reading just the first chapter of such books, many people will abandon all idea of mountaineering. I admire the mountain explorers of the past, setting forth into a world

they knew nothing about. In a way they were fortunate because that very ignorance offered them more adventure.

Patagonia covers a vast area between latitudes 38° and 52° south. The mountains of Patagonia mark the southern end of the Andes and are characterized by extremely poor weather with huge quantities of precipitation. The tail end of South America reaches out toward Antarctica, toward the Palmer Peninsula. Some experts claim that these mountains continue on into Antarctica, re-emerging as the Vinson Massif. Similar rock types have been found there along with the remains of plants that are said to have thrived on both continents in a geological era when it is thought they were still joined together. The constant winds blowing off the Pacific bring clouds that are heavy with moisture. These clouds collide with the high peaks, rise, and cool down, causing the moisture to condense and be released over the mountains as snow and rain.

In Patagonia the Andes rise above 9,800 feet for the last time. And the harsh climate means that the weather, even at 3,300 feet, is comparable to the conditions prevailing in the Western Alps at 9,800 feet. The Patagonian mountains have intriguing shapes; spiraling towers usually encrusted with huge mushrooms of snow often spell a premature end for an attempted ascent. The climbing itself is tremendously challenging, not least because of the sudden, vicious changes in the weather, which is poor throughout the summer when there are only a few bright days. The winds that sweep across the Patagonian mountains reach speeds of up to 125 miles per hour, carrying with them snowflakes and sleet that cover the rock faces in a thick layer of ice. Yet sometimes, with a mild southerly wind, the sky above the Patagonian mountains clears, and then the scene is one of unparalleled beauty. "Patagonia is exceptionally beautiful," Royal Robbins once wrote. "Go there to hike, go there to photograph, but if you want to climb seriously you need to be a masochist with unlimited time on your hands!"

People often think that these days there aren't any little corners of Earth yet to be touched by humans. But that doesn't apply to Patagonia. Maps of the Patagonian Andes are still fairly poor and lacking in detail. The small white patch marking the Hielo Continental doesn't say a great deal to someone; but in reality, this ice cap is 280 miles long and 31 to 56 miles wide, stretching from the Baker Fjord to Seno Union. Miles from the nearest civilization, the mountains that adorn this vast expanse are for the most part unconquered, mainly because the weather is so bad, but also because of the long and complicated approach routes. So it is perhaps understandable that the early conquistadors first simply gazed at the Patagonian mountains from the pampas, the grassy, sandy flatland that stretches more than 300 miles all the way to the Atlantic coast. Mountaineers did not arrive in Patagonia until very late.

When Mallory and Irvine were climbing toward the summit of Everest in 1924, Fitz Roy, the highest peak in Patagonia, was still called Chalten, "volcano" in the language of the Patagonian Indians. That name derived from the fact that the mountain is always shrouded in cloud. Later, while measuring its height, the topographer Perito Moreno renamed the mountain Fitz Roy, after the English Captain Fitz Roy who was the first person to properly explore the coastal area. The first real explorer and conqueror of the Patagonian mountains was the Salesian priest Alberto Maria De Agostini. He organized the first mountaineering expeditions to Cerro Mayo (7,809 feet), Cerro Electrico (7,405 feet), and Cordon Moyano. These peaks were first

climbed around 1930. In 1936 an Italian expedition made the first genuine attempt on Fitz Roy, although they got no farther than the start of the face.

It was not until 1952, with France still rejoicing over the conquest of Annapurna—the first 8,000-meter peak to be climbed—that Guido Magnoni and Lionel Terray became the first men to set foot on the 11,073-foot summit of Fitz Roy. Terray's description after completing the expedition spoke of the enormity of the feat: "Of all my climbs it was in conquering Fitz Roy that I came closest to the limits of my strength and courage. It is not just the accumulated pitches of extreme difficulty that make Fitz Roy a major ascent. Climbing on Fitz Roy is highly complicated, risky, and exhausting, even more so than climbing the most difficult Alpine faces. Fitz Roy is a long way from any major human settlement and experiences bad weather almost all year round. The upper part of the rock face is covered with a layer of ice, and, worst of all, the climber is threatened by deadly storms."

Fitz Roy is far from being the only peak to provide an extreme challenge to climbers in this part of Patagonia. Not far away looms the intriguing 10,177-foot Cerro Torre, literally meaning "tower peak," an apt description, because "mountain" is almost too insubstantial a word. Following the conquest of Fitz Roy, the great battle for Cerro Torre began. In 1958, Italian mountaineers made their assault on the mountain from both east and west. Walter Bonatti, approaching from the west, was forced to turn back just 394 feet below the summit, though he did discover that this side offered the most logical access to the summit. But the real dramas unfolded on the eastern side. It seemed as though Cerro Torre had to be conquered—at any price. In those days the style of an ascent was unimportant; the only thing that mattered was reaching the summit. The consequences of this attitude are still evident today. Climbing standards at that time meant the east face was still too tough a nut to crack, and with the techniques used, this ascent was really stolen from the future.

The first climbers to reach the summit from the western side were Mario Conti, Casimiro

> But mountaineers are only different in the activities we choose because we have found, within ourselves, something that all are seeking. It is hard to live without that feeling, once experienced. Perhaps we are only different from those who have the dreams—but do nothing about them.

Ferrari, Daniele Chiappa, and Pino Negri in 1974. Theirs was also the first documented ascent of Cerro Torre. By this time all the 8,000-meter peaks in the Himalaya had long been conquered. Slovenian climbers did not reach the summit of an 8,000-meter mountain (Makalu via the south wall) until 1975, and we were latecomers in Patagonia, too, missing out on the pioneering years of first ascents. Yet despite the fact that the main peaks had been climbed, some of the more difficult faces remained untouched. And this is what my friends and I were seeking.

In 1983 Janez Jeglic, Franc Knez, and I eagerly anticipated our departure for Patagonia, to that *terra mystica*. Our main goal was the East Face of Fitz Roy, and if that's not enough, we thought, the East Face of Cerro Torre as well. But we were soon brought rudely back down to Earth in the face of Patagonian realities. No sooner had we got off the plane at the airport in Rio Gallegos than we were almost blown down the runway by the powerful wind. We then had the long journey to the point where the road ends beneath the Patagonian mountains. Here, Argentine soldiers helped us cross the mighty river using horses, and then it was on to base camp at the tree line.

At home we had worked out our ascent plan, which was to be a combination of fixed ropes and alpine style climbing. The plan was to use fixed ropes for just over half of the 3,280-foot face, and then make an alpine-style push for the summit in two days. We would have an equipment dump in a snow cave just beneath the face. It was an excellent plan and in good weather could have been carried out very quickly without major difficulties. Unfortunately, there isn't much good weather in Patagonia and, on our trip, the conditions didn't favor us. Nevertheless, we made good progress in setting up the fixed ropes, and soon the day arrived when we started up the face in alpine style. We climbed all day and in the evening set up a makeshift bivouac some 490 feet below the summit. A beautiful starry night promised good weather. But by three in the morning the situation had changed dramatically; snow was falling and the wind was strengthening rapidly.

We held on until first light and then began our descent. Our climbing route ran through a major dièdre, which in bad weather is quite dangerous because of the risk of avalanche. We had serious problems on the descent with poor fixed

> When I'm climbing I forget about everything else
> and function automatically, like an animal,
> and I only become "normal" again once I've left the face.

ropes that were damaged in several places. A shortage of money for the expedition meant that we were using homemade ropes that hadn't been tested. But luckily they held. After a few days the weather improved and on December 8 we completed our first new route in Patagonia. For the time being we had had enough; but even as we were leaving this *terra mystica* we were already dreaming of new goals—including Cerro Torre and Torre Egger.

Anyone who has not been in a similar position would probably wonder how we could be dreaming about new adventures while we were still tired and beaten from the first. But mountain climbers find it hard to live without dreams and goals. We were gripped by the idea that we were seekers and conquerors of a barren land, doing things that a "normal" person would not envision. But mountaineers are only different in the activities we choose because we have found, within ourselves, something that all are seeking. It is hard to live without that feeling, once experienced. Perhaps we are only different from those who have the dreams—but do nothing about them.

In the mid-eighties we three musketeers tried once again to realize our dreams and found ourselves on the east face of Cerro Torre. On January 16, 1986, we stood on the summit and looked down on nearby Torre Egger, not knowing then that it would be our next goal. That summer I was in Pakistan, climbing Broad Peak, but by November the three musketeers were once again heading across the pampas towards Torre Egger. We quickly climbed a new route on the southeast face, accomplishing the third ascent. Our style was very elegant, using only a few fixed ropes. Torre Egger is a little lower than Cerro Torre but it carries the reputation of having the highest degree of difficulty. On the evening of December 7, we stood on the summit, enjoying the magnificent view of Cerro Torre, where we had been 11 months previously.

It has been said that the summit of Cerro Torre looks like a half-opened champagne bottle. And it is that magnificent peculiarity of the Patagonian peaks, where most of them are covered in a mushroom of ice and snow, that causes the main problem for climbers. There have been many cases where climbers have had to turn around just a single pitch below the summit. And the descent from the summit is dangerous because the snow is often too soft to set up good protection. On Cerro Torre we managed by leaving an ice ax on the summit from which to descend. But on the summit of Torre Egger the snow was much too soft, so the last one of us had to climb down.

Each new ascent in Patagonia opened new horizons for me, and each time I could see farther. By the time Janez Jeglic and I agreed to attempt the south face of Cerro Torre, we had gained a lot of experience. But, to succeed, it is not enough just to have the experience and the desire. A strong will is also vital, and for the south face of Cerro Torre we had to be tremendously determined. This was, after all, the only unclimbed face on Cerro Torre, and also the longest. It was 1987 and we were back in Patagonia. Again three of us, but in place of Franc Knez the third member of our party was Janez's wife Irena. Recently married, this was their "honeymoon."

That new route via the South Face of Cerro Torre is one of my greatest mountaineering feats and one in which I came closest to the limits of my strength, courage, and endurance. We carried a 16-mm camera to record the exploit and made a short film. Janez Jeglic and I had done something similar to mark ten years of climbing together when we set off for our greatest climbing adventure on the West Face of Bhagirathi III (20,982 feet) in the Gharwal Himalaya. We climbed a 5,250-foot wall alpine style in six days and descended to base camp via the other side of the mountain.

After 1990 our views on mountaineering changed. I had not been to Patagonia for a few years, and I was no longer attracted by the climbing style we had used in the eighties. I suggested to Janez that we attempt a new route on Cerro Torre in alpine style, but he wasn't interested. He did go to Torre that year, completing a short ascent on the south face with some other friends, but using fixed ropes. Personally I wanted something new, something different. All the time I've been climbing I've wanted to be as fast as possible. While it isn't necessarily true that greater speed entails greater danger, if you want to be fast you must limit the gear you carry. And if you don't have sufficient equipment it can be dangerous when the weather closes in.

Climbers are often faced with the dilemma of being quick and successful, although the risk is somewhat higher in the event of unforeseen difficulties—or—of being better equipped and better prepared for the unexpected, but also slower and

perhaps unsuccessful. In 1996, I made a number of rapid ascents in Yosemite: El Capitan's Salathé Wall in 10 hours and Half Dome via the direct Northwest Face in 11 hours, 20 minutes. I came to realize that the most difficult shift was in the mind—in changing my way of thinking. When you achieve this, the climbing itself is no longer so difficult.

When we climbed the Salathé route we began at first light. After ten pitches we overtook an earlier party still sleeping at the Mammoth ledges. Of course, those climbers were surprised. If you intend to climb for several days you are slower, lazier, and less concerned about time. They, too, could have climbed a few pitches in those early hours of the morning, but they didn't do it for reasons of comfort. They had set out with a different mind-set and were prepared for several days of climbing. If you only intend to climb for a single day, however, you have to make use of the whole day, from first light. Come the evening, when we had already returned below the face, the others were still only preparing their second bivouac.

We had a similar experience just below the summit of Half Dome, when we overtook a dozen climbers on a ledge, sheltering from a storm. Although the storm was raging around the mountain, with driving snow, rain, and sleet, the two of us continued on toward the summit in complete control. We simply had no other choice. That is the most important thing about this sort of climbing. You must be decisive, although sometimes you also have to grit your teeth. To succeed with this approach, you must have a partner who thinks like you and is also good. And Aischan certainly was, though later he unfortunately had an accident.

In 1997 I met up with Rolando Garibotti in Yosemite. It was as if we'd been climbing together for ten years. Everything went superbly and, on top of it all, we were quick—climbing like a well-oiled machine. Rolando is from Bariloche in Argentina but has lived in Colorado for some years with his wife. Years ago, when he came from the Argentine pampas directly to Yosemite, he shocked the local climbers with his audacious, rapid ascents. He also knows his Patagonian homeland well, gaining his first real climbing experiences on Cerro Torre at the age of 17. And at the age of 15 he was climbing Aguja Guillaumet. We soon recognized that together we would set our sights on Patagonia.

At the end of January 1999, Rolando and I met up in Patagonia. Our goal was the west face of Fitz Roy by the Ensueño route, first climbed by Italian mountaineers in 1995. Their alpine-style ascent and descent took six days. Rolando and I were counting on climbing the route in a single day. This was a fresh challenge and I was enthusiastic.

As we walked toward the face in the early morning I was quite nervous. I wasn't sure that we were capable of climbing such a long and difficult 5,250-foot route in a single day. But by the time we started climbing, my frame of mind had changed completely. When I'm climbing I forget about everything else and function automatically, like an animal, and I only become "normal" again once I've left the face. I can push aside my fatigue and remain concentrated until the end. I only get tired once I've returned to the glacier. By four in the afternoon we had climbed the 37-pitch route, taking ten hours, and were back on the glacier just after midnight. We were very pleased, and after this ascent we looked even farther.

In November we were back. This time we climbed a new 2,950-foot route on Punta Herron and then, in a few hours, made the first ascent of the unclimbed Punta Filip. We ended this trip with an ascent of Fitz Roy via the longest face, 7,550 feet from the Torre glacier. The first ascent was made in 1983 by a Slovakian team climbing in expedition style with fixed ropes, but they avoided the lower 2,625 feet of the face. We planned the climb for a single day and pared down our equipment to a minimum: no cooker, only 100 ounces of water, a few sweets, and our technical gear. We didn't even take proper bivouac gear.

Just after four in the morning we left our little tent, and by five we had already begun the ascent. We proceeded to climb without rest until ten o'clock in the evening, when we made the decision to bivouac at 10,170 feet. We were simply too tired to continue through the night. In 17 hours we had completed 6,550 feet of demanding and delicate climbing. The bivouac was arduous—at minus 7° we shivered through the night in just our clothes. And our breakfast consisted of a small packet of crackers and a little water. The following day it took us four pitches to reach an easier section, and we arrived at the summit shortly before noon. Descending via the south face to Rio Blanco, we continued from there to the Torre valley, arriving at two in the morning. We were as happy and joyful as a couple of kids leaving Disneyland.

Overcoming a myth in the mind can be difficult, but you have to try!

It is hard to say if this marks a breakthrough in the development of mountaineering in Patagonia. More than anything it is a different approach, and one in which you need a lot of experience. When I first started mountaineering, we did a huge amount of climbing with great enthusiasm. We were crazy and headstrong. Nowadays I compensate for this madness with experience. But above all I have come to realize that to do something more quickly and differently, you first of all need to change your way of thinking. I cannot say that I am now physically stronger than I was some years ago, but when faced with the toughest challenges, I am able to convince myself that I am up to the task. The most important thing is to have alongside you a climber who has the same attitude and is a top climber himself. He has to be the sort of person you can trust completely. The rule is that in critical situations a bad partner becomes even worse and a good one even better.

In 23 years of mountaineering I have climbed with four excellent climbers. The first was Franc Knez, a man who was way ahead of his time. He is the most talented climber I have ever seen, and it was a great honor for me to have learned my trade alongside him. With Janez Jeglic I did my most audacious and crazy climbs. And with Franc and Janez together, as the three musketeers, we accomplished many successful feats. In the nineties I met the Swiss climber Aischan Rupp. We roped up together for a number of rapid ascents in Yosemite, which gave me a fresh insight into climbing. Rolando Garibotti is ten years my junior and a man with strong ethical principles, something I value greatly. Together we transferred the rapid, light alpine style from Yosemite to Patagonia.

In the early days of mountaineering the equipment was very modest and technology was little used. It only came into the equation when climbing became more mainstream. At the time, some people grasped at technology as if it alone could take mountaineering forward. But quite the opposite was true, because mountaineering was increasingly losing its soul. The climbing style was no longer important. This was the era of the commercial expedition, when success had to be guaranteed. Climbers slowly began to lose sight of the real reason they climbed in the first place.

Exactly where we are today, and where mountaineering is headed in the future, is hard to say. There are as many different views about mountain climbing as there are climbers. Personally I believe that mountaineering must return to its roots. Of course, it is always difficult to go back. But we must recognize that mountaineering did not begin with us, and it will not end with us either. We are a generation who, like all other generations before us, inherited something and will leave something behind. It is important that we are aware of the tradition and the identity of mountaineering, but

it is no less important that we move with the times. Back in the eighties I didn't know what I'd be doing in the nineties, and nowadays I am happy that I can make, to the best of my ability, climbs that the next generation will climb more quickly and even better. But equally, I have great respect for the generations of the past, because they accomplished great feats for their time. And of all the mountaineering feats, I value most highly those that were achieved in the manner that is closest to my heart—the simple alpine style.

The Patagonian wilderness still conceals a great many enticing mountaineering challenges. Most of the peaks have been climbed, but many routes still wait to be tackled and a lot of the well-known and attractive routes still await their first repeat ascents. There are even some unclimbed peaks to be found. You just need to put in the effort and delve deeper into the interior of the Hielo Continental. And great traverses have yet to be executed. All that is needed is the vision, the idea, and the determination. Everything else is already here. The great Patagonian storms will continue to rage, helping future generations to return contented from Patagonia, full of the adventure that this *terra mystica* has to offer.

Born in 1960, Slovenian climber Silvo Karo has distinguished himself on big walls, particularly in Patagonia. He started climbing in the Julian Alps of Slovenia, where he put up several new routes, including several in winter.

By the early 1980s, Karo was already traveling abroad. He went to the U.S. and made his first trips to Patagonia, where he climbed a 3,300-foot new route on the East Face of Cerro Fitz Roy called Devil's Dihedral, ED+ (6b/A2), and a 1,312-foot new route on the East Face of Aguja Val Biois called D.E. Route, TD+.

He continued climbing many new routes in the Julian Alps, the Dolomites, the Austrian Alps, and in Croatia, but it was in Asia that he cemented his formidable reputation: Yalung Kang (27,905 feet); Broad Peak (26,402 feet); Lhotse Shar (27,560 feet); Bhagirathi III (20,982 feet) by a new route on the West Face, climbed alpine style in six days; and Mount Everest by a new route from the Western Cwm to the West Ridge.

Karo kept returning to Patagonia to chart his course on unknown and untraveled vertical ground. Some of his most notable recent accomplishments there include a 3,773-foot new route on the East Face of Cerro Torre called Devil's Directissima (7a+, A3); a 3,100-foot new route on the South Face of Torre Egger called Psyco Vertical, (6c/A3); a 1,640-foot new route on the North Face of El Mocho called Grey-Yellow Arrow, ED (7a+/A0); a 3,935-foot new route on the South Face of Cerro Torre (6b/A4); the first free ascent of the 5,250-foot Ensueño on the West Face of Cerro Fitz Roy, ED+ (6b+), in a record time of ten hours.

In his search for new ground, Karo also traveled to Greenland to complete a new route on the left-hand tower of Nalumasortoq called Muscle Power. Rated ED+ (7a/A3) and 2,460 feet, the tower was climbed alpine style in three days.

Silvo Karo was on the international film jury at the Banff Mountain Film Festival in 1997. He was honored by the Trento Film Festival for his contribution to climbing in Patagonia.

ROLE MODELS

THOMAS HORNBEIN

ROYAL ROBBINS

JACK TACKLE

HEROES:
PERSONAL PONDERINGS

THOMAS HORNBEIN

When I was in my teens Everest hadn't been climbed yet. James Ramsey Ullman's *High Conquest* was like the magic mirror through which I could climb into a fantasy world of high mountains and audacious human aspiration. Could a person survive up there, I wondered, much less climb? To exist in such a seemingly inhospitable setting seemed scarcely imaginable. Those who attempted to do so seemed somehow greater than life. Now Everest has been climbed by a cast of a thousand (I among them).

Heroes were simple back then. George Leigh Mallory was one of them. He was a dreamer with a passion to reach the highest point on Earth, a commitment that seemed to transcend all other ties to our usual world, one that included the willingness, it seemed to me, to gamble with his life to accomplish a great and glorious goal.

As I near the eighth decade of my life, I find myself thinking more about heroes. Two things have provoked these thoughts. The first is the realization that I still need heroes, that they are not fuel only for youthful dreams. The second is occasions when someone comes up to me and says, "Oh, it's a thrill to meet you. You've been a hero of mine for...." After the moment of feeling flattered, followed by one of feeling undeserving, leading to the one questioning the judgment of

the admirer, I confront a disconnect in my own logic. Mallory was, for me, a hero. OK. So how am I different? If I could have heroes of my choice, who am I to judge others' choices? But these moments have gotten me to thinking about heroes in a way that never troubled a younger, less reflective Hornbein. What makes a hero? Who decides? Why do heroes matter?

WHAT IS A HERO?

I headed toward the *Oxford English Dictionary* to give me a jump start on this question. Here's a bit of what it said about "hero." After the definitions about great heroes of mythology and war, the one that best captured the essence for me was:

"A man who exhibits extraordinary bravery, firmness, fortitude, or greatness of soul in any action, or in connection with any pursuit, work, or enterprise; a man admired or venerated for his achievements and noble qualities."

My personal concept of hero now seems narrow compared with the way the term is used in our modern society. I am not so much into sports heroes, war heroes, entertainment heroes, or most political heroes (though occasional political figures display a capacity for heroism).

Certain attributes are important to my concept of hero, though not all apply to all my categories of hero:

Ability to risk, to tolerate uncertainty.

Courage, though courage alone does not

a hero make, even though it seems an essential ingredient.

Volition: Commonly acts of heroism involve confronting a choice. An action compelled by another doesn't qualify, though going above and beyond the call of duty certainly does.

Selflessness, a distinguishing characteristic of some but not all types of heroism. The risk to self is an important element.

As I examine those who are my heroes based upon these attributes, I find that most of them fit into one (or more) of three categories that comprise my present domain of heroes.

THE HERO AS SAVIOR

Although selflessness and sacrifice don't appear in the *OED*'s definition, those who voluntarily risk their own well-being to aid others are, to me, heroes. These are the heroes of the heroic act. We hear and read about them in the news regularly: those attempting to rescue someone from a raging river or a burning building. Sometimes they fail; sometimes they pay with their lives. Often, when the rescuers, if they have survived, are praised for what they have done, they shrug it off. They weren't thinking about being heroes. Indeed, often they will claim they weren't even thinking at all; they were only doing what was needed.

Then there are those who perform such feats after ample time to contemplate and clearly realize what they are putting on the line. Many such moments can be found in the history and fiction surrounding war or disasters. One touching and exalting fictional example is the hunchbacked painter of birds, Philip Rhayader, in Paul Gallico's poignant tale, *The Snow Goose*. Rhayader left all he loved and what might have been to sail off in his tiny boat across the Channel to rescue soldiers trapped on the beach at Dunkirk, not unaware of the risk from heavy bombardment. It was something he had to do. And another example, in real life, is displayed over and over again in the efforts of many northland Norwegians to assist, at risk to themselves and their families, in carrying Jan Baalsruud safely to neutral Sweden, as told in David Howarth's *We Die Alone*. These acts represent a kind of heroism that stirs my

soul, and maybe troubles it as well, as one perceives the distance between such an act and one's own daily life.

Nor does our world of mountaineering lack for examples. One that comes to my mind took place on K2 in 1953 when Art Gilkey developed a pulmonary embolus high on the mountain. In the course of attempting to lower him to safety in a makeshift litter, one member of the team fell, pulling off, one-by-one, all the others except for Gilkey, whose makeshift litter was attached by a rope to an ice ax belayed from above by Pete Schoening. Sometimes things happen that fall outside our realm of comprehension. Often we call them miracles. However that may be, somehow the ropes of the falling climbers became entangled in the litter and their fall to certain death was arrested by Schoening's ice ax belay. The feat seems superhuman in some ways. Was Schoening a hero? In his eyes it was nothing more than doing what he had to do (a common element in heroic acts). In his companions' eyes, though, it's likely another matter. To him they owed their lives, and "My hero!" would not be an understatement.

But in terms of acts of heroism, what Schoening did, without choice or time for reflection, is overshadowed by what the whole team did with choice—that is, the election to try to bring the ailing Gilkey down off the mountain under immensely difficult and dangerous circumstances. In a sense they, too, perhaps had no choice, or at least, I suspect they did not in their essential humanity feel that they did. And one wonders, speculating beyond what's on the printed page, might Gilkey, while his companions were regrouping from their injuries after the fall, have taken the opportunity to disconnect himself from the mountainside to which he had been secured? He knew that his companions' efforts to get him down had put them at immense risk, had nearly killed them all, and that there were still miles to go. Would that be the ultimate heroic act among heroic acts?

Examples abound of such selfless courage and sacrifice, not only to assist others but also to defend deeply held beliefs and principles and even one's own integrity. That most of us will ever have to confront such choices seems maybe more improbable than it really is, but as a model of how we would hope to act, they have precious value.

HEROES OF GREAT FEATS

Here is where the dictionary definition fits most naturally into our world of mountaineering and exploration. Examples are Mallory and his companions in the days before Everest was climbed. And at least some of those seeking the geographical poles fit this same category: Peary, Cook, Scott, and Amundsen are all examples, all humans with very human frailties; each was driven by a passion to explore, whether it be for fame and fortune or for something burning inside. Can one really regard these ventures as heroic? Each required commitment, courage, and vision. Each of these individuals commands admiration, even while one may be critical of competence or integrity or other weaknesses. Each can seem remote from the realities of our day-to-day lives. Selfless sacrifice is not a component of this form of heroism, if indeed we choose to call it that.

Pioneering a new route, William Unsoeld and Thomas Hornbein pause at 24,200 feet on Everest's West Ridge, which spans the border of Nepal and then forbidden Tibet.

Climbing mountains seems to be about as far from selfless sacrifice as one can get. While the attendant uncertainties of the challenge of the endeavor may shape the lives of each of us who indulge, even in ways that affect how we may influence the lives of others, the act itself seems to be inherently selfish. While heroic acts as savior can always occur along the way, as they can in less exotic settings, the essence of climbing a mountain is hard to justify to loved ones and others who hold some stake in the climber's continued existence.

Perhaps because I am too close to this particular form of endeavor now, the magic it held when I was a teen in awe of Mallory has lost some of its luster. But Mallory and his legend have undergone no essential change and certainly no diminution in the public's eye after the recent discovery of his high resting place. Therefore it is I, and my view of heroes, that must have evolved in the intervening half century. I know many, including myself, who are not unlike Mallory in what drives us to search for adventure. Perhaps that familiarity and sense of identity take a bit of the luster off Mallory as hero. Even so, he remains one for me, but in a different way now. My admiration for the accomplishments of these adventurers is undiminished, particularly for those who have brought new vision to traveling on new ground. Maybe my expectation of hero status has risen as I have grown more reflective and the once seemingly impossible feats have become more and more our daily fare.

Success is not a necessary criterion for heroes, at least if success is measured by accomplishing the goal originally defined. Look at Mallory. Other examples of heroic failures shine forth. At the top of my list, steadfastly a hero among heroes for many decades, is Ernest Shackleton. I carried Alfred Lansing's paperback version of *Endurance*, the classic account of the journey of Shackleton and his men, with me to Everest in 1963. What the team set out to do—to make the first traverse of the Antarctic continent—is almost forgotten as one relives the events of their months of imprisonment in the drifting ice, and the dramatic escape in tiny boats, to ultimate survival of every member of the team. What shines through most of all is the impelling force of Shackleton himself, a rare kind of leader (not unlike Lincoln but with different capacities for different demands). As with K2 in 1953, luck played a tremendous role. But as a Nepali dignitary told me after Everest in 1963, "Luck is what you make it." Ernest Shackleton, by a rare personal quality of leadership ("the boss" to his men) pulled it off. In him dwelt elements of all three of my kinds of heroes: the great feat, the savior, and the survivor.

THE HERO AS SURVIVOR

I have another type of hero where elements of selflessness and volition might seem less relevant at first glance, but it is just those aspects of the style of coping with adversity that defines the heroism of these ordinary heroes. There is a quote I've cherished for some years now, from the foreword by Dr. John Young to a book entitled *Options*. The book was written by Barry Corbet, one of my companions on Everest's West Ridge. He wrote it for others who, like himself, have sustained a spinal-cord injury (he got his in a helicopter crash):

"What drives them? Whence comes their superhuman motivation and courage? ...Only after years of peripheral involvement in their lives, including some deep friendships, did I realize that they are heroes [the Gimps and Crips], but only in the sense that all human beings have the capacity for heroism, particularly when they have no other choice. To this day, I have never ceased to be amazed at the ability of common, ordinary people to overcome adversity."

For me, though Corbet doesn't buy it—which adds challenging seasoning to our friendship—he is a model for my hero as survivor. Barry's been a paraplegic for the second half of his life, and it's never a life that's easy. But you get on with it. Currently he is editor of *New Mobility*, a magazine for the many others who share spinal-cord injury or similarly confining disabilities. What he has done is not unique, but he has pulled it off with style and creativity that adds to my admiration for him, even as I cannot truly imagine what it would be like to be in his place. When we talked recently about heroes, Corbet had this to say: "To me, a hero is someone who makes the world better or sacrifices his own interests for a greater, nobler cause. By that definition, we're all heroes some of the time, but

almost none of us consistently. And by that definition, mountaineering is pretty much nowhere." Yes, Barry!

As an anesthesiologist, I occasionally confront similar heroism in my patients. Some are coping courageously with fear; some with the fear of going to sleep and not waking up again, some with the fear that they may awaken to a diagnosis that is their sentence of death. The ones who amaze me the most are those who live with an incurable, imminently fatal illness, yet who touch me, their caregiver, with reassurance, with a reaching out to teach me that the process of dying is an act of living. Their gift is one I would hope to be able to give should I one day be in their place. They, like Corbet, are both heroes and role models.

GREATNESS

Lincoln, Gandhi, Mozart, Einstein, and so on—the list could fill pages. They didn't feel quite like heroes to me; they were something different, something more. In due course it occurred to me that their distinguishing characteristic was greatness. By greatness I mean that they have, in significant ways, not just enhanced my life but they have altered the world in which we live for the better. They have had a major effect on the shape and quality of our collective destiny as a society—as a human race. I admire them as I admire heroes, but the relationship is more distant, less immediate to my own dreams and aspirations.

Then there are those who are my role models: my mentors, teachers, colleagues, and friends, and others who may not know me. They have had major influences on how my life has unfolded. They have served as models to the shaping of my beliefs, my morality, and my approach to science and medicine and mountains and relationships and untold more. They are less remote than many of my heroes, yet with a more palpable impact on the shaping of who I am.

WHO DECIDES?

Heroes are in the eye of the beholder. You have yours. I have mine. At times we may share common heroes, sometimes for common reasons, sometimes not. Sometimes one person touches multiple lives as hero, even whole populations, but numbers don't define a hero. One alone will do.

ON BEING A HERO

I embarked upon this journey into heroland to better understand my own place in it. Being seen by others as a hero was uncomfortable, even though satisfying. Yet heroes—yours or mine—are not a rare, endangered species. So how does one act when on the receiving end of this hero thing?

We have a tendency, at least a wish, to see our heroes as a bit bigger than life in all aspects of their lives. Yet ultimately heroes are just people. One can see how the modern images of Peary, Cook, and Scott are affected by this expectation. Ed Hillary, who with Tenzing Norgay in 1953 was the first to reach the "third pole," the highest point on Earth, was recently interviewed for an article in *Sports Illustrated*. The article called his first ascent of Everest and Roger Bannister's four-minute-mile one year later their most "favorite feats" of the just-ended century. Hillary put his own celebrity into what I thought to be a fitting context, noting, "If someone wants to believe I am a heroic figure, fine, but for me, I did a reasonable job at the time. I didn't get carried away then, and I never have."

So what do you do when you become the target of such esteem, whether you are Hillary, Corbet, Hornbein, or someone else? For a while, my approach was avoidance: Pass over the compliment, redirect the conversation. In due course I came to accept that we "heroes" are not unique, but that we can positively affect the dreams and aspirations of others, just as we were affected by the acts of our heroes. The solution I have found simplest and most comfortable is to thank the person for sharing their feelings, then use the opportunity to learn a bit more about what has created this bond between us. One of the most precious venues for such exchange is a class of young students, for they don't yet see boundaries. Sometimes I see a small, quiet boy whose ears are a bit outsized for his head; he rarely asks a question but it's clear he's listening. It's an eerie feeling, because in my imagination I'm looking back into the mirror of time.

WHO NEEDS HEROES?

Who needs heroes? Well, I do, for one. But I think that perhaps we all do. What's the hero's place in our lives? The wisdom and experience from the world around us, most notably from other human beings, nurture part of our own capacity for growth and change. Admiration for others—who they are, what they contribute, how they extend our horizons—fertilizes our own growth from where we are to what we might become. Friends, mentors, loved ones, and even strangers all help mold our clay. These role models influence who we become in powerful ways.

Where do heroes fit in? In a way, they are the stuff of dreams. For me, they occupy a special summit a bit less accessible, a mountain peak that in my mind's eye has grand walls of rock and brilliant ice, clouds veiling an elusive, lonely summit. It is not a mountain I can climb, and never will, but one I nonetheless dream I might.

Thomas Hornbein was born in 1930 in St. Louis, Missouri, where, at a young age, he began his climbing career on neighboring trees and the slate roof of his family home. Later, at the University of Colorado, he began to pursue climbing more seriously. His experiences with mountain rescue and teaching first aid prompted an interest in medicine, which led to the physiology of breathing.

In May of 1963, he and Willi Unsoeld became the first climbers to ascend Mount Everest via the West Ridge and complete the first traverse of the world's highest mountain. Through the years, he has continued climbing, with ascents of Masherbrum, Paiju and Masherbrum La, Ulugh Mustagh, Kangkarpo, and Long's Peak in Colorado, in addition to daily ascents to his 14th-floor office.

He has received many awards throughout his distinguished career, and he is currently Professor and Former Chairman of the Anesthesiology Department at the University of Washington. He was on the jury of the Banff Mountain Film Festival in 1999.

Standing on
the Shoulders:
A Tribute to My Heroes

Royal Robbins

The future may be unclear but I can't imagine that, as of the new millennium, all of the old laws of the universe will have been put to rest. It seems certain to me that whatever men and women have always needed, and need today, they will need in the future. And it seems certain to me that whatever forces have driven or pulled men and women toward the heights in the past, and compel them upward in the present, will be at least as forceful in the days to come.

To my mind, two such forces stand out. One is our need for the natural world. We are made to be part of nature. Our connection to that world is our connection to sanity. Henry David Thoreau famously said, "In wildness is the preservation of the world." That seems intuitively right. Can anyone imagine keeping one's sanity in a world where nothing existed but New York and Los Angeles? But what is it in wildness that fills that crucial need in the human spirit? What is that soothing balm? I can't say it's God's presence. We all experience that differently. But we could say it's God's handiwork. The natural world is soothing and refreshing because it is God's creation—yes—but more important, it is God's creation unsullied by human invention. It is the presence of Divine Creation along with the absence of human contrivances that soothes and delights the soul, and

that provokes the soul to say, "I have come home."

On TV, in films, in picture books, and through virtual reality in cyberspace, we can reproduce nature with uncanny exactitude. But to what benefit? It's all "wonder-full," and intellectually and emotionally stimulating. But it's not the same and will never be the same as the real thing. A cyberflower and a cybersunset only make us yearn for a real flower and a real sunset. Nothing man can do or make can approach the majesty of a real mountain, a real Half Dome, a real Matterhorn. Ultimately if our world were only steel and glass and cyber happenings, then a single tree, a single leaf, or a single blade of grass would be a wonder because it is not man-made. It is natural.

The other need that isn't going to evaporate is the thirst for personal challenge. This craving drives men and women to climb mountains, and so to discover who they are and what they may be. We are the spawn of ancestors whose daily lives were struggles for survival. We need adventure. It's in our blood. It will not go away. The mountains will continue to call because they uniquely fulfill our need for communion with nature, as well as our hunger for adventure.

That's about all I can see of the future, that the human needs for nature and adventure will not become obsolete. They will be filled. The drama will be played out. I would rather talk about the past, for what's past is prologue. And the ideals and spirit that moved the earliest and greatest climbers will continue to motivate climbers in the future.

My first hero was my scoutmaster, Phil Bailey. The Boy Scouts introduced me to climbing when I was 12 years old. I dabbled for several years, until my fate as a climber was sealed at age 15. It was not a mountain that provoked my commitment to vertical strife and vertical striving, but the words of a book—a history of mountaineering by James Ramsey Ullman. The title, *High Conquest*, sets the stage, and the book captures the romance of mountaineering in a way that recent histories fail to do—they have too much polish and too little innocence. Written in 1941, Ullman's book looked forward to the end of a world war, when men would again raise their eyes skyward, not in fear of planes coming to drop bombs, but rather to seek the high summits that would draw them to a different type of conquest—High Conquest.

And what was this "high conquest"? In answering that question, the book struck a deep responsive chord in my soul, for Ullman wrote not about the conquest of the large chunks of rock pushing upward out of the Earth's crust, but rather about the mountains inside the mountaineer. A quote from George Leigh Mallory leads us to the conquest that is the true subject of the book: "Have we vanquished an enemy? None but ourselves." And so I came to see that the mountains we conquer are not those on the horizon: supreme, cold, and taunting, but rather those within us: of fear, weakness, and ignorance. These were the true high peaks. And, when we could stand on top of them we would indeed be "on top of the world."

To a 15-year-old, unsuccessful at school and seemingly everything else, this promise of the mountains being the anvil upon which the climber could forge his character was powerful and convincing. I saw my destiny: I would become a climber! And so it was that the ringing words of Ullman and the inspiring epigram of Mallory combined to seal my fate, to provoke a lifelong commitment to the craft of climbing.

I was now pointed at climbing literature, and my second book was a novel by Andre Frisson-Roche, about a young apprentice guide in the French Alps who, after the death of his father in a lightening storm on the Petit Dru, grows to strength and maturity as a climber. After reading

First on the Rope I knew that was where I always wanted to be—at the sharp end, finding the way.

My first heroes were these authors and the characters in their books. After that I was inspired by other heroes of the quest for summits—by Herman Buhl, Anderl Heckmair, and Heinrich Harrer; by Gaston Rébuffat and Lionel Terray; by Emilio Comici and Riccardo Cassin; but particularly by the great Italian climber Walter Bonatti. Bonatti created a range of sterling climbs, but his solo, first ascent of the Southwest Pillar of the Dru stands out magnificently as an inspired achievement. Here was a granite buttress, over 2,000 feet high, accessible only after facing the dangers of the Dru Couloir. No solo of this sort had ever been done in the western Alps. It was a steep, difficult, technical rock climb, exceeding anything that had yet been done—even in the comparatively friendly and sheltered environment of Yosemite Valley. And it was carried out over a period of six days in the violently stormy French Alps, high on an isolated mountain above the dangerous Dru Couloir.

The Bonatti Pillar is a masterpiece, a shining example of the truth of Geoffrey Winthrope Young's dictum, "It isn't getting to the top that counts. It's the way you do it." This ascent, even with a partner, would have been a terrific accomplishment. To do it solo added hugely to the feat. My solos of the Leaning Tower and El Capitan owe much to Bonatti's early example, but they don't rise to his level because he was so far ahead of his time. I was only imitating. Absent Bonatti's example, my climbs would have been more visionary and daring. I was standing on the unseen shoulders of my great predecessor.

I never met Walter Bonatti, but I met and climbed with a couple of my other mountain heroes, Joe Brown and Don Whillans, two legends of British climbing. Joe and Don and others like them grew out of the English working class after the Second World War. When I first met and climbed with Joe in North Wales I found him affable and cheerful, a friendly and ebullient spirit of the crags. Tom Patey's song about Joe contains the stanza,

> In the shadow of Dinas Cromlech,
> Where luckless leaders fall,

The Corner it was towering high,
And Joe uncommon small.
But his heart was as big as the mountain,
And his nerves were made of steel—
It had to go, or so would Joe,
In a monumental peel.

Of course, Joe did make the first ascent of Cenotaph Corner, one of his superb test pieces in Britain. I climbed it with him in 1964. It was too hard for me that day to take the sharp end, so I was treated to a performance by the master on one of his finest routes. He climbed with an economy of effort that left me breathless—never a wasted move. The only other person I have seen climb with such grace is Chuck Pratt. Brown inspired me as a supreme artist of the crags.

Like Joe, Don Whillans was "uncommon small," but the smart thing was to not refer to Don's size in his presence. Apart from his notorious pugnacity, Don was one of the world's leading climbers, both on pure rock and in alpine conditions. His routes on rock were often described as, "like Whillans, short and tough." He was the master of vicious little climbs, easy to fall off, and frequently lacking protection.

What I particularly admired about Don was his granite-like common sense and his supreme calm in the face of danger. Like all climbers, he must have been a romantic at heart, inspired by the siren call of the summits. But when he was on the mountain, Don was the ultimate realist. He saw the situation with perfect clarity and never let his emotions, his dreams, or his ambitions get in the way of lucid thinking and crisp decision-making. I often thought that if the going in the mountains got tough, and I found myself in a grim situation with survival the issue, the man I would most want to be with was Don Whillans.

The remaining heroes on my list are Americans. The first is John Muir: immigrant Scot, explorer, mountaineer, conservationist, and bard of the American outdoors. Muir is, of course, more famous for his poetic pleas to save our natural heritage than his mountaineering exploits, but he was a true mountaineer. Who can forget, after having once read it, Muir's gripping description of his hairbreadth escape from death during an unroped solo ascent of Mount Ritter in his

beloved Sierra Nevada? Picture him, frozen into immobility in a steep corner, unable to advance or climb down, desperate, terrified, and about to accept the inevitability of death in hot blood when a sudden inspiration, as if sent by a guardian angel, enables him to escape alive. His account is now a classic of mountaineering literature. But Muir's biggest impact upon the American climbing world has been not through his climbing writing; it has been through his message of the sacredness of the natural order and the desirability of leaving it natural and unsullied.

American climbers have long lived by this principle. The American Alpine Club's mission statement includes as a goal, "the conservation and preservation of the mountain environment." When I joined the Sierra Club, I learned right from the start, "to leave it as you found it." This applied to trail, camp, and picnic spot, but especially to the rock on which we climbed. That meant pitons were not left in place. They were removed.

In Europe it was otherwise. The Alps were (and are) studded with pitons. But American climbers, under the goad of Muir's eloquent articulation of the "leave no trace" philosophy of resource stewardship, became committed to leaving the rock as much as possible in its natural state. They removed pitons, partly to preserve that quality of naturalness in and of itself, but also because they valued the exploratory qualities of the first ascent and wanted, as nearly as possible, to reproduce and relive the original adventure. Americans took great pride in not leaving a single piton even on an extended climb. Ultimately this commitment led to the conversion, in American climbing, from destructive pitons to rock-friendly artificial chockstones.

Another American who has deeply influenced me is John Salathé, who came to America from Switzerland at the age of 45. He was a blacksmith, allowing him to respond creatively to a need he perceived in following the Muir ethic while scaling the great Yosemite walls—hard steel pitons. Salathé dreamed of doing continuous big-wall climbs, which would require hundreds of pitons. Carrying a rack of 20 or 30 pitons meant some might be used dozens of times. The soft iron pitons available at the time (imported from Europe or purchased at Army surplus stores) simply were not adequate. They quickly became deformed and useless.

Seeing a need for which no tool existed, Salathé hand-forged hard steel pitons out of, as legend has it, the metal used in the axles of Model A Ford cars. This invention would revolutionize American climbing. Salathé then proceeded to put the pitons to good use in scaling the three hardest routes in the country—routes on which the technical difficulty at the time probably exceeded anything in the world. Among these were the Lost Arrow Chimney and the North Face of Sentinel Rock.

These climbs were great leaps forward—multiday ascents requiring extreme physical fitness, commitment, determination, and great technical skill in placing pitons for direct aid. Salathé excelled in this latter skill, possessing an uncanny ability to get pitons to stick in almost nonexistent cracks. But in addition to his great technical skill, and indeed abetting and supporting and fostering it, was a sense of style that would set a standard for generations of climbers to come.

In those days Yosemite climbing required the occasional bolt, or sometimes a string of them, to overcome truly blank sections of otherwise climbable rock. Always present was the temptation to get out the drill before it was absolutely necessary, to take the easy way out, rather than screw up one's courage and work tirelessly and inventively to find a way to get up without resorting to the detested expansion bolt.

Amazingly Salathé never succumbed to this temptation. His bolts were always deemed by later parties to be "justified." How hard that is to do. How remarkable that he did it in his day, without the goad of competition. No one would have faulted him for placing twice as many bolts. He was competing only with himself. What was he thinking? Where did he get this sense of style? Why did he set these almost impossibly high standards for himself? We don't know. He didn't write or talk about these things. His eloquence on such matters was pure action and his actions were, to us, spellbindingly persuasive. American climbing would have been quite different had those of us who followed in Salathé's footholds not been so deeply impressed by the courage and commitment to excellence of this thoughtful, taciturn, Swiss

blacksmith who came to California and taught Americans a thing or two about climbing. On his shoulders, so many of us have stood—reaching for higher holds.

There are three other men I admire for qualities I would like to possess. The first is my climbing companion Chuck Pratt. I have said many times that Chuck was the best climber of our generation. I was always in awe of Pratt's ability to float effortlessly up the hardest off-width jam cracks. But he was not just a jam crack specialist. His mastery extended to face climbing, slab climbing, and aid climbing. Pratt could do it all, as well as balance on chains between fence posts and juggle half a dozen items at once. He was also the best writer of our generation. His masterpieces *The View From Dead Horse Point* and *The South Face Of Mount Watkins* are classics of climbing literature. I admired and enjoyed and attempted to emulate Pratt in all of these areas. Although failing, I was nonetheless prodded to higher achievement by the example set by Charles Marshall Pratt.

But beyond and above these deeds and talents, Pratt is my hero because of the kind of person he is —the very best of climbing companions: jovial, keenly witty, with a sense of humor that has a laser beam focus on the absurdities of the universe and the hands we are dealt in the cosmic poker game. I once heard the phrase, "Only the pure climb gracefully." I know Pratt would wince at being called "pure," being as much a sinner as the next man. But when it comes to climbing itself, well, that is almost sacred to Chuck. Pratt, more than perhaps anyone I have known, has always climbed, first and foremost, and last and finally, for the climbing experience itself, for the rewards that come directly from the dance of man and rock. Climbing for Chuck is a life-giving elixir, and he has always wanted to keep it as pure as possible: uncorrupted and unalloyed by gain, fame, or ambition, or any sort of debasement. Chuck has kept his integrity.

Another friend in this class is Tom Frost. Along with Chuck, he was my closest climbing companion in the golden age of Yosemite climbing. I guess I looked at climbing with Tom as more of an adventure than with Pratt. With Pratt along, success was more certain. But nothing was lost in companionship or laughter being with Tom. His optimism and high spirits were infectious and always uplifting. Tom is the kindest and gentlest and most generous person I have ever met, with never an ill word to say of anyone. He is also a man of courage and leadership, as witness his recent vanguard role in the effort to save Camp IV in Yosemite. And he continues to possess the true spirit of climbing. Just a couple of years ago, at age 60, with his son, he climbed three big El Capitan routes, one of them the North America Wall.

My last example is a young contemporary less than half my age. He is a Canadian named Peter Croft. Peter has been my hero for many years, ever since he came blazing out of nowhere with his stunning free solo ascent of Astroman on Washington Column in Yosemite. Tom Frost and I had made the second ascent of this route, mostly with direct aid in the early sixties. That one could climb this route without resorting to direct aid was impressive. To do it without a rope was astonishing. But such was Peter Croft's level of mastery. That it was mastery, and not mere daring, was proven by a string of free solos of similar stature, executed to perfection. This mastery was also shown in, among other feats, his ascent with John Bachar of The Nose of El Capitan and the Northwest Face of Half Dome in one day. This was far ahead of its time in American climbing.

To be one of the great climbing stylists in the world and to remain unassuming, modest, generous, and always in touch with the essential joy of climbing; to always seek in one's climbing to reproduce that first original wonder that got us hooked, as Peter does, is to add to achievement the qualities of the human spirit that create a person about whom one can say, "That is a man."

I have looked back rather than forward because looking forward is to "see through a glass darkly," in St. Paul's noted phrase, and I have gotten my ideas and inspiration from the past. But there are some observations about the future I think we can make, based upon the lessons of the past. As I said earlier quoting Shakespeare, "What's past is prologue." But just what is the past? However far the future extends, we shall always need the natural world preserved and available as the natural world. And we shall need the opportunity to play out the drama of personal conquest that mountains provide.

The qualities of the climbers who inspired me will be needed as much in the future as they have been in the past. It will remain true that getting to the top is not the main thing, but rather the tools and methods we use to get there. With the proliferation of climbers and growth of population, it will be even more important to leave as little evidence of our passage as possible. We shall still need vision and boldness and courage and prudence. A sense of style will never go out of style, and standards, so high that we reach and maintain them only by striving mightily, will always be part of the climbing game. But we may also expect that, among other things that will go marching into the alpine future, there will be camaraderie. Yes, conflict and cross-purposes among climbers are a natural part of the human condition. But overall, and in the long run, the brotherhood of the rope has prevailed. Fellowship among comrades who share danger and who trust their lives in each other's hands has always been a powerful impulse in the climbing world. This fellowship, this brotherhood of the rope, or, for those who wish a more gender-neutral term, this Spirit of the Rope, lives and breathes and never dies. It is a powerful force. It has love in it. We have often heard of esprit de corps. What of Esprit de la Corde, that unseen thin line connecting climbers, through time and through space? Viva Esprit de la Corde. Long live the Spirit of the Rope.

Royal Robbins is an internationally famous climber and adventure kayaker. His climbs include many first ascents in North America and in the Alps. In 1957 he made the first ascent of the Northwest Face of Half Dome, and he has made first ascents of the three great faces on El Capitan in Yosemite Valley. His river runs include first descents of 30 rivers in California and Chile.

Robbins has consistently assumed a leadership role in whatever arena he is working. To recognize that commitment, he received an Outstanding Leadership Award from the Outdoor Industry in 1993. He and Liz, his wife and partner in adventure, created and run the Royal Robbins Company. He appeared at the Banff Festival in 1995.

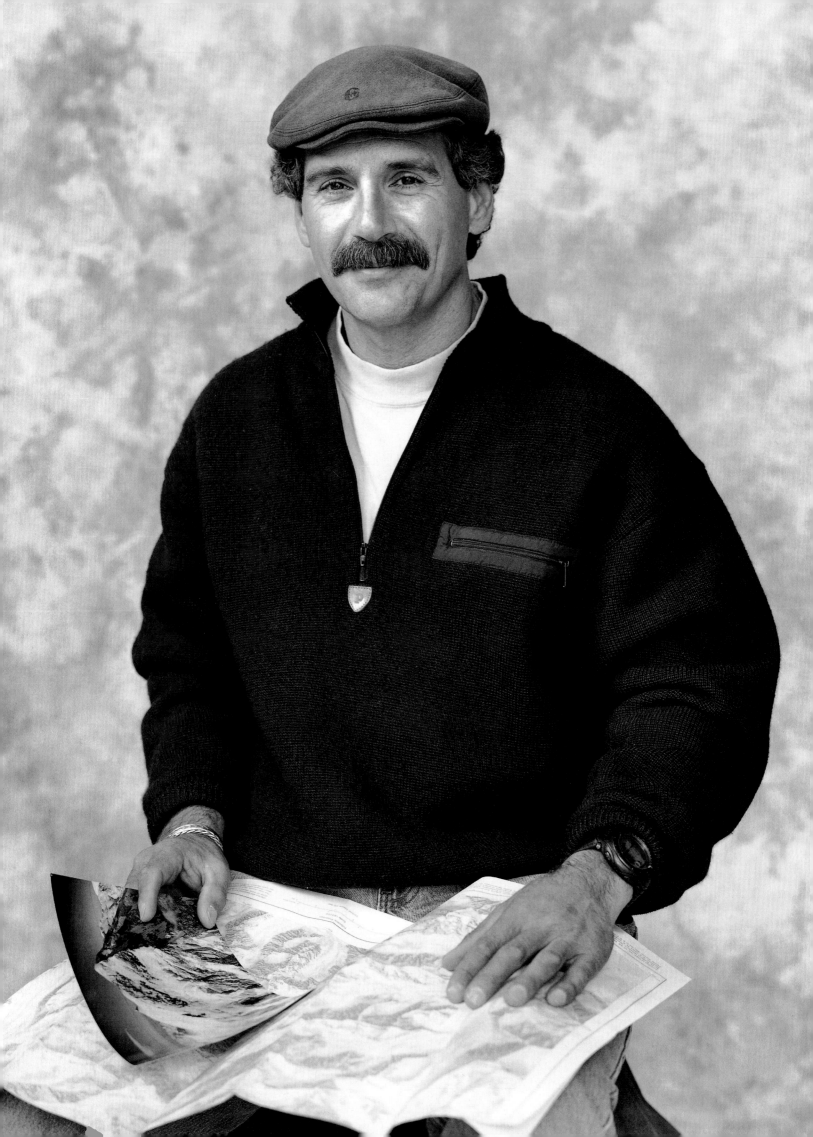

The Accidental Mentor

Jack Tackle

It's 2:00 a.m. on May 7, 1979. Mount Huntington looms ominously behind us. The air is heavy, like the olive-colored calm that precedes a tornado. Ken Currens and I are in a remote cirque, entering the second day of our alpine-style climb; we are 2,000 feet up the virgin Southeast Face of Denali. Ken is leading, appearing only as a speck in the distance, the rope stretched out almost all the way. He labors beneath his heavy pack. Belaying in the dusky light, I am amazed at the wonder of this place—an unclimbed 8,000-foot face on the highest peak in North America.

Suddenly, from above comes a short cry. Instinctively I glance up and see Kenny falling backward, cartwheeling down the ice toward me, ice tools clanging, hardware rattling, rag-dolling down the wall. Time freezes—what is about to happen? One Chouinard ice screw, 30 feet above me, is Ken's only piece. Seconds seem like an eternity as Ken passes me and falls into the mist below. I envision the ice screw above me ripping out, then being catapulted from my stance. I see myself falling, tumbling, just like Ken into the abyss below. A voice inside me speaks with utter resolve, "So, this is what it's like just before you die." Kenny disappears; the ropes draw tight, singing like piano wires as they stretch. Then the inevitable impact. The force is unbelievable, slamming me into the wall and jerking my body upward. The ropes twist tightly around my right arm and upper chest, cutting off my circulation. My pack hangs underneath me with my two anchors dangling below, 15 feet higher than where I placed them. Everything is quiet. I am still alive.

A 250-foot leader fall—onto one screw—held by a hip belay. This is not your optimal situation on a new route in a remote part of Alaska. I shout repeatedly to Ken. There is no response! Again, I beg. Nothing! I feel incredibly alone. Ken is not in view because he is hanging below a lip of ice above a crevasse, 120 feet below. Pinned to the wall like a butterfly in an insect collection, unable to move, I am desperate. The tangled web of the belay makes extrication impossible. Fearing the single anchor that holds us in the balance will fail from the stress, I yell frantically again, "Kenny! Are you all right?" Ken must be dead. A fall of this magnitude on 60-degree ice with a 50-pound pack leaves little chance of survival. I fear he is dead weight at the end of the rope and I am a captive counterweight.

Incredibly, I hear him respond: "I think I broke my leg!!" "Jesus, he is alive!" Hearing my own voice confirms that it's real. I plead with Ken to get his weight off the rope. Until I can free myself from his weight, we are helpless. Without telling me, Kenny takes out his Swiss Army knife as he is twirling in space, upside down, and cuts himself from both ropes. The umbilical cord is severed. He drops ten feet into the crevasse, with a fractured femur and a severe head wound. Ken has set me free.

Regrouping, I realize I need to climb up to, and then rappel off of, the single piece of gear that held the fall. Staring at the ice screw 30 feet away, I mutter, "It looks okay." Quickly, I reorganize my mind and my gear, then set off for the anchor. Halfway there, a huge spindrift avalanche roars down the flutings of the face above me, and a moment later I'm engulfed. Screaming, " No!" I hang onto my two ice tools, head down, eyes closed, praying not to be swept away. Everything goes dark for a few moments, then slowly it becomes a constant flowing river of powder snow, in which I am suspended. Finally it stops. I reach the screw and prepare the ropes for the rappel. Since the ropes and screw have sustained the huge fall, they must still be good. I clip in and go. One hundred twenty feet lower, I lean out over the crevasse lip and spy Kenny lying almost completely buried in the avalanche debris. The snow mixed with blood is the color of cotton candy as I sweep it away from Kenny's face and legs. He is lying helplessly on his side in a cocoon position, his fractured leg held with one arm. "You're going to be okay. We're going to get you out of here in one piece." Kenny grimaces, then nods his head at my reassuring words—wanting to believe them, even though they have no basis in reality, given our predicament.

The bond that can exist between two partners, engaged in the goal of climbing an uncharted, large scale, alpine route, is stronger than steel but more fragile than a gossamer. When adversity strikes, that bond is either strengthened or broken. Ken and I become one spirit, with one goal.

His broken femur demands the methadone. My knife cuts 40 feet off of one of our 9-mm ropes, and I splint Ken's legs together. We go through the painstaking and traumatic process of elimination, trying to find out what movements he can and cannot bear. "Mostly everything" is what he cannot do. Lowering him is out of the question.

Finally we choose a strategy. Ken faces out, holding an ice ax in each hand like an outrigger as he sits on top of my forearms. I face into the ice, down-climbing ever so slowly on my front points as we move, inch by inch, toward last night's snow cave. There is no rope, no belay, no anchors—only trust and hope. Often I move too abruptly and

Ken screams in pain, writhing on top of my forearms. "I'm sorry, I'm sorry," I say. We rest. We go again. The refuge of the cave beckons. Now the methadone is starting to kick in, so we make better progress. I have no sense of time until I look at my watch and realize it has taken us four hours to descend 400 feet to the entrance of the cave. Inside, the simple task of getting in his sleeping bag is even more difficult than the precarious descent. Eventually I enclose him in the warm down chrysalis.

My next task is to chop snow blocks and set them within Ken's reach. I give him all but a few candy bars of my food. He has the stove and all the fuel—maybe ten days worth. Standing outside the cave, I yell into the radio, "Mayday!!! Mayday!!!" Silence. We cannot sit here and hope that someone will fly by and hear our plea for help. I look him in the eye and say, "I'll be back soon, my man. You can last in here for days. I know you can." His inner strength and resolve is inspiring. "I'll be here. I'm not going anywhere," he says with a momentary smile.

Down-climbing 2,000 feet to the glacier from our cave, I ponder the daunting prospect of skiing unroped down the glacier—the very route Ken and I skied up, safely tied together, only two days before. I know I will see Ken again. I ski ten miles down the West Fork of the Ruth Glacier and out into the amphitheater, determined to find help. I lose count of how many times I hear a *whoomph!!!!!* behind the tails of my skis. I look around and see charcoal-colored holes in the snow with ski tracks running out from both sides. Suddenly and serendipitously, Cliff Hudson flies overhead and we make radio contact. Minutes later we are airborne in the orange 185.

When Cliff and I arrive in Talkeetna he radios ahead to let the park and others know about the need for an immediate rescue effort. A huge storm is approaching the Alaska Range; the clock is ticking. Although I feel that Kenny can survive for many days, I think that his being trapped indefinitely in the cave is tempting fate more than we already have.

Immediately after landing, the phone calls are flying among the National Park Service, the media, and myself. "Please don't call the military in from Anchorage," I argue, making my case to Bob Gerhardt, the chief climbing ranger at McKinley

Park. I believe climbers should be responsible for their own rescues. "What would work best is just a few climbers who are skilled in this kind of environment going back in and helping me get Kenny."

In the midst of the fire storm, fielding phone calls and questions, the minutes that are tantamount to Kenny's survival are ticking away. In a strange way I feel alone in the maelstrom of this moment—like the loneliness you can feel in the middle of a large crowd. This rapid staccato of life-threatening decisions is stressful, but the task at hand is to get Kenny safely off the face now, not tomorrow!

All of a sudden from around a corner of the TAT front office, two rugged, recently arrived climbers lean over to me and say, "We can help." One is tall and has a chiseled chin and a look of confidence and skill that is apparent in his calm and understated nature. His partner is not as imposing physically, but he has that reserve and confidence of the mountaineer who has "done the deal" and knows what to do when the stakes are high. The tall, muscular individual is Mugs Stump and his quiet, competent partner is Jim Logan. They are in Talkeetna to attempt the yet unclimbed East Face of the Moose's Tooth. Unselfishly setting aside their goals—climbers helping climbers—the three of us immediately start formulating the rescue plan.

Thirty minutes later we are flying back into the Ruth. We land at the Mountain House in two different 185's—Cliff's and Jim Sharp's. A Hughes 500D helicopter ferries us to the upper West Fork in two stages—first Mugs with Jim—then me. Numerous well-intentioned people try to talk me into staying put. "Mugs and Jim can take care of Kenny by themselves," they say. Even though I have been up now for 30 hours I refuse, pointing out that I know where Kenny is in his cave of despair; they don't. Most important, I remember the look in Kenny's eyes when I left. An unspoken promise to again see his battered but courageous face remains to be fulfilled.

The snow emits a squeaking sound underneath my feet. I struggle to keep up with Mugs as we approach the base of the face. I keep thinking to myself: "How can this guy be this strong?" He is breaking trail as he drags most of the hardware and gear needed to lower Ken from the cave, yet I can barely keep up with him. "Mugs, the pace is a little steep for me. Can we rest for a second?" I say. Jim turns to me and says he usually can't keep up with him either. It's a kind gesture.

I feel the presence of this man's powerful energy that, in turn, fuels me, even though my tank is near empty. *Crunch, crunch, crunch.* He places his crampons softly on the névé with perfect and methodical technique—efficient, intelligent, disciplined. Watching his enormous shoulders strain under the load, I am inspired by both his physical strength and his silent devotion to the task. Mugs never says much. Instead he acts, knowing what needs to be done. Months or maybe years later, I came to realize the impact these moments were to have on my life. Still, at that moment I knew this was someone I could learn from and be inspired by to continue to climb. The accidental mentor!

The three of us ascend the 2,000 feet to the cave without incident. It is the middle of the night. The sky is darkening now, even more so than the dusky, anthracite sky that normally accompanies an approaching storm in early May. We reach Kenny only 11 hours after I had left him. The three of us chop him out of the cave, place him in the litter inside two sleeping bags after pulling traction against the sled, and start the series of 600-foot lowers. Mugs is in charge of running the anchors while Jim and I stabilize the litter as we slide down the face to the glacier below. Jim and I anchor off to pickets when we reach the end of the 600-foot rope. Mugs quickly and calmly down-climbs to us and sets up the next anchor rig. Five hours pass as we repeat this process over and over again. We reach the glacier at 5:00 am and the sky overhead is lowering its black canopy. Jim Okonek is waiting for us in the Hughes chopper, an example of his stalwart character. Cliff has been judiciously flying cover over us all night, monitoring our progress and relaying to Jim. With Kenny still in the litter, we stick him sideways in the backseat of the chopper, and the three of us blast down the West Fork to Cliff and his waiting 185. A quick transfer and we are off for Anchorage's Teamster Hospital. We land 36 hours after Kenny's leader fall.

Kenny's courage and fortitude were paramount to his survival. Mugs Stump's and Jim Logan's generosity of spirit and physical effort were not only key to the success of the rescue but also a shining example of how other people can change your life forever through the simple act of helping another human being in need.

There are many reasons and motivations to do big walls and new routes in the great ranges of the world as many as there are climbers who are willing to enter that hostile crucible known as " the alpine arena." The primary reason why I found myself on this obscure feature of Denali, which I successfully climbed later in 1982 with Dave Stutzman and named the Isis Face, was because of a beautiful and detailed work of art—a black-and-white photograph by Bradford Washburn.

For a period of 15 years or so my relationship with Brad was only over the phone or through written correspondence, as I anticipated the arrival of the most recent plates I had ordered for my next project in Alaska. Numerous phone calls were placed through the years to his private office at the Museum of Science in Boston, most of them intercepted by his personal secretary. But sometimes I would be surprised with the unanticipated, "Hello, Brad Washburn here!"

The ensuing flow of energy and enthusiasm was simply astonishing. Accurately, he answered inquiries about the route in question, the weather he experienced when he was there on Mount Kennedy in 1935 or 1966, or the condition of the glaciers and crevasse systems that year. Was Brad really able to recall, with the detail and accuracy the energy of his voice conveyed over the phone, 40 or 50 years earlier, as if it was like yesterday? Absolutely.

After all those years of correspondence, I finally met Brad Washburn in May of 1992. I had just gotten off the Kahiltna, having spent most of May doing time by myself on the West Buttress of Denali and its environs. I had soloed a couple of the standard routes, and then I did one new, small route with a visiting Scotsman, alone like myself as a result of last-minute partner attrition. As I was flying out, Jim Okonek told me that Brad and Barbara Washburn were in town. They were doing a promotional tour of their new McKinley book with David Roberts, in the midst of their yearly pilgrimage to Alaska. I was filled with excitement at the prospect of finally getting to meet both of

them after all this time. Talkeetna was only so big so, if they were still in town, I would find them. I quickly showered and shaved. I slid into my refreshing clean clothes. They fit much more loosely than they had weeks earlier, thereby improving my self-image immensely. I headed for the Fairview for that greatest of Alaska Range traditions—the first beer—with the hope of improving my self-image even further.

One of the few lessons I have learned well is the danger of meeting, face to face, one's heroes. What assurance did I have that Brad would remember our last phone conversation with the same significance and clarity that I had? I felt only great expectations and angst. He probably felt neither. Why should he? My lessons with other "heroes" stuck vividly in my mind. In their cases, the book was definitely better than the movie. Alpine filibusters were fraught with language barriers, other agendas, and late-night drowsiness that completely deflated years of wanting to bask in the presence of their greatness—to somehow gain knowledge, insight, and skill by osmosis. Be careful what you wish for. More succinctly, the only two tragedies in life are not getting what you want—and getting what you want. Which tragedy would it be with Brad?

The great thing was that it was neither. I had finally met a mentor of mine, a hero of generosity, not just a heroic figure without a personal connection. His handshake was firm and youthful. The light in his eyes was filled with enthusiasm, and we quickly adjourned to the cabin where he and Barbara were staying. I had much I wanted to ask and didn't know where to start. Brad was so approachable and made me feel so comfortable that we both lost track of time.

That evening will stand forever as the greatest example of Brad's generosity and his attitude about helping the climbing world in general. Every question was answered with humility and detail. I relayed a story about seeing a wolverine on the Ruth Glacier with Jim Donini in the Great Gorge. He, in turn, told me about the same mammal completely destroying their camp with more vengeance than a grizzly on the Muldrow in the fifties. I asked selfishly for more and more information, and it just kept flowing. All of a sudden it was 1:30 a.m. We had been talking for hours, unaware of the time because of the midsummer light. I remember saying, "Brad it's so late, I should let you go to bed." "I can always go to bed. I can't always talk to you," he replied.

Then I asked Brad who his heroes had been when he first started to climb. He thought for a minute and replied, "I didn't really have any. I learned a helluva lot from my guides, Charlet and Coutet." I pressed, " Well, what inspired you to go and explore all these unknown places?" His answer hit me squarely in the face: "Pictures—I would look at pictures of all these vast, remote, and beautiful places and want to be there." It was the perfect answer, for it was Brad's pictures that inspired my dreams. So, the sharing of knowledge—the gift of mentoring—continued until 5:00 a.m.

I have never liked the phrase role model. It's a cliché. Heroes are impersonal fantasy figures to whom we often look for inspiration. When I was in high school, Dick Butkus was my hero because I played football, and middle linebacker was my passion. Some may have described him as my role model. I am sure I spoke of him as my hero. I remember watching him play with the Bears and absolutely dominating the emotional intensity of the game. I could actually feel it through the television screen. That part was real. But how had he gotten there and what sacrifices had he made? None of that was something I could share in, because it was impersonal. It lacked an essence; personal caring and attention, a shared goal, and a shared interest.

Mugs shared that part of himself with Ken and me on Isis, simply because he had a generous heart and was willing to help us in our time of need. Brad Washburn's immense contribution to my life, much less my climbing, continues to inspire and motivate me.

The personal impact of these two individuals would never have been as significant without my having the great fortune to get to know them. I am sure they had little or no idea of what influence they had on my life, especially at the time. It was probably the last thing on Mug's mind when we were lowering Ken down the face. Brad's thoughts were, just as surely, on our conversation that night in Talkeetna, not on how he was changing my life.

A friend of mine taught me the true definition of an optimist: "An optimist is a person who believes the future is uncertain." Think about this. We all know that there is only one certainty in this life, and that is death. If we adhere to the certainty of death, then the future is in fact totally predictable and that portrays pessimism, not optimism.

My responsibility is to remember how I was made to feel by Mugs and Brad. Respect, and finding time to share with others, is a responsibility that we sometimes overlook and forget. A hero of generosity is a mentor. Mentorship is the responsible act of giving to someone else the same gifts of time and knowledge that you received from the people who helped you along your own chosen path.

On November 1, 1999, after a slide show in Banff, Alberta, a boy and his father approached me cautiously. The young man, maybe 12 years old, said, "Your slide show really inspired me. Would it be possible to have my picture taken with you?" I asked him his name and he replied, "Alex." I said, "That's a very good name. That's a great name, a very strong name", thinking of my recently departed dear friend Alex Lowe. "I would be happy to have my picture taken with you."

I believe I understand how much that evening might have meant to him. He may never know how much it meant to me to hear his words: "You inspired me." Remember, the future is uncertain.

Over the past 25 years, Montana-based Jack Tackle has pursued all types of climbing, but always with an emphasis on alpine-style ascents of new routes. Although he has climbed extensively in the Himalaya and South America, he is best known for his climbing in Alaska, where he has made 23 trips since 1976.

His climbing accomplishments include the first ascent of the 8,000-foot Isis Face of Denali, first ascent of the Diamond Arête on Mount Hunter; a new route on the South Face of Trapecio in the Cordillera Huayhuash; the Cobra Pillar on the East Face of Mount Barille in the Ruth Gorge; a new route on the Southeast Side of Mount Foraker called the Viper Ridge; first ascent of the Elevator Shaft on Mount Johnson; a new route called Arctic Discipline on the North Face of Mount Kennedy; and the Fitz Roy Super Caneleta route in a 72-hour push.

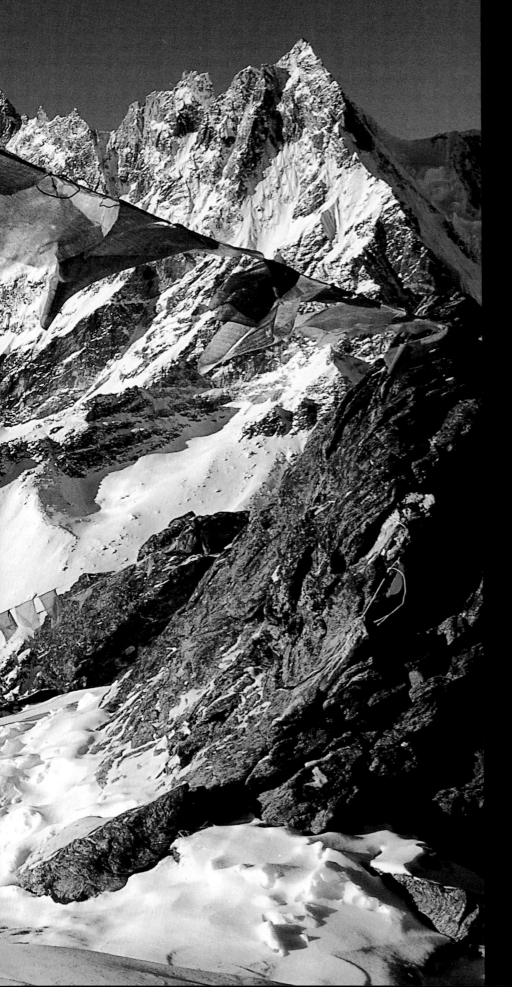

THE CHRONICLERS

DAVID BREASHEARS

AUDREY SALKELD

ED DOUGLAS

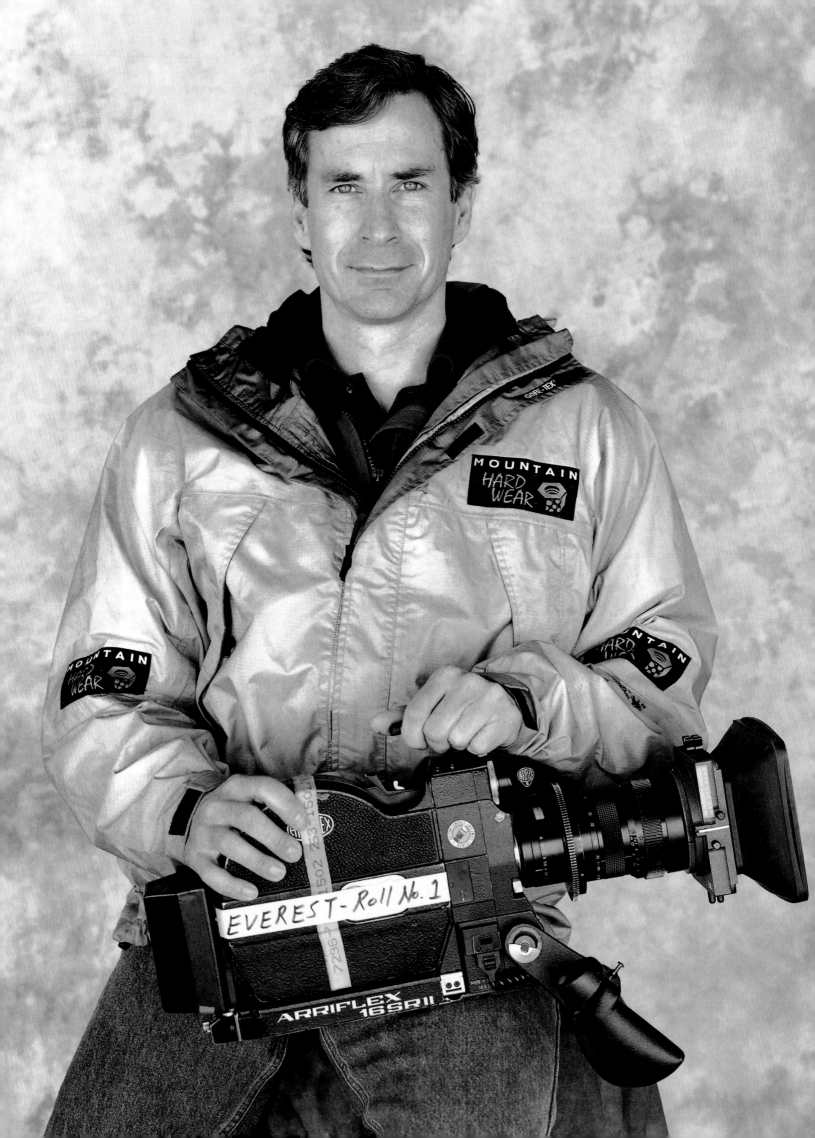

THE POWER OF AN IMAGE

DAVID BREASHEARS

He climbs toward me dragging his ice ax, shuffling each exhausted leg a little higher. Behind him mist streams from the massive cornices overhanging the Kangshung Face. I wonder how he manages to keep moving. He seems so weary, bent like an old man moving in a trance, a black-and-white figure only 20 yards from the summit of Everest. The long climb from the South Col had taken its toll; twice we nearly turned back after floundering in waist-deep, drifted snow, but the tug of Everest pulled us upward. I open my eye, the eye that is not pressed against a black-and-white video viewfinder, and see that the straggling climber is dressed in blue. I close my eye and concentrate on the figure in the camera's frame and on controlling my breathing. I've run out of bottled oxygen and need to constrain my heaving chest; the camera must be steady while I transmit the first live images from Earth's highest point. And that's how I've witnessed much of the Himalayan experience, staring intently through a viewfinder, trying to get it right, trying to breathe, trying to tell a story.

That shot of Larry Nielson slowly, stubbornly trudging toward me—I was on top with Gerry Roach, Peter Jamieson, and Ang Rita Sherpa—is one of the most memorable of the images I've recorded. Larry was becoming the first American to climb Everest without supplementary oxygen. He's a shell of a man at that moment, a body that has lost most of its life force, but he feebly hoists his arms skyward in a victorious gesture. To me, the way he moves in *Ascent of Mount Everest*, which I documented for ABC's *American Sportsman* in May 1983, expresses everything about the triumph and the fatigue of that experience. It communicates much of what I felt when I first saw Edmund Hillary's famous photograph of Tenzing Norgay on Everest's summit, his flag-adorned ice ax raised overhead in triumph. I admired the conviction of Tenzing's stance, the sense of purpose, and weariness, that it conveyed. It struck me as dignified, perhaps heroic, but it didn't happen in a flash, it took hours of scrutiny before my 11-year-old mind began to understand the message that it carried.

When Hillary released his camera's shutter, he created an iconic image and a hero. He also had a hand in shaping my passion for mountains. I was too young to comprehend the power of an image to influence a life, to fathom that I could someday catch up to my imagination as it traversed the globe and ascended high mountains inspired by a single photograph. But I did sense that there were discoveries, rewards, and merit in the climber's life, and that climbing mountains wasn't what normal people did. I became a climber who never carried a camera until I needed a way to express myself that couldn't be found in my climbing.

~ . . . I've witnessed much of the Himalayan experience staring intently through a viewfinder, trying to get it right, trying to breathe, trying to tell a story.

I initially became interested in filmmaking because it offered a more appealing way to earn money than the menial jobs I took to support my climbing. It also offered an opportunity to learn a new craft in the mountains. During the mid-seventies, I briefly worked on an oil rig near Gillette, Wyoming, climbing rock during my time off. My job was to stand at the top of a derrick, on a metal platform called the "crow's nest," and hoist or lower pipes and rods in and out of a wellhead. It was grim work in a culture of frustrated, violent men. The winter temperatures were often minus 20° F and lower, and I handled the thick metal pipe with thin gloves or none at all. That winter I learned how to take care of my bare hands in the unforgiving cold of the windswept plains of northeastern Wyoming, an experience that would serve me well years later.

Using a motion-picture camera was something I learned through observation and in visits to the editing studio. My sense of visual composition came through trial and error. With a little experimentation I learned how to craft an image and a scene using different camera angles and focal lengths. Sitting in screening rooms, I listened to the editors' reactions to my footage and heard their criticisms: "If only we had a tight shot of a windblown ridge," or "If you had a wide shot of the climber's point of view, I could use that." I watched, I listened, and I asked a lot of questions, but, most important, I learned how to tell a story with a camera.

My first Himalayan filming experience was on Ama Dablam, not Everest. I begged my way onto an expedition led by Tom Frost. He said they couldn't afford my transportation costs, so I paid for my own ticket and worked as a volunteer load carrier and assistant cameraman. Ama Dablam is 22,494 feet high, a ruggedly beautiful, sacred peak towering above the Thyangboche monastery 15 miles from Everest. It was the spring of 1979 and the mountain had not been climbed since its first ascent in 1961.

As load carrier and assistant cameraman I essentially performed the role of Sherpa for the film crew. It was a humble job but one with responsibility; the film team needed their loads and delivering those loads at 15,000 or 22,000 feet was a task I enjoyed immensely. I relished the simple ritual of the load carrier and sometimes let my imagination elevate the importance of my work: Surely there was no role more important than dispatcher of unexposed film and guardian of exposed film. During the approach march to Ama Dablam my gaze was often fixed on Everest's wind-raked summit, a small triangular patch of rock and snow peeking over the long horizontal ridge of neighboring Nupste. Leaving the mountain after our summit success, my steps carried me away from those mighty mountains but closer to Everest and a life with a camera.

The great visionary mountaineer Reinhold Messner stressed the importance of passing from one level of accomplishment to the next. His alpine style ascents of 8,000-meter peaks and climbing Everest "unmasked" grew out of his previous hard-won experience. I was fortunate to be surrounded by talented climbers and filmmakers who stressed this path of learning—the path of apprenticeship. Mastery of craft led to excellence and achievement, I was told. For many years I was hired to work on films because of my competence and experience as a climber, not a filmmaker. But I felt privileged that renowned mountaineers trusted me on their rope. It was important to them that I understood their experience and that my presence was never a hindrance or a liability. After a few years I grew as comfortable with the camera under my arm as with the ice ax in my hand. I was satisfied with the title of mountaineer/filmmaker, and frequently without work.

There is creative joy and fulfillment in choosing the images you use, the details from the camp, and the cliff that will best tell the story of a climb. An expedition cinematographer is often left to his or her own devices for long periods, with little oversight from the director, if there is one at all. This gave me the chance to be the principal storyteller; the images exposed on the film in my camera were my opinions of the events that best depicted the climber's world.

The hardships and rewards of working in high places are foreign to most, but it's a life that has allowed me a role of observer, documenter, and participant. I found a way to express myself and show others my world in an oddly autobiographical manner. When perched on a ridge peering through a lens, the experience unfolding before my eyes and captured in my camera was my experience, my world, the climber's life.

I chose, for the most part, a life behind the camera. I gazed spellbound, 33 years ago at the image Hillary framed of Tenzing Norgay, the greatest tableau of the mountaineering world. I often marveled at the lack of a Hillary summit photo; had they forgotten, had they run out of film, or had Hillary felt it unimportant? My young mind considered the absence of a Hillary summit photograph as almost intentional, as if Hillary was choosing to say "this is Tenzing's moment;" Tenzing had helped pioneer the route with the Swiss the year before. I was also certain that it was the act of a humble man, a man who felt it more important to record his companion's triumph than his own. I admired the man behind the camera.

How did that image shape my life? Have my images influenced a life? On May 23, 1996, a 42-pound IMAX roared to life on Everest's summit as Robert Shauer and I documented Jamling Tenzing Norgay's triumph 43 years after his father's. It was an affirming end to a tragic season: Jamling Tenzing Norgay was in front of the camera with me behind it, framing for the world the son of the man whose image standing in the same place spurred me to thoughts of the mighty Himalaya and the climber's life.

Like many very talented climbers, David Breashears describes an adolescence as a skinny and scrawny kid not very successful at team sports. As soon as he was exposed to climbing, though, he focused on it and was intelligent in his approach to training and ambitious in his dreams. He quickly became known for his abilities—and also for his boldness on signature routes like Eldorado Canyon's Perilous Journey.

An opportunity to work on a mountain film as a safety person opened up a whole new world for Breashears. Being an intensely curious person, he immediately saw the possibilities in filmmaking—combining his love of climbing with a way of communicating the experience to others.

Filming opened up the world's great mountain ranges for Breashears, and the Himalaya, particularly Everest, became his second home. He has received four Emmys for his films and numerous awards from mountain film festivals. He has reached Everest's summit four times. His IMAX film Everest *brought the triumph and tragedy of the Everest experience to millions of people around the world.*

His first venture into writing was his autobiography High Exposure, *which won an award at the Banff Mountain Book Festival in 1999. More recently he teamed up with his good friend and mountain historian Audrey Salkeld to write an historical account of George Mallory's Everest expeditions,* Last Climb. *He has appeared as guest speaker, filmmaker, and jury member several times at the Banff Mountain Film Festival.*

THE CRITICAL OBSERVER: SIFTING THE EVIDENCE

AUDREY SALKELD

For the purposes of this essay, I am considering the observer not an eyewitness, necessarily, but an informed "watcher"—rather like a "China-watcher"—someone who notes events and developments over time and then endeavors to make sense of them. I won't go into what I see as a deep human need to "get to the bottom" of things, and I won't discuss the arrogance of each generation in rejecting the conclusions of earlier chroniclers and examining everything afresh. Nor will I ponder what purpose is served by history or what part myth plays in building history. We comfort ourselves with the belief that an understanding of the past teaches us to avoid present and future pitfalls, helps predict likely outcomes. History repeats itself, we like to say. Sounds dubious. Maybe those who consider historians to be no more useful as prophets than tipsters are nearer the mark. We'll leave it there. My own interest—as an "observer"—is in retrieving what's there to find, trying to reconcile "on the record" and "off the record" accounts, building up the fuller picture. I enjoy sifting clues and blending newly discovered detail into the existing body of evidence. I can think of no more apt illustration of this detective process than to examine the consequences of the discovery of George Mallory's body on Mount Everest in 1999.

"You can't make theories out of whole cloth,"

Tom Holzel used to like saying when we began investigating the Mallory and Irvine mystery back in the mid-1980s. What he meant, though maybe he didn't always stick to it, was that every postulation, every leap into the unknown should be from (or to) a referrable point. Creating stepping-stones of supposition, without something, however tenuous, to link one with the next, was inadmissable. But that's what's so hard. Too often all you have are marooned facts, and how else can you relate them without giving imagination full rein? The main thing is to differentiate clearly between incontroveritable evidence and conjecture, while remembering that intuitive conjecture—based on a sound understanding of the characters and circumstances involved—is quite different from pure fancy.

Working toward a supportable hypothesis means putting aside what you want to have happened, removing all temptation to bend evidence to fit. I'd love to think Mallory and Irvine climbed Everest before perishing even while professing that the summit is not all important. It would seem fitting recompense for their boldness and sacrifice, but it's an irrational desire and has no place in critical investigation. With no foreseeable way of ever being able to prove that Mallory and Irvine did not succeed in their quest, and no present evidence to support that they did, all we can explore here and now are levels of probability.

Have the 1999 finds changed what we know of their last climb? Let me say—wearing my "critical

> *Perhaps we should question why*
>
> *so much importance is attached to finding out if*
>
> *Mallory and Irvine could have reached the top.*

observer's" hat—that I have been staggered to see how woolly-mindedness and wishful thinking informs many widely held convictions. "We know Mallory got to the top because there was no photograph of his wife in his pocket." We do? Family legend certainly supports the notion that George wanted to bury a picture of Ruth on the summit, but his intention isn't spelled out in any surviving contemporary document, so far as I know. On the other hand, in one of his letters home (April 19, 1924), he scolds Ruth ("Naughty girl") for not sending him a picture of herself. So, not only don't we know if Mallory set out on that last day with his wife's picture in his pocket, we can't be sure he even had one. Similarly, because a flashlight was found in his top camp in 1933, it is often assumed that Mallory and Irvine climbed on their last day without a working torch between them. We can't say that. Irvine may have had one; Mallory could have had another, only to drop it when he fell in the dark. If that's what he did. The goggles found in his jacket pocket suggest an accident in darkness. But he could have taken them off in the snow squall we know hit the mountain around two o'clock that afternoon; or he could have carried a spare pair. And so it goes. We're not able nor obliged to decide which of any speculations is "correct" because none of them can be at this stage. We are all free to conjure our own scenarios.

Every item discovered with Mallory's body tells something of what was involved in climbing high mountains within the knowledge and technology of the 1920s. Seen together, the man and his accoutrements, they represent a unique time capsule or snapshot of one day in June 1924 when the most famous climber of his age set out to climb the world's highest mountain with his young partner.

Prior to 1999, the main clues guiding our interpretation of events on the pair's last day were: Odell's glimpse of them climbing adroitly somewhere high on the summit ridge; the ice ax retrieved in 1933 a little below the First Step and believed to be Irvine's; and reports of an "English dead" found by a Chinese climber in 1975. Of these, the ax is concrete enough, though it's actual position is debatable within a few feet. Odell's sighting, perhaps the most poignant image in mountaineering history, is sadly vague in its detail and impossible to corroborate. He was never able to pinpoint where the men were, leading some of his contemporaries and climbers of later generations to question what he had seen, or indeed whether he saw anything at all. And what of the Chinese find? This hinges on the recollection of Ryoten Hasagawa, the Japanese companion to whom Wang Hong Bao confided his discovery, four years later and in the absence of a shared language. We may feel inclined to accept that Wang (now deceased) found a body at 27,000 feet, as Hasagawa understood; but we cannot treat the fine detail—a seated figure in disintegrating clothing with a hole in his cheek—as beyond dispute. An element of innocent misunderstanding could have been introduced. Chinese whispers. You see what a killjoy business it is, being a critical observer!

Thus, before last year, we had only one firm clue: the ax. This meant we could not positively place Mallory and Irvine higher on the mountain than the vicinity of the First Step. Has that changed?

A 1924 oxygen bottle has been recovered from close to the ice ax site, and at last we know where Mallory came to rest—more or less in a vertical line beneath it. These are the additional hard facts. Unfortunately, they still do not move Mallory and Irvine more than a foot or two higher on the mountain. Again, that's not to say we can't assume they went higher, toward the summit. Just that we cannot prove it.

Nevertheless, there are further clues and intimations to work with. We know their past performances, their intentions, the route possibilities open to them; we can estimate a likely climbing rate and how much oxygen they had at their disposal. We shouldn't exclude from the equation what we have learned of the mountain since 1924, the topography of the face and the Northeast Ridge, the experience of subsequent climbers over this ground. Above all, we should take into account what we know of Mallory and Irvine's fitness as the expedition reached its final phase, their characters, the experience they brought to the climb, and the snow and weather conditions pertaining on that day. It gives almost infinite permutations for making a success or failure of their bid to reach the summit.

The position and condition of Mallory's remains are of utmost significance, and it's a great pity they could not have been seen by a trained pathologist. Hitherto, it had been widely assumed that the ax, up near the ridge, marked the site of a slip by one or the other climber. Yet all those who saw the body last year doubt this. They are convinced that it had not fallen so far. Other corpses that fetched up on the same snow terrace, and which obviously had come down from the ridge above, were hideously mangled. Mallory was intact and his pose looked adopted. Even so, his injuries were many and serious, particularly a fracture to the temple, which almost certainly killed him. Sustained in the fall, this would have rendered him immediately unconscious. How then do we explain the ordered arrangement of the body, as if he had been attempt-ing to arrest his slide, or to assume a less agonizing position? Although, on the face of it, these factors contradict each other, there is one way Mallory could have been alive when he came to rest and still have died instantly from a blow to the head. That whole slope is a stone chute. We assume the two men fell together and the clues suggest that Irvine fetched up slightly higher on the mountain. Mallory could have arrested and at once looked up to see what had happened to his friend. The slithering of two bodies would have triggered showers of stones. One catches Mallory on the temple and at least saves him from a lingering death.

Holzel believes that the striking cruciform attitude of the body is the result of its having been rolled over—deliberately. He speculates that this was done by Wang in 1975. An interesting idea, this glosses over the fact that even in the mild summer of 1999 the body was immovably frozen into the mountainside; you would expect it to have been as firmly anchored in 1975. Equally, if it had lain half a century on its back and only a quarter of a century on its front, why wasn't the clothing on the front of the body more tattered? Mallory's back was stripped bare by wind and weather, but his day bag and the contents of his pockets were protected beneath him. If you wanted to allow the possibility of a rollover—and the idea was suggested to Holzel by a Harvard Professor of Neurology, based on the body position—you would need to be asking: Could anyone else have done it? What about Irvine, if he survived their fall? Knowing he could not bury his dead companion up there, might he not do the next best thing: roll him over to protect and conceal his damaged face? On any scale for intuitive theorizing, this construct sends the needle veering toward the fanciful, I think.

What more can the clothing tell us, beyond its "time capsule" value? Despite its inadequacy compared to modern fabrics, it is intelligently layered. Mallory was wearing the buttoned, close-woven, windproof gabardine jacket that was standard issue to the expedition. Made by Burberry's it formed part of what was known as the "Shackleton outfit," though it is interesting to see from the 1924 group photograph that none of the climbers illustrated had opted for a smocklike top, as worn by Shackleton himself. They all chose the draftier, buttoned version, which the slimmest among them (like Mallory and Norton) wore belted. If benighted, it is inconceivable Mallory could have survived in what he was wearing, reinforcing the assumption that he died on the day of his summit attempt.

I think the photographs taken of Mallory's boot are among the most poignant of all. The nailing patterns adopted by climbers were very much down to individual choice; they could be mixed and matched from a wide range of hobs, clinkers, tricounis, and the like to cope with whatever terrain was expected. Mallory knew what to expect, and he remarked to Longstaff how he regretted they had "no crampons for the last bit—or only the heavy sort." Yet, unless he lost them in the fall, he appears to have selected a combination of nails that gave him very little "bite" around the edge of the boot sole, just where you would think he needed it most.

The personal items found with Mallory comprised an "odd collection," it seemed to Conrad Anker, who discovered the body: Penknife, small pencil, scissors, safety pin, beef lozenges, a sticky bit of Kendal Mint Cake, needle, thread, well-squeezed tube of petroleum jelly, and matches. An altimeter and a watch both had hands and glass missing; there was a strap for attaching Mallory's oxygen mask to his helmet, his snow goggles, a pair of mittens that looked unused, several handkerchiefs, and a cache of notes and letters. For those unfamiliar with it, mint cake is a traditional energy-giving candy made in the English Lake District. One manufacturer in Kendal claimed that 40 pounds of its confectionery went to Everest in 1924, requiring two mules to carry it. Mallory and Irvine were the chief consumers, it was said. Mallory, in fact, had such a sweet tooth it was necessary to keep an eye on him during the journey across Tibet because he would get up on one of the mules and help himself.

The research team could find no trace in Mallory's pocket of the crystal or hands of his watch and concluded it was probably broken before the accident. Jim Curran has remarked that the most likely time for a climber to damage his watch in this way is when he forgets to take it off before attempting a wide jamming crack. Like that of the Second Step? Nice one. But how do you explain the missing glass of the altimeter?

Jochen Hemmleb has done a sterling job in deciphering the various notes and lists of stores found with Mallory. In particular, by marrying the new documents with the expedition record and estimating porter capacity, he believes at least seven bottles of oxygen could have been available to the pair at Camp VI. (This is not including the four somewhat smaller bottles we know Finch left on the ridge above his Camp V the year before, and which could have been retrieved.) The detail of the lists shatters the myth of George Mallory as disorganized scatterbrain; clearly he could be methodical and ultraprepared when it counted. But if we gain an insight into his intentions, we still have no proof of what the pair actually did that day. We know Mallory kept all options open till the last minute, telling Odell the day before the attempt, that "we'll probably go on two cylinders." To Noel he said, "...start looking out for us either crossing the rockband under the pyramid or going up skyline...."

The question of oxygen gives us the freest rein for new speculation. Most historians in the past—apart from Holzel and Hemmleb—have dismissed its use as a side issue to the main story of endeavor. Any mention tends to dwell on its "experimental" and "unreliable" nature or how "unwieldy" and "heavy" it was. Partly, this can be traced to the attitude of the 1924 climbers themselves. To most of them artificial oxygen was an anathema, and no one felt this more so than the official "Oxygen Officer," Noel Odell. He wrote a damning report on its performance and likely efficacy. We are told of Irvine's endless refinements to improve its function and lessen the weight, but sadly—somewhere over the years—the "Mark V" model brought home to illustrate his modifications has been lost or dismantled. Irvine was a "mechanical genius," so everyone maintained, and we can assume his diligent work with the apparatus would have formed the basis of his university thesis once he got home. Yet, because his surviving companions lacked understanding or appreciation of his work, we were left with the unworthy suspicion that perhaps he made some vital mistake, or "tinkered" the apparatus to death. This would certainly have been the line taken by the system's manufacturers, had it come to open discussion. Better not to investigate further, everyone thought then.

Mallory was not an unbeliever, however, nor yet impractical when it came to mathematics and machinery (he had been in charge of howitzers during the Battles of the Somme). His natural aversion toward the apparatus had been completely dispelled by Finch's 1922 performance using it. In March and April 1924, Mallory's correspondence reveals how much the problem was exercising him. It is important to go back to these documents and see how he argued to influence Norton's plan of campaign to include one and possibly two summit attempts with oxygen. Norton remained skeptical and could not refrain from insinuating into the revised bundobust a remark to the effect that if the summit was gained, the achievement "would be a triumph of organization and of the Sherpa, who, without oxygen, carries loads to 27,000; but the climber who does the last 2,000 with oxygen cuts a poor figure."

En route to India on the R.M.S. California, George Mallory and his climbing partner Andrew "Sandy" Irvine sail toward destiny.

Norton recognized the tenuousness of the enterprise. An accident to man or instrument, the breakdown of a climber, impossible weather conditions, or an unexpected climbing obstacle would probably spell "failure for this year," he allowed. But Mallory, as he embarked on his third expedition, was not contemplating failure. Height records alone no longer interested him. "We're going to sail to the top this time & God with us," he promised Longstaff, "or stamp to the top with our teeth in the wind."

So absolute was Mallory's conversion by this time, he even advocated using oxygen for reconnaissance and the preparation of campsites above the North Col. Moreover, climbers in Camps V and VI could stay fresh at night by breathing it, he said. This insight into his thinking helps explain the urgency he felt to get a third attempt going after the first two "ill-prepared dashes" without oxygen had failed (as he'd predicted they would). Equally, it demonstrates why Odell would have been utterly the wrong partner for him on such an venture. Odell was deaf to any advantages the equipment offered and had patently never listened to the many and interminable discussions on tactics. When he reached the top camp while Mallory and Irvine were away on their summit attempt, never for a moment did it occur to Odell that the oxygen bits and pieces scattered inside the tent could indicate that the two had been sleeping on oxygen, as Mallory recommended. Instead, he jumped to the conclusion that the apparatus had developed some fault and delayed their start. The only other explanation he could come up with was the bizarre one that Irvine was inventing for himself some problem to solve, to keep him occupied in the hours before his last climb!

A full bottle of oxygen in 1924 weighed 8 pounds and provided between 3 and 4 hours' supply. Even after Irvine had reduced the valves and pipework to save up to 5 pounds, the apparatus still weighed 4 or 5 pounds. Thus, with three full cylinders in the carrying frame, the complete system came to at least 28 pounds and gave up to 12 hours' assisted climbing. Going on just two, would still present "a bloody load for climbing."

Almost certainly Mallory underestimated the lateral distance from Camp VI to the summit, and the speed at which they were likely to cover this high ground. This is hardly surprising when both Finch and Norton, who'd led the two highest attempts before him, felt that from the point they turned around, the summit was within reach. They'd just needed to be a bit fitter or luckier on the day. If he and Irvine could get an early start, Mallory must have felt confident of doing better.

Critically speaking, we don't have enough fixed figures to determine Mallory and Irvine's climbing rate. We can base calculations on the newly discovered oxygen cylinder (and assume it to have been empty) and on the time of Odell's sighting, 12:50, making adjustments for whether we think this was at the First, Second, or even Third Step. But all is academic without knowing at what time the pair started out. Most analyses assume this to have been at first light, between 5:00 and 6:00 a.m. But if we believe Mallory intended pulling out all stops this time, that he was unwilling to go home without the prize, then again we should pay more attention to his original recommendations. He wrote to Longstaff on April 19 that he wanted to "start an hour or more before daylight," which would hopefully give him "full moonlight and windless air." Mallory was no stranger to long days, remember. At the height of his Alpine career, it was nothing for him and Winthrop Young to be out for 20 hours or more, with a predawn "Alpine start" taken for granted.

Mallory, at the time of this letter, was estimating that climbing with oxygen could give them a vertical rise of up to 400 feet an hour (the figure he believed Finch and Bruce achieved in 1922). From Camp VI to the summit incurred a height gain of 2,200 feet, so for each man to be carrying six to eight hours' supply of oxygen in two bottles may have seemed to Mallory just sufficient to get to them to the top and headed down again. But if the first of these cylinders was changed where Eric Simonson's team recovered the bottle below the First Step, and with the long ridge (or traverse) still ahead of them, would it still have seemed possible to Mallory that the distance could be covered with only one cylinder? Too late then to nip back for a third. This bothers me.

Their ultimate choice of route is a puzzle, too. Mallory's note to Noel, written on arrival at Camp VI on the day before the summit bid, indicates they were still undecided between ridge and the traverse. When were they going to make up their minds? On the hoof? Here is where I feel forced to formulate out of "whole cloth," or almost so. Be warned!

Captain Noel, in his book *Through Tibet to Everest* (1927), says Mallory and Irvine moved their top camp higher on the day they arrived up there. He bases this on the understanding of Lakpa, one of the Sherpas who accompanied them to the camp. Few attach much credibility to the idea. We know Mallory was ever impatient for action. He plotted, fretted, worked, and reworked his plans. We suppose he and his party reached Camp VI around the middle of the day. What do we think happened for the rest of that day? We can picture Irvine fine-tuning the oxygen in preparation for a very early or not-so-early start next morning. But what of Mallory? He's unlikely to have sat and watched and we don't believe he moved the camp. Could he have continued climbing toward the ridge to get a feel for the terrain and determine which would be their best line of approach? And if he set off straight-away, before the Sherpas headed back down, could that account for Lakpa's confusion?

It appears from Hemmleb's estimates that there would have been enough oxygen in camp to spare some for this recce. (Remember: Mallory advocated using it for reconnoitering toward the ridge, and he was then on what amounted almost to a mission to prove his original conception of the problem was the right one.) Moving alone and fast, how quickly could he have covered the distance towards the First Step, where he would gain a good view of both route possibilities? Was the cylinder Simonson discovered from this penultimate day, perhaps? Could Mallory have carried two cylinders even, and stashed the unused one up there for the summit day?

Mallory's preference for the ridgeline is well known. Yet we can assume this would have looked the harder option for the inexperienced Irvine. If we discount Odell's sighting or place it at the First Step only, we have no way of saying which route was finally settled upon. When Wyn Harris found the ice ax in 1933, some 250 yards east of the First Step and 60 feet below the crest of the Northeast Ridge, he was astonished that it was lying on such easy-angled ground. Nevertheless, he reasoned, it could only have marked the site of an accident because, if dropped from the ridge, it would have been an easy matter to clamber down and retrieve it. Supposing Mallory, on his hypothetical reconnaissance, found this "easy" way onto the ridge that Wyn Harris identified later—could the ice ax have been left by him, Mallory, as a marker for the following day? (The flaw in this argument, of course, is that we are convinced from its markings that the ax was Irvine's. Still, it was one of the expedition-issue axes and, if picked up in hurry, would look much like any other.

I am not asking for "critical" weight to be given to this scenario. My point is to demonstrate the open-endedness of the possible, given the clues at hand.

Let us look for a moment at Conrad Anker's near-free ascent of the Second Step and his conclusion that Mallory could not have climbed it 75 years earlier. Anker rated the top pitch as "probably a solid 5.10." He refers here to the steep crack (overhanging slightly toward the top) that the Chinese ladder now occupies. The likelihood that Mallory attempted an alternative crack to the right was dismissed by Anker because the rock there was rotten and the exposure too great.

I agree it is unlikely Mallory and Irvine climbed this step on June 10, 1924, but I don't follow the same reasoning. Looseness and exposure would not have deterred Mallory from the alternative crack or elsewhere (though Irvine may have balked at it). Heights never fazed George at all, and he had supreme self-confidence in his ability and sure-footedness. From the age of seven he clambered blithely about on the roof of Mobberley Church, where his father was vicar. Many of the rock routes he put up in Wales and the Lake District have never been positively identified by later climbers who find it hard to see where he found a line across such dubious and overhanging rock. British climber Martin Crook has been repeating some of Mallory's known routes and describes them as

aesthetic and brilliant, with the outcome unsure to the end. He characterized their key ingredients as length, seriousness, loose rock, and technical difficulty. I feel certain Mallory could have found a way up the Second Step; I just don't believe he would have taken Irvine up there.

Perhaps we should question why so much importance is attached to finding out if Mallory and Irvine could have reached the top. If they did, surely that would imply Mallory had pushed beyond the limits of wisdom, had not allowed sufficient time to get down in daylight, and had not put Irvine's welfare above ambition or a perceived sense of duty. It could indicate that he was, as Captain Noel believed, possessed by Everest; he had lost his reason to it and had blocked from his mind the family he loved and the great plans he held out for his new career. By the same token, if they turned back before the summit, Mallory's sound judgment would be vindicated. The fall is just as fatal, but the balance between boldness and irresponsibility, mischance, and misjudgment is subtly altered.

When Holzel and I embarked on our researches, frequently we had to explain who Mallory and Irvine were. Mountaineers knew of them, of course, but saw little point in raking over old evidence. Now, with all the publicity and the many books and films, hundreds of people are hooked on the mystery. Before long, Irvine may be discovered also. Then our understanding will once again be turned on its head. Or, we may never know more than we do now. But so long as these Everest pioneers fascinate and inspire, then speculation over their fate has validity. And our understanding grows.

That, I suppose, is the purpose of history.

Audrey Salkeld is a highly respected and experienced mountaineering writer and historian from England. She is author of The Mystery of Mallory and Irvine *(with Tom Holzel) and* People in High Places *and has translated books by Reinhold Messner and Kurt Diemberger.*

Her most recent book is Last Climb: The Legendary Everest Expeditions of George Mallory, *which she co-authored with David Breashears. In 1996, her book* A Portrait of Leni Riefenstahl *won the Boardman Tasker Award for Mountain Literature. She has written scripts for television documentaries and edited a number of anthologies, including* Great Climbs *with Chris Bonington, which was the Grand Prize winner at the Banff Mountain Book Festival in 1997. She has appeared several times at the Banff Mountain Film Festival as a jury member and seminar participant.*

Manchester in January. Sweat dripping from our brows onto the slick painted walls, my friends and I would storm round the room, forearms bulging, eyes popping, backs flickering between each wire-taut strand of muscle as we moved.

There was little chat. There would be grunts, shouts, complaints. Someone, his fingers opening into impotent claws, might shout: "Weak bastard! You're pathetic!" And then, when the lactic acid had been massaged away, he would get back on the wall and start all over again.

No wonder I was frightened. I had grown up reading Gaston Rébuffat and Maurice Herzog. I was in it for the poetry, for the romance, and for getting to feel slick about myself with the minimum of effort. I wanted to float effortlessly up sun-soaked rock, perched heroically on my toes while scanning the route ahead. The titanic self-discipline I could witness on a daily basis was as alien to me as attending all my lectures or getting a decent job.

It would be difficult to overestimate the influence of Margaret Thatcher on rock climbing in the 1980s, even though it's never been recognized. The former prime minister certainly lives on in determined ignorance of the debt I owe her, how she made everything so clear for me.

Mrs. Thatcher had told us there was no such thing as society. To Americans, used to the cold truths of über-capitalism, it might not have been a surprise. But to those of us who believed in socialism, admittedly without ever understanding what it meant, she seemed like the devil incarnate.

But the devastating consequences of her government's policies had some interesting by-products. In the mid-1980s, with unemployment in the north of England a seemingly insoluble problem, welfare was easy to get and keep. If a few climbers made capital out of this by remaining permanently unemployed, few questions were asked.

Later, as the government squeezed out the opportunities for scamming the system, or more cynically found ways to massage the unemployment figures, climbers prospered by setting themselves up as professionals, claiming £40 a week on the Enterprise Allowance Scheme rather than the £25 they would get on the dole. You got the money for a year, and then you went back on the dole.

Some of my friends stuck it out, living on next to nothing to carry on climbing. It was more than just a sport, a pastime to help you relax after work. It was like a religion, a whole way of life outside that being mapped by the government and then later by the media. I don't suppose there were many who thought of it in those terms. They were just doing what they enjoyed. But it was undeniable that the things we were told would make us happy and fulfilled—house, job, car, new hi-fi, designer clothes—could be easily surpassed by the cheaper and nonproductive alternative of going climbing.

I think again and again of those words by the 19th century's greatest art critic, John Ruskin, words that Mahatma Gandhi said changed his life: "There is no wealth but life." Promiscuously bearded, sexually dormant, and politically naive he may have been, but Ruskin nevertheless maintained a strenuous grasp on what it is that makes us human. And he knew mountains too. A member of the Alpine Club from December 1869, he had discovered the Alps long before that, in 1833 at the age of 14. The sight was a revelation for him:

"I looked up and lo! Seven thousand feet above me soared the needles of Mont Blanc, splintered and crashed and shivered, the marks of the tempest for three score centuries, yet they are here, shooting up red, bare, entirely inaccessible, snowless, the very snow cannot cling to the down-plunging sheerness of these terrific flanks that rise pre-eminently dizzying and beetling...."

You get the picture. This isn't the kind of stuff that crops up regularly in the pages of *Climbing* and *Rock and Ice*, but it's ironic, given that we view Victorians as a rather stuffy bunch, that Ruskin's gushing adoration of the mountains should seem so ludicrous to our let-it-all-hang-out generations.

He climbed mountains, not to have his name recorded in the annals of the Alpine Club, but to understand the mountains better. He wanted complete knowledge of geology, glaciology, ethnography, botany. He could and did write scientific papers on geographical issues, while illustrating them with his own drawings. He wasn't just a romantic, responding emotionally to the pull of the mountains; he had a deep, structural understanding of the different aspects of their nature, from the rocks themselves to the people who lived among them, which combined to give what he said about them such a profound weight. And in doing so, he makes our specialized and limited age seem more plodding than usual.

On those clear autumn days in Manchester, as I dragged myself unwillingly to the lecture hall or a tutorial in the faceless modern building that housed the arts faculty, my eye would be drawn inevitably to the low ridge of purple hills that ringed the east side of Manchester. The weight of the city, of all those people moving on their own tiny arcs across its concrete streets, would be lifted for a moment. That place, over there in those hills, was somewhere I could feel alive, where the moment of release could give me the clarity to understand unconsciously that poetry, prophecy, and religion are all one. Fingers on rock, or fingers in the till? It seemed an easy choice. Of course, nobody told me that climbers could have fingers on rock *and* in the till. I only figured that out later.

John Ruskin, of course, saw it very clearly. In *Sesame and Lilies*, he berated the mountain climbers for their smug self-importance, for imagining that reaching the top of a mountain was somehow worthy of renown; in fact, it was reductionist, turning the sublime into the ridiculous, yet another arena for the futility of human ambition. "You have despised nature..." he wrote, "that is to say, all the deep and sacred sensations of natural scenery. The French revolutionists made stables of the cathedrals of France; you have made racecourses of the cathedrals of the earth."

The mountaineers batted Ruskin's hot-aired blast to one side comfortably; it was wildly overstated. But now, in our age, his criticisms have finally been realized in the very place he held so

Climbers brave the Tyrolean Traverse on Gugiea Edmondo de Amicis, Switzerland, first ascended by Praz on July 17, 1906.

dear—Chamonix. Our generation queues to board the *téléphérique* to the Aiguille du Midi station, pushing aside the crowds on the balcony to finish that mountain's *Cosmiques Arête*, driving with growing despair from one full campsite to the next, and jostling in the climbing boutiques for our next purchase.

Of course, it's the local population that has ruined the Alps, not mountaineers. It's draping the mountains in cable cars, drilling railway tunnels, constructing huts, and marking paths, marketing the attractions of the area so heavily that they are lost in a blanket of people. Skiing is an industry literally constructed on the back of environmental degradation. Had the old man seen what has been done in the Trois Vallées, his beard would fall out.

You might think that the Swiss and the people of Haute-Savoie would be content to leave it at that, to continue counting their money and praying for the off-season, which I suppose is now reduced to November. Think again. Mountaineering, which they may once have thought was at maximum capacity, is now being shoehorned into the role of mass tourism.

The only way to do this, given that the Alps are actually quite dangerous, is to offer safe climbing. The burghers of Chamonix and Interlaken read climbing magazines too, and they have noticed the huge growth of sport climbing in Provence and Spain. They understand perfectly well that climbing is no longer a walk on the wild side; it is a reasonable pastime for traders at the Bourse or lawyers in Milan, providing it is safely managed.

The Swiss Alpine Club funds the retro-bolting of those areas not at capacity in order to keep their huts going and the punters coming through the turnstiles. Senior members of that club argue that climbing should be made safer through the use of bolts. The magazine *Alp* supports a campaign to re-equip popular rock climbs. Guides add bolts to routes that are on their regular list, to make taking clients on them safer and quicker. New huts are built to increase the popularity of hitherto "underused" routes like the Zmutt Ridge on the Matterhorn or the Mont Maudit approach to Mont Blanc from the Cosmiques Hut. It's easy to see how this process will be extended: Put bolts in the Tacul couloirs and other popular ice routes to boost winter alpinism; add more campsites; and improve access through the construction of cable cars and better roads.

The motif for climbing in the 1990s, the immediate context for the age we now live in, is consumerism, which is not so much a philosophy as the absence of one. It doesn't matter why we want new video recorders or climbing harnesses, just as long as we do. You can follow the rise of consumerism in climbing through advertisements in the magazines. *Mountain Craft* in 1963 ran an advertisement for a Scarpa boot called the Super Scoiattolo—catchy, eh?—which reads: "A moderate weight climbing boot designed for mountain excursions."

By the mid-1970s not much had changed. Sporting an impressive quiff and an insane grin, Don Whillans was recommending that we wear Topp Togs that are "produced from the revolutionary BROLLIBOND® process." (Who was Reg Brollibond? Does he sit home drinking and cursing the name W. L. Gore?) Nor had boots changed much. Advertising the Sella 107— "a great little number" according to manufacturers Berghaus—we were told that it was "a top-selling lightweight boot because of its exceptional lightness." In those days, tea ladies apparently did the copywriting.

Well into Mrs. Thatcher's decade you could sense a change in emphasis. Gone was the charmingly archaic copy and painting-by-numbers graphics, the monochrome images of men with beards. In their place was a brave new world full of clean-cut kids who were not afraid to show the rest of us the contours of their legs. The camera lens now picked out the body, muscles ripped big in the center of the frame. The context had shifted from man in the environment to individual achievement and superficial appeal.

By the mid-1990s, Scarpa wasn't telling us that their boots worked; they were telling us that "you can't tame it so you might as well unleash it." It's ironic that the safer some aspects of climbing get, the more extreme is the language used to describe them.

In the last years of the decade, as we cast an eye back while turning to the future, I saw this advertisement in an American magazine. Most of the page was taken by the image of a pale young woman with straight blonde hair and huge gray eyes, the pupils dilated so wide you'd swear she'd been caught by the camera's flash in a pitch-black room. Her chin was narrow and pointed, and she inclined her head forward slightly, making her forehead seem enlarged and rather oppressive. In small type next to her photograph were the following words: "Beth Rodden. 16 years old. Loves ice cream. Gets straight As. Kick-ass climber." And right at the bottom of the page, by the name of the company using this intense young woman to shift its product, was the pay off. "The future," it read portentously, "is now."

Beth didn't look like the kind of person who would kick anyone's "ass." Make their heads spin round maybe, but not something so direct and pleasurable as giving someone a kick up the backside. But it's not Beth that irritates me. It's the grim, unforgiving, reductionist, smug, and competitive worldview espoused. "Not only," the copywriter is telling us, "does this woman climb hard, she's successful at school and is innocent and youthful enough to admit to liking ice cream." There you have it. Winsome and intelligent athleticism in one all-American dream; not only can you climb 5.14 and be a brain surgeon, you can be cute, too.

You may think that it's all nonsense and no more, that how advertisers choose to sell a client's product makes little difference to the fundamental nature of a sport. Maybe so, but it shows how a market has matured, how climbing companies have grown from being a way for enthusiasts to make a living from what they love, to reasonably sized businesses where the accountant's rule is law and not the simpler truth that if it's no good, it won't sell.

Climbing may reflect the preoccupations of

society, but it also offers a release from those preoccupations, a sense of freedom, a return to childhood. As another guru, the Yogi Sklarananda, put it: "Climbing may be hard, but it's easier than growing up." Mountains are harsh and hostile places, but they are also, paradoxically perhaps, good for the soul.

That is why the shadows of fascism that fell across alpine climbing in the 1930s seemed so abhorrent, because the mountains are family and should have been beyond such oppressive notions. You believe instinctively that mountains, with the banality of modern life stripped away, should illustrate how much we share and not how much divides us. Finding that our spiritual home has been absorbed by such vicious ideas is shocking and uncomfortable. And, in a way, consumerism presents similar problems.

This has proved Mrs. Thatcher's lasting legacy to mountaineering. She eased the passage of the consumer society, where success or failure is measured not in the depth of your understanding, but in the depth of your wallet; not by how you change your outlook, but how often you change your car. The steelworks and coal mines of the north are gone and have been replaced by shopping malls. Hitching to the crag, driving beat-up cars, and dossing in caves don't hold quite the same cachet. The antiestablishmentarian quality of climbing got lost around the time McDonalds sold its billionth hamburger.

Ruskin spent a lot of his time bemoaning the lot of ordinary working people in the 19th century—and being roundly condemned for it. He hated that they lived and died in unsanitary conditions, that their lives were hard and often short. He would not have begrudged them the massive advances in material wealth that have occurred in the developed world in the last century.

He would have welcomed, I'm sure, the explosion of interest in the mountains he so loved among the working class. He would have understood that, in turning their backs on the city on their Sundays off, the hiking clubs of Manchester provided the kind of freedom that politics or economics couldn't offer alone. The climbers who emerged from the city before and after the Second World War seemed to be saying: "This is mine, this is what freedom is for."

Ruskin died a hundred years ago, in 1900. Nobody reads him much now, and nobody thinks much about the trainloads of people who, like me, escaped from Manchester to do something that made them feel human, to be able to believe that the only wealth is life. Most of them are now dead. By the time I arrived there, in the battered fragments of what was left of Manchester's boom years, God was also dead, and the idea of a British nation tattered and derided. It was every man for himself again, and only fools and idiots would get left behind.

No wonder I looked for somewhere to belong; no wonder I wanted something... other.

Years ago, when I was still living in Manchester, we climbed into a rusty old Ford and drove slowly to southwest Wales and the white, rugged cliffs of Pembrokeshire. There were plenty of good climbers down there, plundering the crags for new lines every weekend. Those on the dole were there full-time, of course, albeit living in straitened circumstances. One of them, one of the best who had added plenty of hard new routes already, had taken up residence in a ditch in a field, and he would catch lifts to the crag from there. From the smug security of a climber's hut, I asked him what he would do when it rained.

"Dunno," he said. "It hasn't rained yet."

It's raining now, fat gobs of water splashing off the window sill outside my office as I write this. In a moment I'll go and give my kids a bath, maybe later watch some TV. In the window I can see only the black night and my own reflection.

Ed Douglas, writer, traveler, and mountaineer, founded the British rock-climbing magazine On the Edge *and is the current editor of the* Alpine Journal. *He has worked, traveled, and climbed around the globe. His most recent books are* Chomolungma Sings the Blues *and* Regions of the Heart: The Triumph and Tragedy of Alison Hargreaves. *Ed Douglas has appeared frequently and been honored with book awards at the Banff Mountain Festivals.*

A Passion for Limits

REINHOLD MESSNER

I am of an age now where I can reflect and look back at the evolution of our sport. I can also project forward to visualize where we might be going in the future. We will be able to save mountaineering for the new millennium if we know exactly which values are important for us when we go climbing.

The most important thing to know is that mountaineering involves risk. If we go to the mountains and forget that there is risk, we make mistakes. Mountains are dangerous! But they are only dangerous if people are there. A mountain is a mountain. It only exists. It is a piece of rock and ice, a beautiful piece maybe, but it only becomes dangerous and beautiful if we are there. We must know how to approach the mountains in the future, and in which directions to take our sport.

In my view, a mountain without danger is no longer a mountain but something else. I have nothing against building indoor climbing walls. These indoor climbing halls have to be safe, so that everybody can experience our sport without injury. But outside in the wild areas, mountaineering must be dangerous so that we can learn. Danger is a filter, which stops people from going where, perhaps, they should not go. Danger has to do with managing fear, gaining experience, and learning hard-won lessons. Without making our own decisions, without accepting personal responsibility for our own actions, we cannot learn to achieve big things.

To understand climbing today we must first look backward. A. F. Mummery was the first person to try to climb an 8,000-meter peak. When he went to Nanga Parbat in 1895, and disappeared, he was a pioneer. Mummery was a famous British climber who became one of the first in history to climb without guides—a *Führerloser* as we say in Germany. He made his own decisions in the mountains.

This principle is also very important for climbers today. We climbers are dreamers. Before starting my expeditions, I always allow dreams to grow in my mind. If these dreams are strong, they grow into action. Then I look for partners and money and, finally, I go. It is difficult and dangerous, but in the end, when it's done, I am my own judge—my own referee. I ask only myself if I did well, if I compromised my values. We climbers do not need referees outside of the climbing scene. We only need ourselves. We climb by our own rules, and each of us has to establish these rules. There are no rules applicable to everybody in our sport. For example, it is not a problem for me that many people want to climb Everest with guides. I think it is regressive for our sport, but it is not a problem. I personally can find many challenges in the mountains and wilderness where I can learn something new about myself.

To understand our sport, I like to study figures like A. F. Mummery or George Leigh Mallory.

I try to understand what was driving them, why they did what they did, and whether we will do the same in another 50 years. What Mummery tried in 1895 is something we can aspire for in this millennium, but what is happening now in the high mountains is exactly the opposite.

Today in the Himalaya, it seems that everyone is using fixed ropes. Not only guided clients but also leading climbers are using them. Some leading climbers, in a parasitic way, use the fixed ropes, tents, and tracks of commercial expeditions. Following the footsteps of others, they seek records—not experience. We bring home memorable experiences only if we are by ourselves. How high, how fast, or how difficult was our climb is not that important.

Somebody who is stronger can go up the high peaks; somebody with less ability can choose a smaller peak. But the most important thing is that we take complete responsibility for ourselves. Is there a real difference between solo climbing a 13,000-foot peak in the Alps or an 8,000-meter peak in the Himalaya? Not if you are alone!

I have nothing against guiding. British climbers in the last century were mostly guided clients and they did great things. But guides should take their clients only where they can survive—not on Everest. No guide is able to control a summit climb of this mountain.

In 1895, when A. F. Mummery tried to climb the first 8,000-meter peak in the Himalaya, this range of mountains was known as the "third pole." In the same period, famous explorers like Robert Peary and Captain Scott were trying to reach the other poles. Both North and South Poles and Nanga Parbat were totally wild. A few years later, Ernest Shackleton, perhaps the greatest adventurer of the 20th century, launched his ambitious Antarctic crossing. Despite his failure, he is my hero: He took complete responsibility for his actions, for himself and his men, and he brought them all back alive.

After the North and South Poles were conquered, it was the turn of the "third pole." For 55 years, nobody could climb an 8,000-meter peak. Two early British expeditions to Everest failed and then, in 1924, George Leigh Mallory and Andrew Irvine disappeared while striving for the summit. A

new hero was born in our mind. From this moment on, the style of high-altitude climbing changed. Millions of dollars were spent. Many died. Why? Certainly not because these climbers were lacking in passion or ability; their experience and equipment were poor. Even so, they went absolutely to their limits. The passion they put into exploring their limits was at least as high as today. Then in 1950, the first 8,000-meter peak was climbed by a French expedition led by Maurice Herzog. He and Lachenal reached the summit by a very dangerous route, but they suffered snow blindness and severe frostbite during their epic descent and would not have survived without the heroic efforts of Rebuffat, Terray, Oudot, and the others. In my opinion, without Herzog's motivation and drive, this team would have had no chance of success on this first 8,000-meter peak.

Next would be Everest! Using the experience of the 1920s and '30s, and learning from the two Swiss expeditions of the early 1950s, in 1953 a British team led by Lord Hunt succeeded by a very dangerous route through the Western Cwm. In the end, the New Zealander Edmund Hillary and the Sherpa Tenzing Norgay were in the right spot at the right moment with sufficient desire to go to the summit. They succeeded using the techniques of the time, which involved the use of oxygen. In doing so, for the first time, they reached the roof of the world.

Especially for the media, this became the ultimate achievement in mountaineering. For these first and subsequent climbers, including myself, an ascent of Everest brought immense prestige. But this prestige involved risk, passion, and months and years of work, training, and suffering. Today, many people think they can buy this prestige without the other investments. Professional guides are offering expeditions to brand-name mountains like Everest, and tourists are buying in with money. Looking for the easiest way, they win their Everest trophy, without gaining the necessary experience or taking personal responsibility. Is this wrong? No, it is only stupid.

Let's move forward with history. During the 1950s, thirteen 8,000-meter peaks were climbed. Why? Because we learned the lessons of the past. We learned how to approach these high peaks, to deal with high altitude and to use new equipment. Putting all this experience together, all the major peaks were climbed in a short period from 1950 to 1964. Then, suddenly, the interest in climbing high mountains seemed to disappear.

As a young rock climber in the 1960s, I was not even dreaming of Everest or Nanga Parbat. But at the beginning of the '70s, when a new generation of climbers approached the big walls in the Himalaya, I wanted to go there as well. After the first ascents by the so-called normal routes, we did not try to walk in the footsteps of the first climbers; we went out to climb the big walls.

The South Face of Annapurna, the first big wall on an 8,000-meter peak, was climbed by the British in 1970. This changed our perspective of the high peaks. In my opinion, the following years were the best ever on the 8,000-meter peaks. We were free to do anything! One thousand and one challenges were there. Able to secure the necessary sponsorships, we could go on expeditions sometimes five times a year. We climbed those big walls and gained experience.

In 1970, after 20 years of climbing in the Dolomites and the Alps, I first went to Nanga Parbat, but I didn't even think of repeating the first ascent route done by Herman Buhl. I dreamed about climbing the Rupal Face. My brother Günther and I reached the summit but were forced to descend the unknown Diamir face, where Günther tragically died in an avalanche.

Above all, what I learned on this first expedition was about death. Also I forgot about flags. During the first period of Himalayan exploration, carrying a national flag to the summit was part of the game. For the Germans on Nanga Parbat, the British on Everest, and the French on Annapurna, the summit shot with the flag was very important. They all carried their national flags for the summit because their nations were behind them, seeking national success. On the summit of Nanga Parbat, I used only my handkerchief, and I am still very proud of it. I used my handkerchief as a flag to salute my personal achievement. We should no longer climb with flags, but with respect for the wilderness. The nationalism shown by flags is misplaced, because the motivation to climb should only come from the passion to pursue our own limits. Each of us has different limits, and in searching for them, we discover human nature.

I was very lucky to be at the right place in the right age. For 30 years I went to the ends of the Earth and I could do it my way. I made over a hundred trips, always focusing on style. Style is much more important than distance or difficulty. I climbed in small groups, reached the top of Everest without oxygen, soloed an 8,000-meter peak, and finally, climbed Everest alone. But the best climbs I had were with one or two partners on big faces in Alaska, the Karakoram, the Himalaya, Tien Shan, Aconcagua, and Hidden Peak.

To be out there in dangerous places, and trying to come back, was everything. I learned that the great moment is not reaching the summit; the coming back is the climax. Before reaching base camp, only halfway to civilization, there is something special. Between wilderness and civilization—at the end of the exposure—that's it! I learned through trying and sometimes failing, not always through succeeding. What is success in the mountains? To return! I tried to climb 8,000-meter peaks on 30 occasions, and I failed 12 times. Without failing, I would perhaps have become not only complacent and self important, but I also would have died.

One of my best climbs was the North Face of Kangchenjunga, which we did in 1982 by a new variation, partly in alpine style. This climb was important, not only for its difficulty but also for the length, the exposure, and the isolation. Exposure, being out there without any hope for help from others, is the base of experience. On a big mountain, exposure can be absolute, and if something goes wrong, you feel like you're on the moon.

Now let's focus on what is happening in the Alps. Many climbers today are against exposure and risk. By putting bolts on routes, by adding infrastructure like fixed ropes and cable cars, more people will come and more people will be at risk from avalanches, from lightning, and of making mistakes. All right! Let them think it is safe, but when we are in the mountains there is always danger. We all are human and we all make mistakes. The easier we make it, the more people will die.

In 1938, when the North Face of the Eiger was

first climbed, it was a major achievement because the danger was high and the isolation real. When those climbers got into trouble, nobody was able to help. But now, helicopters can rescue those who make mistakes. Consequently, today's North Face of the Eiger is not the same as that of the 1930s, 1940s, or even the 1950s. Likewise, climbing 8,000-meter peaks no longer represents the same kind of challenge that existed in the 1960s, when the high peaks were being climbed for the first time.

The 8,000-meter peaks are still difficult and dangerous if we approach them on our own, or by a new route. But climbing between commercial groups, which some leading climbers are now doing, using established trails, fixed ropes, tents, and sometimes even stealing food and oxygen bottles from others, is a strange sport. Are they not like parasites? Recently, I read in the papers that many people have climbed Everest solo, only to find that they reached the summit with 20 or more others. How is it possible to solo Everest with so many other people, I ask myself? Maybe they are superhuman and fly above the others.

In the Karakoram some time ago, armed with a permit for the Gasherbrums, I approached Base Camp. There were 200 people waiting to climb. Some came up to me and said, "It's too bad. It's not like in your time. Everything is really spoiled." And I asked, "Why are you here?" "I wish to do an 8,000-meter peak," was the answer. "But now you're part of the spoiling," I replied. "If instead of following others you would go on your own by your own route, you could be alone. There are still many possibilities." But they all wanted to climb the Japanese Couloir on Gasherbrum I or the classical Austrian Route on Gasherbrum II, after somebody else had put in the fixed ropes. None of them tried to do a variation or a new route. Why? Because they were looking for the easy way for "success" by any means, for prestige. For me there was a simple solution. I left base camp and did my own climbing on a smaller peak in alpine style. This was the approach of the pioneers. We must reintroduce it to the high mountains in this millennium.

Great difficulties on smaller peaks are much more fulfilling than fighting with 200 people for the "trophy" of an 8,000-meter peak. The reward is not to stand on the summit of an 8,000-meter peak, but to experience the return from danger, exposure, and difficulties. If we face danger in difficult situations, we become another kind of human being—perhaps more animal than human—but open for reality. The moment we realize we did it, we survived, and we are coming back is the beginning of a new life. Endurance, fear, suffering, cold, and the state between survival and death are such strong experiences that we want them again and again. We become addicted. Strangely, we strive to come back safely and, being back, we seek to return, once more, to danger. Climbers are schizophrenic.

The problem with the commercially guided expeditions of today is that the moment of full accountability, of returning from danger and coming out of exposure, is never for sale. People who go to Everest with guides on a commercial expedition are not really experiencing this moment of "coming out of exposure." They think they can buy something that should not be for sale. They are cheating themselves. But let them do so. I don't feel bad if people are doing Everest this way. I know they will never experience the climax we get when we put ourselves at personal risk—when we take complete personal responsibility on our own shoulders and when we, step by step, day by day, strive for survival.

The art of climbing in all its forms consists of surviving. It is an art, because being in the mountains is very dangerous and climbing is difficult. The exposure on high mountains is such that, even today, nobody can come to our immediate assistance. In particular, this is the reason I am against guided groups on Everest. There is no help when a big storm hits, an avalanche occurs, or we make a mistake. I ask whether anyone has the right to say, "Come with me to Everest. I guarantee that I know how to handle it. I will take you up and I will bring you back down safely." No. Nobody can make this guarantee. Some years ago I had an offer to guide Everest. An American who owned an airline told me his dream was to climb Everest, and I would be able to guide him. He was willing to give me a part of his airline. I did not do it and I am happy about that. First, I was not sure I could even climb Everest myself any more. Second, I would not go on Everest with oxygen, because I have never used oxygen in my life and as a guide it would have been better to use it. But third, I could never take the responsibility for a client on Everest. It is simply too dangerous. Everest is a very dangerous mountain, especially from the south side.

We all need only a few elements to survive: water, air, food, soil under our feet, light, and warmth. We need nothing else, except—for some of us—the challenge of the unknown. As a rock climber, the soil under my feet was missing. At high altitude, oxygen was missing. Once I tried to cross Greenland during the winter and failed: It was always dark; the light was missing. I crossed deserts; water and food were missing. In whiteouts, orientation was missing. In all of these situations—surviving the dark, the cold, the vertical exposure, the high altitude—we deal with death. Mountains and wilderness are not made for human beings and we feel the isolation. We experience it on Everest, we feel it on El Capitan, and we know it at the North Pole. We are so happy when we take the last step out of these places because we know that, once again, we have avoided death.

The deepest experiences in mountaineering involve facing death. We all know that. We have to die. Every time we expose ourselves to dangerous places, death is a possibility. But we use all of our ability, our passion, and our instinct to avoid it. After succeeding, we feel great and are so deeply affected that we need such an experience again and again. Perhaps this becomes the biggest danger that we face.

We will probably never know exactly how our deep internal feelings occur. But we can constantly strive to seek and learn, by going out and also by studying climbing history. No, we no longer need to go to the Himalaya or the Dolomites to make maps: A satellite can do it. But we can still use the mountains as a medium for the study of our internal maps. Look at the face of Herman Buhl when he returned, back from the edge, after having climbed to the summit of Nanga Parbat in 1953. Our faces are like maps, especially after our adventures.

So now to the bottom line: Danger, exposure, cold, and difficulty are part of our mountain experience. These are what we fear and enjoy, and from them we learn. And we will continue to learn in this millennium if we defend these values. Don't sell them out. It is so easy to sell out by building a cable car in the mountains, but by doing so, we steal isolation and exposure from the mountains.

What's important? At the end of our lives, it is not important if we are rich or wealthy. At the end of our lives, it is important how many experiences we have lived through. For me, mountaineering is one of the best activities from which to become rich with experiences. We should not discuss ethics. We should save values. Mountains without danger are not mountains.

We should not make rules for others. I have rules only for myself. First, I will never go where others are going. I climb on my own or with a small group. Second, I push myself only to my limits, never above them. Passion for limits is my motivation, and this could be a good slogan for mountaineering in the new millennium. The third thing is that I don't leave any infrastructure behind: no bolts, no fixed ropes, no camps.

In my entire life, I have never placed a bolt and I never will; if I cannot do it without one, I don't go. I have never used oxygen bottles; if I cannot climb without supplementary oxygen, I don't go higher. It's not a difficult decision. And I will never carry a telephone or have a handset with me in the wilderness. To do so would mean destroying the sense of isolation and exposure that I seek. If I can call out, I am no longer on the edge. These are my self-imposed rules. Now, getting older, I simply dream of climbing lower mountains and skiing across smaller ice caps or deserts. I try to do so with less and less support. After my political life as a nomad, I will spend half a year or more in the wilderness with only a rucksack—and nobody will know where I am going.

Reinhold Messner made a swift two-man ascent of Hidden Peak and the first oxygen-free ascent of Everest with Peter Habeler, followed by solo ascents of both Nanga Parbat and Everest. He was the first man to climb all fourteen 8,000-meter peaks, but he considers the first traverse of two of these in a single expedition—Gasherbrum I and II, with Hans Kammerlander in 1984—as his supreme Himalayan achievement.

(1976 — 1980)

The High Point on Banff's Cultural Calendar JOHN AMATT

Looking back over the past 25 years of the Banff Mountain Film Festival, I'm amazed by how far we have all traveled. It was a cold, blustery day in 1975 when Chic Scott, Evelyn Moorehouse, and I sat down on Ev's basement floor to discuss an afternoon of film entertainment to be sponsored by the Banff Section of the Alpine Club of Canada. Both Chic and I were aware of the Trento Festival of Mountaineering and Exploration Films in Italy, the oldest event of its type in the world. In 1966, I had climbed Nevado Alpamayo in Peru and assisted Ned Kelly in producing his film, *The Magnificent Mountain*, which later won the Mario Bello Trophy for mountaineering films at Trento. And Chic had visited Trento while working with Dougal Haston at the International School of Mountaineering in Leysin, Switzerland. Given our location in the Canadian Rocky Mountains, it seemed logical to start a similar festival in Banff, which would become the first in North America. Equally logical was the sponsorship of

(Above) Below the Ramparts *Directors: Harold Tichenor/Albert Karvonen* *(Right)* Adventure filmmaker Mike Hoover

the Alpine Club of Canada, which has continued to this day.

That first year our goals were to gather together, on an annual basis, the best mountain and mountaineering films and to record the sources of such films, so that others might be able to acquire them for later use. Our intent, then as now, was primarily to create an event for the enjoyment of outdoor enthusiasts, but also to provide a platform for adventure filmmakers to showcase their work to the world. At the time, I was heading up the fledgling School of the Environment at The Banff Centre—which subsequently was to become part of The Banff Centre for Management—and was in the ideal position to undertake the organization of the 1st Annual Banff Festival of Mountaineering Films, which took place on Sunday, October 31, 1976.

That one-day event proved to be a greater

EL CAPITAN
A FILM BY
FRED PADULA

El Capitan
Director: Fred Padula

success than we dreamed possible. We had planned to use the 250-seat Margaret Greenham Theatre, but an hour before the screenings were to begin we found ourselves with an overflow crowd of 450 people struggling to gain admission. Fortunately, we were able to transfer to the larger Eric Harvie Theatre and the four-hour program unfolded without a hitch. Classics such as Mike Hoover's *Solo*, the dramatic *Abimes* re-enacting Roberto Sorgato's fall on the overhanging North Face of Cima Ouest di Lavaredo in the Dolomites, and the British film *Roraima—The Lost World*, in which Joe Brown, Don Whillans, and Hamish MacInnes slog through slime forest, torrential rain, snakes, scorpions, and spiders to climb a sheer rock wall in Guyana, riveted the audience. Many who attended can still recall Joe Brown's dry response, "It's not one of my top ten favorite hikes," when asked in the film whether he was enjoying the experience.

Reviewing the Festival in the *Banff Crag and Canyon* newspaper, local critic Jon Whyte wrote that "I can scarce think of a film orgy that developed in the audience a better communal feeling. If John Amatt can manage to gather a program half as good as this next year, he'll have to hire security to handle the mobs." Reflecting back today, it is interesting to note just how close to the truth that prediction has become.

The Festival became competitive for the first time in 1977, with a national panel of judges selecting winners from 19 films entered primarily from Britain and Canada. In total, ten films were screened before an enthusiastic audience of 700 people. The highlights were the Grand Prize winning film, *Descent*, depicting National Ski Team member Dave Murray training and racing in Europe, and Jon Whyte's *Jimmy Simpson: Mountain Man*, a sentimental journey through the memories of one of the

BILL MASON
(1929–1988)
Filmmaker, Artist, Canoeist

~

Bill Mason was born in Winnipeg, Manitoba, in 1929 and displayed exceptional artistic talent from an early age. He graduated from the University of Manitoba School of Art in 1951 and, after working as a commercial artist, came to filmmaking almost by accident. In 1958, he was an actor-canoeist in Christopher Chapman's film, *Quetico*, and it was during the making of this film that he realized that live-action filmmaking would best allow him to share his thoughts about the land, its creatures, and the Creator.

Water Walker

Bill enjoyed a long and distinguished career with the National Film Board of Canada, during which he earned 67 national and international awards. His first two films, *Paddle to the Sea* and *Rise and Fall of the Great Lakes*, each won ten awards at festivals held at diverse locations in Italy, Iran, Argentina, Sri Lanka, England, Uruguay, Israel, Canada, and the United States. And his later films *Blake*, *Death of a Legend* and *In Search of the Bowhead Whale* became classics that were shown in every Canadian classroom for a generation.

Bill's association with the Banff Mountain Film Festival began in 1977, when the National Film Board entered one of his *Path of the Paddle* series. This was followed by *Song of the Paddle* in 1979 and his final film, the epic *Waterwalker* in 1984. While not strictly "mountain" films, Bill's work was always immensely popular with festival audiences and captured the strong adventure and conservation ethic that was to dominate his life. Not surprisingly, he became an avid supporter of the festival and was subsequently a jury member in Banff on four occasions.

With the completion of *Waterwalker* in 1984, he returned to the painting and writing, which was his primary love. Bill Mason died prematurely of cancer in 1988, and his paintings were published in the large format book, *Canoescapes*, which was described as "the culmination of a lifetime of creative work influenced by the beauty of the natural world."

The Man Who
Skied Down Everest
Crawley Film Limited

early pioneers of the Canadian Rockies. The 1977 festival was also notable for the first screenings of the *Path of the Paddle* canoeing films, marking the start of Bill Mason's long association as a friend of the festival.

The 3rd annual event was noteworthy for two reasons. For the first time, the festival was expanded to two days and took place over the weekend of November 4-5, 1978, thereafter establishing the first weekend in November as the traditional date. And the legendary film producer F. R. (Budge) Crawley of Ottawa joined us as Chairman of

the judging panel, bestowing on us the credibility of his reputation and outstanding achievements in the industry. In 1975 Budge had won an Academy Award for his epic large format documentary, *The Man Who Skied Down Everest*, which chronicles the frightening descent and fall of the Japanese skier Yuichiro Miura from the South Col of Everest into the Western Cwm. In his opening remarks, Budge talked of the Oscar as being "an American award for a Canadian film about a Japanese skier on a Nepalese mountain," which neatly paraphrased the international attention that the festival was receiving. Outstanding films that

LEO DICKINSON

Adventure Filmmaker Extraordinaire

With over 60 films produced since 1969, Leo Dickinson is unquestionably one of the world's leading adventure filmmakers. He has won Grand Prize at the Banff Mountain Film Festival on three occasions with his films *Dudh Kosi—Relentless River of Everest* (1978), *The Cerro Torre Enigma* (1981), and *Eiger* (1984). In 1978's *Everest Unmasked*, he filmed Reinhold Messner and Peter Habeler making the first ascent of Mount Everest without oxygen. In 1991 he organized and filmed the four-man team that made the first hot-air balloon flight over the world's

Ballooning Over Everest

highest mountain. This outstanding achievement was recorded in his acclaimed film, *Ballooning Over Everest*. Leo's films have won awards at every major mountain/adventure film festival, including Telluride (USA), Les Diablerets (Switzerland), St. Hilaire (France), La Plagne (France), Trento (Italy), Kendal (England), San Sebastian (Spain), and Banff.

Leo is an experienced mountaineer, having climbed the fiercely overhanging Brandler/Hass route on the

Cima Grande di Lavaredo, the Phillip/Flamm route in the Civetta, and the North Faces of Piz Badile, the Matterhorn, and the Eiger. In addition, he has climbed to 24,936 feet on both sides of Mount Everest. But along with his wife, Mandy, he is also a world-class sky diver with over 3,500 jumps, many with cameras attached to his helmet while making eight documentary films on the sport. In the process, he has been involved in establishing several world records. Since 1981, Mandy has worked with Leo on all his projects, and in 1992 the couple filmed *BASEclimb*, an epic climb and free fall off the vertical Trango Tower in Pakistan. More recently, in 1996 they both sky dived onto the North Pole, and two years later they worked together on a BASE jumping film off Angel Falls in Venezuela.

Leo has authored three books describing his adventures: *Filming the Impossible, Anything is Possible,* and *Ballooning Over Everest,* and his photographic work has been published in major magazines including *Life, NATIONAL GEOGRAPHIC, Paris Match, Stern,* and *GEO*.

Annapurna—A Woman's Place
Directors: Dyanna Taylor/Marie Ashton

year included Bob Godfrey's *Free Climb: The Northwest Face of Half Dome*, depicting Jim Erickson's 12th attempt to make the first clean ascent of this Yosemite classic, and *Dudh Kosi—Relentless River of Everest*, the Grand Prize winner described as "one of the most exciting whitewater canoe adventure films yet made." This was the first of many award-winning films that Leo Dickinson would continue to enter, his support being typical of that of many independent filmmakers who would contribute to the event's success in the early years.

One of the festival's most memorable films won the Grand Prize in 1979, Fred Padula's lyrical *El Capitan*, which depicts a three-day ascent of the thousand-meter (3,281-foot) Nose route on this Yosemite landmark. Many who saw this masterpiece can still recall the majestic close-up of the moon as it passed behind the shadowy profile of climbers on the vertical wall. "Amongst climbing films, *El Capitan* is without peer in poetic beauty," the jury wrote that year. There were now 25 films entered from seven countries, and a noticeable trend was developing for "adrenalin" films, depicting high-risk sports. The amusing *Sky Dive* had little to do with mountains, but the audiences loved the free-fall parachute jumping and the 3,000-foot plunge off a vertical rock wall in California. Similarly, *Fall-Line* captured a former surfing champion transferring his skill in one of nature's most powerful arenas to other areas of challenge: powder ski-

ing and hang gliding. No one really knows what happened during the fifth year in 1980, but it's fair to say that the festival exploded. In total, 58 film entries were received from as far away as New Zealand, Japan, Britain, Spain, France, and Switzerland, and also from the United States and Canada. For the first time, sellout crowds flooded the Eric Harvie Theatre and the event was described as "one of Canada's most unique movie events" and "the high point on Banff's cultural calendar." One of the best mountain feature films ever made, *Mort d'un Guide*, won the Grand Prize. This epic suspense-filled drama tells the story of two guides who attempt to regain their reputations by making a new route on the West Face of the Dru, near Chamonix, France. One guide dies and the other is rescued, only to return later in an attempt to finish the climb. And in the Mountain Sports category, *Once in a Lifetime: The Underground Eiger* captured everyone with its footage of cave divers exploring the world's longest known underground river in England.

From the overwhelming response of festival audiences and independent filmmakers alike, it was evident that the Banff Mountain Film Festival had now assumed a place as one of the leading adventure film festivals in the world.

Descent
National Film Board of Canada

1981–1985

This Festival is for Mountaineers JOHN AMATT

In the spring of 1981, due to time spent organizing the first Canadian expedition to Mount Everest slated for the following year, I handed the responsibility of Festival Coordinator to Patsy Murphy, who had been involved with the event since its beginning. Subsequently Patsy, Mary Christie, Pat Farrand, Bart Lewis, and Denise Lemaster were all to play critical roles in the evolution of the event over the next five years. For the first time, a multi-image slide presentation workshop was featured and a "Best of the Festival" cross-country tour was launched in major cities with the cooperation of the seven Alpine Club of Canada sections from Ottawa to Victoria. Leo Dickinson again won the Grand Prize, this time with his film *The Cerro Torre Enigma*, which investigated the controversy surrounding the 1959 first ascent of this extremely difficult Patagonian peak. In the Mountain Sports category, Jasper resident Wendy Wacko made her adventure film debut winning with the popular *Challenge—The Canadian Rockies*, which recorded thrill-seekers kayaking local rivers, powder skiing in the backcountry, and climbing the 3,000-foot ice pillar of Slipstream

(Above) Un Pic Pour Lénine
Director: Bernard Germain
(Right) Challenge — The
Canadian Rockies
Director: Wendy Wacko

near the Columbia Icefield. Writing his annual critique in the *Crag & Canyon*, Jon Whyte commented that the Festival "was getting bigger without diluting itself, a neat finesse. From year to year there is a common (theme), but the variety of styles, presentations, moods and particular interests keep the festival from atrophying."

The 7th Annual Banff Mountain Film Festival in 1982 was notable in that a Friday night guest speaker was scheduled for the first time. Doug Scott presented his "Himalaya— Alpine Style" slide show, initiating a tradition of opening night guest speakers that remains one of the most popular features to this day.

Some 60 films were now arriving from 12 countries and over 4,000 people attended from as far south as Los Angeles. Filmmakers were also invited to participate and to introduce their films prior to screening. Top honors went to *Kangchenjunga*, a Czechoslovakian film about climbing the world's third highest mountain, while Laszlo Pal's *Everest North Wall*, the story of the 1982 America-China expedition to Tibet walked away with Best Film on Mountaineering. Like previous coordinators before her, Patsy Murphy survived two ten-hour days in a dimly lit room working with the festival jury. "At times the noise level really got to me," she later described, "with four judges discussing the finer points of a movie and trying to reach consensus over the whirling of

Winds of Everest
Director: Laszlo Pal

projectors and the film sound track. But it was great fun."

Under Mary Christie's direction, the 1983 festival was the greatest success yet, drawing media coverage from New Zealand, France, and throughout North America. The perennially popular Sunday evening Awards Night was launched, creating a session for Banff locals who often have to work during the weekend. And a Festival Social was offered at the cele-

1985 Guest Speaker Dick Bass on the Summit of Mount Everest

GERHARD BAUR—MASTER OF DRAMATIC RECONSTRUCTION

Hailing from Bavaria, Gerhard Baur's influence on mountain filmmaking and mountain film festivals was worldwide. Banff was no exception.

His first entry at Banff was *The Eiger—Conquering the Killer Wall* in 1983, an example of what Baur became famous for: historical reenactments of significant mountaineering incidents. During this re-creation of the 1969 Japanese climb of the North Wall of the Eiger, Baur's time spent on the wall filming and climbing was some of the most dangerous of his life.

A more renowned re-creation by Baur appeared at the Festival in 1988; *The Grandes Jorasses North Face* won the Grand Prize that year in Banff, and at almost every other festival where it appeared. The story of the 1934 first ascent of the North Face of the Grandes Jorasses by German climbers set a standard for dramatic reconstruction. As Grand Prize winner of the festival, *Jorasses* joined the cross-Canada tour that year. Bernadette McDonald, who accompanied the tour, recalls that the accident scene in the film was as gripping during the tenth viewing as it was during the first.

Baur returned to the festival several more times with consistently beautiful films shot in China, Tibet, Bavaria, and the Dolomites. But he is probably best remembered by audiences and professional filmmakers alike for a 13-minute film called *Die Entscheidung (The Decision)*; it won a special jury award in 1986 and was featured at the 20th Anniversary. Baur conveyed the decision-making process, known by all extreme athletes, in a way that resonated profoundly—and all without one word spoken.

Die Entscheidung (The Decision)

9th Annual
Banff Festival of Mountain Films
November 2nd - 4th, 1984

brated Banff Springs Hotel, which Jon Whyte described as "one of the best bashes ever held in Banff." Looking at the animated conversations taking place around him, Bruce Henrickson, a film producer from Denver, noted that this festival is unlike any other: "This festival is for mountaineers. They're really into it. They like what they're doing and we like what we're doing. Together it's great."

Controversy reigned when the festival jury, selected a cycling film for the Grand Prize. But the film *Coors International Bicycle Classic,* depicting a race in the Rocky Mountains of Colorado, was beautifully filmed and clearly stood out against the competition. As guest speaker, Jeff Lowe showed clips from his films, providing an entertaining look at the often conflicting behind-the-screen priorities of climbers and filmmakers. In his review, Jon Whyte commented: "The Mountain Film Festival is one of the few instances I'm aware of where exuberance, accomplishment, love of the Earth, aesthetics, vitality, and grace can come together to be celebrated." Another writer commented, "One can sense in the cresting waves of enthusiasm the swell of an almost tribal emotion."

Initiating what would evolve in the future into the highly popular festival seminars, free lunchtime programs were introduced in 1984, with the Parks Canada mountain rescue team offering a harness-and-rescue workshop and Banff Ambulance Service presenting a first-aid program. Opening night guest speaker was Austrian mountaineer Peter Habeler, who kept the audience spellbound with the story of his first oxygenless ascent of Everest with Reinhold Messner in 1978. For the third time in seven years, Leo Dickinson won the Grand Prize. His film *Eiger* records Eric Jones's solo climb of the forbidding North Face and is interspersed with interviews of the 1938 first ascent climbers, Anderl Heckmair and Heinrich Harrer. And Bob Godfrey's *Sherpa*, an insightful look into the impact of Westerners on the culture of these indigenous people of the Solu Khumbu region of Nepal, was awarded the Best Film on Environmental Issues.

By now, attendance at the Festival Social at the Banff Springs Hotel, featuring a very impressive buffet of international cuisine and refreshments, had doubled to over 900 people and was in danger of becoming a victim of its own success!

To celebrate the tenth anniversary of the festival, the focus in 1985 was a "Best of the Best" event, with cash awards being offered for the first time to entice the nine previous winners of the Grand Prize, as well as producers of new films, to submit their films in two separate

(Above, right) 1984 poster for Banff Festival of Mountain Films (Below, left) 1982 Grand Prize Kangchenjunga *Director: Ján Piroh (Below, right)* Tibetan Death Rites *Director: Norman G. Dyhrenfurth*

The Fragile Mountain
Director: Sandra Nichols

competitions. The judging took place during the week prior to the festival itself, with an eclectic jury of Bruno Engler, Bob Godfrey, Hans Gmoser, Lito Tejada-Flores, Jon Whyte, and David Breashears struggling to reach consensus. Because of the superb collection of films entered, the top prize in both categories was shared between two films. In the "Best of the Best" competition, Leo Dickinson's *Eiger* and Bob Godfrey's *Sherpa* shared the Grand Prize, with Fred Pedula's *El Capitan* as runner-up. In the new films arena, Robert Fulton's *Wilderness—A Country in the Mind* (dedicated to the late, great photographer Ansel Adams) and Mike Hoover's hang-gliding film *Up* were chosen.

A third theater was used, for the first time, for panel discussions entitled "Extreme Sport—The Next Ten Years" and "Mountain Film-Making—A Perspective." Fresh from his Seven Summits achievement, 55-year-old Dick Bass and Emmy award-winning camera-man David Breashears spoke on the opening evening, marking David's first visit to Banff, a pilgrimage he was to repeat on many occasions.

In an interview before the festival, I offered my opinion of what made the Festival unique: "Most film festivals are primarily for film-makers. Our festival is for the public, although we try to incorporate the best of both worlds. We offer the filmmakers exposure and credibility by winning an award in a competitive event and at the same time provide a social, entertaining program. There's a kind of culture attached to this event, if you like, that we're careful to maintain." After ten years of evolution, the Banff Mountain Film Festival was firmly established and looking forward with optimism to the next decade of development.

EXPEDITION EXTRAVAGANZAS

During the late 1970s and early 1980s, festival audiences were exposed for the first time to the made-for-television documentaries of large expeditions to Himalayan big walls and 8,000-meter peaks that educated and informed about the expedition way of life. Audiences were introduced to the exotic world of Kathmandu, the colorful culture of the amazing Sherpas, and the long caravans of yaks traveling for weeks through the magnificent Nepalese landscapes to base camp. Amazed by the dangers of Himalayan icefalls and the extreme weather, and in awe of the debilitating illnesses and physical deterioration suffered by the climbers, viewers were thrilled by the summit successes and shocked when tragedy sometimes struck.

Chris Bonington's expeditions led the way at the festival in 1977 with *Annapurna South Face*, an enthralling account of an exceptional climb of this 3,000-meter (9,843-foot) face, and the summit reached by legendary British climbers Dougal Haston and Don Whillans. In *Everest— The Hard Way*, Dougal Haston and Doug Scott cemented their growing reputations with their triumph on the Southwest Face of the world's highest mountain. At the 1980 festival, Leo Dickinson's *Everest Unmasked* told the story of Reinhold Messner and Peter Habeler's climb of Everest without oxygen and received a Jury Award

To the Ends of the Earth
Director: William Kronick

for Best Expedition Film. But the Best Film on Mountaineering that year was *Antarctica*, an ABC/American Sportsman production relating a two-month trek across this vast continent by four adventurers aspiring to climb a virgin peak.

As China opened its doors to world mountaineering in 1980, we saw climbers riding camels to base camp in *Kongur*, the story of the Bonington, Boardman, Tasker, and Rouse team, which made an alpine-style ascent of this unexplored 25,326-foot summit in the Chinese Pamirs. But the following year, a non-climbing film won the Best Expedition Film award: The epic *To the Ends of the Earth* recorded Sir Ranulph Fiennes's 52,000-mile odyssey around the planet via both South and North Poles.

By the early 1990s, filmmakers and festival audiences alike had had enough of this repetitious recording of expedition life, and new trends had started to evolve.

(1986–1990)

Moving Onto the International Stage

BERNADETTE McDONALD

My first job with the Festival was working with the international jury in 1986. They awarded the Grand Prize to Wendy Wacko from Jasper, Alberta, for her feature-length film *The Climb*, a dramatic reconstruction of the famous 1953 first ascent

Bruno Engler, First Summit of Excellence Award Winner

of Nanga Parbat by Herman Buhl. The film emphasized the perils of group dynamics, exaggerated in the rarified environment of high, thin air. She later said that winning the Grand Prize in Banff was the highlight of her professional filmmaking career.

Hamish MacInnes, deputy leader of the successful 1975 British Everest Southwest Face

expedition, was the guest speaker; he regaled the audience with his seriously funny stories of mad rescues in the depths of winter in northern Scotland.

The marketing background of festival coordinator Denise Lemaster contributed to the growing amount of publicity and awareness the Festival was receiving. Headlines like "Fantastic flicks" and "Banff Mountain Festival enters second decade a strong winner" were complemented by a "Media in Adventure" seminar featuring some very respected editors: Michael Kennedy from *Climbing*, Bruce Patterson from the *Calgary Herald*, Bart Robinson from *Equinox* and George Bracksieck of *Rock and Ice*. Greater international participation from the Europeans and Asian filmmakers added a cosmopolitan flavor.

One of the beauties of this grassroots festival was that it evolved in a natural way, always responding to the needs of the community. Each year at the Festival, there seemed to be another feature, adding to the richness of the experience. 1987 saw the introduction of the Summit of Excellence Award, which was to be awarded annually to an individual who had made a significant contribution to mountain life in the Canadian Rockies. Over the years, it was to become a much coveted and highly prized award, because it represented recognition by one's peers. That first year it went to Bruno Engler, transplanted Swiss guide, photographer, and raconteur, who became a close friend of the Festival.

There were other local heroes honored that year. Sharon Wood and Dwayne Congdon, who were local residents, members of the "Everest Light Expedition," and Everest summiteers, were the opening-night speakers. The audience response was warm and full of pride for these two mountaineers who had made it onto the international stage, performed well, and survived.

Wood and Congdon's unassuming style stood in stark contrast to the polished, media-savvy style of another alpine athlete—Christophe Profit, a French climber profiled in *Trilogy pour un homme seul*. Documenting a daring enchainment-like approach to three formidable north faces in the Alps, with helicopter-assisted descents and television cameras monitoring every move, the film offered a glimpse of the cutting edge of mountaineering in the Alps at that time.

The Festival leadership changed hands in 1988 when I was appointed festival director. My primary goal that first year was to change nothing for fear of interfering with what was obviously a very successful format. But of course that was impossible. Evolution can't be stopped.

There were two new additions to the festival that added depth and personality in very different ways. For the first time, the festival joined forces with the Whyte Museum of the Canadian Rockies to bring a significant mountain exhibition to the valley. It was Galen Rowell's "Mountain Light" photogra-

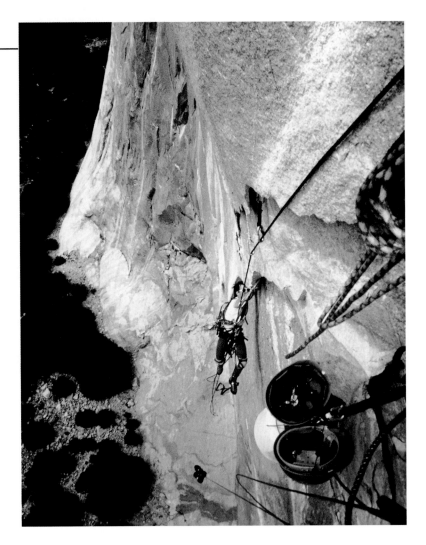

phy exhibit. Described by those who saw it as "luminescent," "dramatic," and "stunning," Rowell's imagery gave us all a glimpse of a master photographer at work.

Rowell also opened the Festival with his impressive presentation on Patagonia, but there was a surprise in store for the audience that night. Two days prior to the festival, the Alpine Club of Canada had hosted the first Canadian Open Climbing Championships and, unbeknownst to the audience, the climbing wall had been set up on the stage of the Eric Harvie Theatre. As the lights came up and the curtains were drawn for the second half of the program, the crowd was astounded to see two climbers racing their way to the top of the wall in a speed-climbing demonstration.

A tongue-in-cheek reference to this new development in the

(Above) Over the Edge
Director: Kathryn Johnson
(Below) Mr. Mike is on the Mountain
Directors: Peter Getzels/Harriet Gordan

Mr Mike is on the Mountain

climbing community read, "Our Brave Mountaineers try the Great Indoors." Reporter Nick Lees went on to describe the scene: "The only hold above was a tiny ledge, barely wide enough to grab...the climber concentrated, reached up and then slowly pulled himself up. The applause in the packed house... was deafening. Applause? Yes folks, a new breed of climber has forsaken the formidable faces of the world and moved the sport to the Great Indoors."

Everyone was thrilled when, in 1989, Chris Bonington opened the Festival, mesmerizing the audience as he drew them into one history-making expedition after another.

The international nature of the Festival was undeniable. More filmmakers than ever were coming to present their films, meet other filmmakers, exchange ideas, interact with the live audience, and see what their competition was doing. Four other mountain film festivals (Telluride, Autrans, Dundee, and Annecy) sent their directors to see what Banff was about and to search for films for their own festivals.

At this time I began working as a jury member at other mountain film festivals, an experience that was gratifying for several reasons. I had

(Above, left) Moving Over Stone
Director: Michael Strassman
(Above, right) Galen Rowell
(Below) Maurice Baquet and Christophe Profit in Le Comeback de Baquet
Director: Nicholas Philibert

the unusual opportunity to see, firsthand, how other festivals operated, and could take the best ideas from each and incorporate them into Banff. I watched endless hours of film, making it possible for Banff to invite the best films in the world into our competition. And on a personal level, the work would take me to interesting places all around the world, working with filmmakers and professionals in the mountain community.

1989 saw one of the best films ever screened in Banff. *Solitary Journey* became the Festival's first triple prizewinner, and no one who was in the audience during the awards presentation will forget the amazed and emotionally overwhelmed director/producer Suzanne Cook as she repeatedly came to the stage to accept Best Climbing, People's Choice, and finally, Grand Prize. *Solitary Journey* was a story of two men and the mountain that brought them together. Dawa Tenzing, Sherpa guide on the famed 1953 Everest

POETRY IN MOTION

ountain films most often portray world-class athletes with a taste for the extreme. But, as the Festival evolved, we have also begun to see filmmakers intent on showing the softer side of that athleticism, recognizing the beauty and fluidity of movement that film can capture so well. Through their eyes, climbing can become a vertical ballet, with individual styles emerging, dependent upon the climbers and the nature of the rock.

One early example of this was *Les Pilliers du rêve*, a climbing film with every step carefully placed, every upward movement effortless. It featured French climbers Patrick Berhault and Patrick Cordier moving gracefully through the fantastic and sacred landscape of the Meteors, a mystical sanctuary in central Greece used by hermits and monks seeking the peace of the mountain tops.

E pericoloso sporgersi (*It is Dangerous to Lean Out*), from French director Robert Nicod, was filmed in 1986 and showed Catherine Destivelle and Monique Dalmasso climbing the vertical walls of the breathtaking Verdon Gorge. But even more breathtaking than the gorge were the two climbers themselves. Nicod chose beautifully colored ropes, and pastel clothing, and camera work that showed off the balletic, graceful, and flowing climbing style of the two women. The film ended with a spectacular and sensual rappel as the two descended through a waterfall.

The Swiss film *Metamorfosi* went a step further, offering a real ballet on the rock. Interpreted—or danced—again by the great French climber Patrick Berhault and set in the picturesque Cote d'Azur and the Ligurian Coast, *Metamorfosi* was a cycle without words, narrated only with gestures and music.

Swiss director Pierre-Antoine Hiroz also featured Destivelle, this time in a short film from 1989 called *Seo*. Destivelle is a European superstar, and *Seo* revealed why. The film combined Destivelle's poetic athleticism with an original musical score based on local rhythms, as she soloed the sun-warmed cliffs of Mali.

Several years later, German filmmaker Gerhard König's film *A Documentary on Impracticality* showcased a world-class athlete in a way that can only be described as minimalist. This fine film featured Beat Kammerlander flowing almost effortlessly up a climb despite it's world-class 5.14a difficulty.

German director Uli Wiesmeier captured the beauty of another sport—hang gliding—in his film *Escape*. The "set" for this film was the vertical limestone walls of the Dolomites, and the "performance" was accompanied by—and seemingly choreographed to—a complex, polyphonic musical score. This was poetry in motion on a grand scale. No longer were cameras mounted on scaffolding suspended from cliff faces; they were suspended from hang gliders, small planes, parapentes, and helicopters, or were perched on the ledges of nearby cliffs.

These films may have been documentaries on "impracticality," but they represented a celebration of the sheer beauty of motion.

expedition, and Lord John Hunt, leader of that British team, related the Everest story from their diametrically opposed East/West points of view. Now in the twilight of their years, both men looked back at their achievement on Everest. Through Dawa's eyes we saw into the hearts of his people, who had been changed forever by this historic event.

Technologically the Festival was changing.

At the beginning, it was truly a film festival with 16-mm and 35-mm films in the competition. But by 1990, three video formats were also accepted. This presented some very real challenges for the festival, because the projection equipment required for video was difficult to find and extremely expensive to rent. But it was a reality, and each year small advances were made to improve the image.

THE MYSTERY OF MALLORY

That great British climber, George Mallory, continues to emerge at the Banff Mountain Film Festival. He is often referred to in documentary films and is probably the most-quoted climber on his reason for attempting Everest: "Because it is there."

His first major profile at the Festival was in 1987 when American mountaineer, Himalayan alpinist, and mountain filmmaker David Breashears brought his entry *Mystery of Mallory and Irvine* to the competition. Breashears's expedition had been assembled to discover the camera of Mallory and Irvine, with hopes of determining if the pair had actually reached the summit. Breashears's expedition was unsuccessful in the quest, but produced a good film.

Galahad of Everest was Grand Prize winner at the 1992 Festival. Directed by John-Paul Davidson, the film is a full-length feature starring Brian Blessed as the intrepid George Mallory, and it progresses through India, Bhutan, Nepal, Tibet, and finally onto the mountain itself. For the 53-year old Blessed, Mallory was not only an inspiration but also something of a personal obsession.

Galahad of
Everest
Director:
John-Paul
Davidson

1999 proved to be the year of Mallory. The world was shocked to see images of his body when his remains were discovered by an American expedition in the spring of that year. Several books were written and at least two documentary films were produced on the discovery—including one film completed in time for the Banff Festival. Director Liesl Clark convinced her producers to allow her to screen a "climbers' version" exclusively for Banff; another version of the program would be broadcast in early 2000. This world premiere mesmerized the audience as they saw, through the incredulous eyes of the expedition climbers, the first glimpses of the outstretched body of George Mallory high on the slopes of Everest. They could sense the awe and respect in the climbers' voices as they wondered, projected, discussed, and hypothesized on the "what ifs" of that fateful 1924 expedition.

The Festival also included a panel discussion on the discovery, composed of many of the world's experts on Mallory.

Trade Show, 1986

Even though we were able to keep abreast of new technologies at the Festival, we had to think about our touring program as well. We had started to get serious about a project that would change the future of the Festival in ways we could not predict. In an attempt to bring the film program to more people, we reinstated an earlier initiative of taking a "Best of Banff" program to Canadian communities. The tour quickly grew from three cities to ten, and then it exploded. It seemed impossible to carry all of that projection equipment around with us, but again, it was a reality and so that is what we did.

The 1990 Festival featured another Brit—although a transplanted one. Adrian Burgess, now living in the United States, brought his own ribald brand of humor to the sometimes too-serious side of mountaineering. He was entertaining, informative, and always amusing.

The number of film entries grew: 140 films from 23 countries made the job of the preselection committee take on epic proportions. One film stood out as special: *Chasseur de miel* was only 20 minutes long, but this French creation by Eric Valli was the predecessor of a filmmaking style we would learn to love. It took an anthropological approach to the brave honey-hunters of Nepal who undertake life-threatening risks as part of their everyday work, gathering honey from bees' nests on cliff faces. We were to see Eric Valli's work repeatedly in the years to come, and it was always magical.

As the quality of entries continued to improve and the reputation of the Festival continued to grow, so too did the Canadian tour. Except it wasn't just a Canadian tour any more. With demand from northern U.S. communities, the tour was now up to 38 screenings in 27 cities. That represented a one-year growth of 60 percent and created a new kind of post-festival life. It was no longer a

three-day event, but a month long "happening." Mountain films were now loved and appreciated from Seattle to Halifax.

The growth of the tour opened up a world of opportunity for the Festival—through sponsorship. Now that the Festival was reaching tens of thousands rather than thousands of people across North America, it became attractive for corporate sponsors, particularly in the outdoor industry. Their loyal support ushered in a period of financial stability for the Festival.

The Festival was starting to become comfortable in its position as a leading mountain film festival and was assuming a new and important role as ambassador for mountain film through its ever expanding tour.

(Above) 1811-1988 — Mountaineering in Switzerland *Director: Victor Wyss* *(Left)* 1990 Guest Speaker, Adrian Burgess

The Track
Director: Michael Christensen

Mountain Legends in Banff BERNADETTE McDONALD

Over the next five years our mission was to ensure that the great, enduring mountain heroes of the 20th century came to Banff and that our audiences would have the opportunity of hearing, seeing, and interacting with these legendary characters. The task was formidable, because many of the great legends were elderly and had stopped traveling years ago. But persistency, combined with the natural beauty of Banff and the growing reputation of the Festival, paid off, and Messner, Herzog, Hillary, Hill, Destivelle, and Harrer all came through Banff's doors.

Opening night of the 1991 Festival featured two French filmmakers who continued to have an influence on the mountain film genre. Eric Valli was back with his latest anthropological entry: *Chasseurs des ténèbres*. Filmed in the Andaman Islands west of Thailand, it profiled a fearless bird's-nest hunter scaling fragile bamboo structures in dark grottoes, high above the ground. An equally adventurous film,

(Above) 1994 Guest Speaker, Sir Edmund Hillary (Right) Height of Courage: The Norman Vaughan Story Directors: Larry Engel and Amy Bucher

Totem, combined superb climbing with a wonderfully quirky sense of humor. Robert Nicod was the director of this fictional story of two climbers going head-to-head with an eagle on one of the soaring towers of Monument Valley, Utah. *Totem* had a successful life, continuing to tour across North America for a long while after the Festival applause died.

A local hero graced the coveted opening-night slot in 1992. Barry Blanchard was a last-minute replacement for the French superstar Christophe Profit, who had an unfortunate double booking. The short preparation time

MOUNTAIN CULTURE FILMS

Although mountaineering, adventure, and mountain sports continued to be the lifeblood of the Festival, an emerging group of filmmakers began to show us something more. This group was profoundly affected by the mountain cultures they encountered in exotic and remote locations and grew extremely skilled at documenting what they saw.

As the Festival received increasing numbers of these films, a new category was added to the competition to represent their work: Mountain Culture. This grew to be one of the strongest categories in the entire competition, with films in the genre often winning the Grand Prize as well. When mountain cultural films began winning the People's Choice Award, it was clear they were truly accepted.

Some of the earliest examples of mountain culture films were those of Eric Valli. *Chasseurs de miel* and *Chasseurs de ténèbres* were beautiful, sensitive documentaries showing indigenous mountain cultures in their environment. In these films, the characters also happened to be doing their jobs—which were extremely dangerous and high-adrenaline adventures!

An interesting example from 1990 was *The Condor and the Bull*. Directed by Harriet Gordon and Peter Getzels, this disturbing film documented the violence and tension that permeated a South American village through the story of the condor and the bull. Equally disturbing and also from that creative duo was *Mr. Mike is on the Mountain*. An expedition film, it broke all the rules in that it told the story of a British expedition to Makalu completely from the Sherpa point of view.

Inevitably, some of the mountain culture films reflected a political point of view. A 1994 entry from David Breashears, *Red Flag Over Tibet*, revealed the impact of 60 years of Chinese rule on the people of Tibet. Another take on the subject was offered by a group of journalists from YTV—led by Nick Gray—who

Chasseurs des Ténèbres
Directors: Eric Valli and Alain Majani

clandestinely entered the country and witnessed the amazing escape attempt by a group of Tibetans trying to leave their life of repression. Their entry was called *Escape From Tibet*.

In a similar vein, *Advertising Missionaries* exposed the manufacturers of such products as soft drinks to remote hill tribes in Papua New Guinea. The whole notion of "progress" was questioned as the film documented the initial stages of cultural disintegration in these "first contact" situations.

One film that successfully combined pure documentation of a remote culture with a compelling personal story was *Behind the Ice Wall*, filmed in Zanskar. The small Buddhist enclave, nestled between Ladakh and northern India, is cut off from the rest of the world in winter, except for a frozen river. The film told the story of a group of children forced to leave their homes in Zanskar and make the perilous ice river journey on foot to Ladakh, where they could attend school. Another entry from the Getzels/Gordon team, this film won the Grand Prize in 1995.

One of the most memorable cultural films took us back to South America. *Les forçats du volcan* was the Mountain Culture winner in 1998 and touched hearts wherever it was screened. It told the story of two groups of people living on opposite sides of a volcano in Colombia, making their living off the volcano in the most horrendous conditions. Villagers on one side climbed to gather sulphur; people on the other side carried ice to the valley below. This entry demonstrated the power of films to move people: The desperate conditions that were portrayed prompted audience members and festival sponsors to donate money and products to the families in order to improve their conditions. The film's Parisian producer, TF1, returned to the area with this assistance.

(Above) Everest—
Sea to Summit
Director: Michael Dillon
(Right) 1994 guest
speaker, Alison
Hargreaves

didn't seem to faze Barry any more than hard climbs do; he was a big hit with the audience. Most people knew about his climbing accomplishments, but nobody could have predicted his poise and storytelling ability.

In addition to the regular competitive film program, the Festival was beginning to program evenings of special-interest films. *Rock Retro*, a feature of the 1992 Festival, aimed at the rock-climbing specialists in the audience. Little did we know that there would be close to a thousand of them! Featuring Canadian solo climber Peter Croft as guest speaker, and some of the best-loved climbing films from the past years, *Rock Retro* was a resounding success.

As the Festival audience became more sophisticated, it also became more discerning. It took something really different to make an impression and *La Escoba de Dios* was one of those films. Directed by John Catto, it was a candid portrayal of a big-wall climb in Patagonia. With very little narration, the film communicated in the language of those who

climbed, and the audience could feel the tension, the fear, the elation, and the humor the small team of four experienced in that inhospitable place.

1993 was a watershed year for the Festival. It had an abundance of everything: fabulous films, great speakers, legendary heroes, local heroes, and controversial seminars.

Reinhold Messner opened the Festival with a presentation that embraced not only the 1,000 people sitting in the main theater but also the

500 additional people sitting in the adjoining theaters. This was the beginning of the Banff "simulcast," something that was to become common in the years to come. Due to the overwhelming demand for tickets, we were forced to simulcast the speakers into nearby theaters, thereby expanding our capacity. Messner was overwhelming. His stories demanded to be heard, his style was utterly compelling, and his personality commanded the entire stage, spilling over into the audience and, through technology, into the adjacent theaters.

An American climbing star was on stage Saturday night. Todd Skinner's "Wildest Dreams" presentation took the audience to vertical walls in exotic places, at climbing grades beyond all of our wildest dreams. His enthusiasm was contagious.

And France was not be outdone. Serving as chairman of the film jury was the Annapurna legend, Maurice Herzog. Everything about Herzog was impressive. He arrived after more than 18 hours of travel, impeccably dressed in a black suit, just in time to enjoy a late dinner. He charmed everyone. Herzog presided over the jury in a distinguished style and, finally, even showed us his humorous side as he attempted to weave his way through the complicated instructions of the closing night Awards Ceremony.

And the films! The Swiss Pierre-Antoine Hiroz was back with his favorite subject—

Catherine Destivelle. The film featured climbing in the American West and culminated with a spectacular solo ascent of Devil's Tower in Wyoming. Australian Michael Dillon arrived with his award-winning *Everest Sea to Summit*. It was a novel approach to an old subject as he followed Tim Macartney-Snape and his wife Ann Ward from the Indian Sea to the summit of the peak. Another Australian, Glenn Singleman, brought a film hot off the press: *BASEclimb* rocked everyone out of their seats. BASE jumping was not completely new to the Festival but had never been seen quite like this before. Singleman, a climber who had never jumped, and his BASE-jumping friend who had never climbed, first taught each other their sports, then proceeded to climb and BASE jump off of Trango Tower in Pakistan. Nobody will forget the footage from the jumpers' helmet-mounted cameras. The stunt came very close to tragic disaster, but they pulled it off and the film went on to be a global success story after winning two prizes in Banff.

Local heroes weren't forgotten either. In honor of the 40th anniversary of the first ascent of Everest,

(Left) L'uomo di legno
Director: Gianluigi Quarti
(Below)
Mustang—The Hidden Kingdom
Director: Tony Miller

Panel speakers (Above, left to right) Leni Riefenstahl, 1994, from the 1994 documentary film Die Macht der Bilder *Director: Ray Müller; Maurice Herzog, 1993; Henrich Harrer, 1995 (Below) 1992 poster*

the Festival invited all successful Canadian Everest climbers to Banff. It was an interesting sleuthing game to find them all; a number of them were known because they were locals, but we had to search from Halifax to Vancouver to find the full complement. It was a success: Six climbers and the widow of Dan Culver walked out on the stage to receive warm recognition of their accomplishments.

The 1993 extravaganza finally ended and I remember, late on Sunday afternoon, wondering what we could do to meet everyone's expectations the following year after such a surfeit of riches. I shouldn't have worried for the parade of legendary mountain heroes continued in 1994, a year that remains a clear winner in the Festival history. Who can forget the sight of Sir Edmund Hillary being regally piped onto the stage, before presenting himself as a true ambassador for the mountains? It is rare that the Banff Mountain Film Festival audience awards a standing ovation, but this was one night they did.

And who could have guessed the rare privilege it was to have British mountaineer Alison Hargreaves at the Festival? As well as opening the Festival on Friday night with her presentation on the "Six North Faces of Europe," she was in the seminars, signing books, in the lobby, on

the climbing wall, and in the bar exchanging stories with everyone. At this point, very few people knew Hargreaves in North America, and many ticket buyers came to Friday night solely on the strength of the Festival's track record. I remember the conversations, "If you think Alison Hargreaves should open the Festival, then I should know who she is, and I'm definitely interested in finding out." Needless to say, all who saw her were charmed; when Alison died tragically on K2 shortly after the Festival, they were even more thankful they hadn't missed her delightful presentation.

Always evolving, the Festival began a series devoted to the history of mountain films. Audiences at European festivals had a good understanding of the old film classics and knew about the important figures in the history of mountain filmmaking. So we launched a series called "Retro Reels," beginning with the German legend, Leni Riefenstahl. A controversial character because of her close relationship with Hitler and the Third Reich, Reifenstahl's films nevertheless influenced generations that followed.

The international jury in 1994 included a film archivist and former Olympic athlete from Prague. Vera Matrasova had worked with me on a jury in the Basque region of Spain several years earlier and had kept in touch. She brought the Best of Banff program to the National Film

Archives in Prague, and now I had invited her to be on our jury. Another jury member that year was Bruno Engler, our first Summit of Excellence Award winner. It was clear to all by the end of the Festival that the two had fallen in love. Vera moved to the valley, they married, and both have remained closely connected with the Festival since.

That year, the jury awarded the Grand Prize to an ethnological film, *Mustang: The Hidden Kingdom*. It was a beautiful, big budget extravaganza, complete with the blessing of the Dalai Lama. Like many films before it, *Mustang* inspired a desire to travel and personally experience a mysterious and remote place.

1995 was the 20th anniversary of the Festival so there was some special programming with the best films from the past 20 years. We also screened what is possibly the first mountain film ever made—from 1901, called *Cervina*. The archival film print was on loan from the Museo Nazionale della Montagna in Torino, Italy, a mountain museum that was becoming a good friend and partner of the Festival.

The parade of legends continued in 1995. American climbing star Lynn Hill spoke on Friday night, and the Austrian legend Heinrich Harrer was the Saturday night speaker. Many Banff patrons claimed Harrer's *The White Spider* and *Seven Years in Tibet* were books that changed their lives. Even though in his 80s, and accompanied by his doctor, Harrer was unstoppable from the moment he arrived. He gave press interviews, held a press conference, delivered a spellbinding lecture, sat on seminars, visited with Tibetans living in Calgary, signed hundreds of books, met with Hollywood representatives working with him on the upcoming film, and dined and socialized with many of his old friends. He was one of the Festival's most animated and energetic guests.

American Antarctica adventurer Norman Vaughan and Polar adventurer Helen Thayer were also part of the Festival. Together with Harrer and Kurt Diemberger, they inspired everyone as they participated in the "Ageless Adventure" seminar.

FRÉDÉRIC FOUGEA— LORD OF THE ANIMALS

There are a few select filmmakers who have consistently directed or produced landmark mountain films, influencing all who follow. None has exceeded Frédéric Fougea of Boréales Production in Paris. At the Trento festival in Italy, this completely unknown director swept in to take the Grand Prize with his *Lord of the Eagles* documentary.

Fougea spent six months in a remote village in Kazakhstan, getting to know a family, observing, and becoming invisible himself. Then he took out his camera to film the ancient use of hunting eagles and to portray the intimacy between father and son and between hunter and eagle.

This turned out to be just the first in a series, "Lord of the Animals," which explored the relationship between humans and animals. In many cases, the relationships we saw on film no longer existed. As progress had moved relentlessly into remote regions, mechanized solutions had replaced the patterns of man and animal working together as a team.

The Gatherers from the Sky, a partly fictional story depicting a relationship between a coconut hunter and his ideal monkey partner, grew around the personality of the hunter, captured by Fougea and the director, Gauthier Flauder.

(Above) He Dances for His Cormorants *(Below)* Lord of the Eagles

He Dances for His Cormorants—one of the most popular films in festival history—was filmed in the Guilin region of China. Through the story of one man and his favorite bird, it intimately told of the ancient tradition of diving cormorants.

The Tsaatan, the Reindeer Riders took us to the outer reaches of Mongolia, where it revealed a partnership between a family and their old, dying reindeer. It told about a hard nomadic life, completely dependent upon reindeer herds.

There were 12 documentaries in the Boréales series. All were featured at Banff, and most won awards, including the Grand Prize and People's Choice. When the Banff Television Festival invited the Banff Mountain Film Festival to showcase a mountain filmmaker for their international assemblage of television professionals, we chose Frédéric Fougea. He mesmerized the audience with fascinating tales of thousand-year-old traditions, intimate relationships, exotic places, and precious moments in time, all captured on film.

(1996 – 1999)

Tackling the Issues

BERNADETTE McDONALD

The last years of the 1990s have seen tremendous growth in the Festival's size and scope, as well as a continuing willingness to tackle some of the topics most important to the mountain community. The Festival became the meeting place for people who are passionate about the mountains, and it was logical that controversial and troubling issues should be examined in Banff. The forum for these issues was the lunchtime seminars,

panel discussions that gathered together some of the leading lights of the mountain community in front of a live—and very active—audience. Again we were forced to use "simulcast" technology because these engaging events far outstripped the theater space.

As audiences continued to grow, the demographic mix began to change. By 1996, the post-Festival film tour had expanded to cover all of North America, most of Europe, and parts of Africa, Australasia and Asia. By late 1999, it included South America. Many attending those Banff screenings in far-off places wanted to have the complete Banff experience for themselves. They were willing to travel long distances to be here. By 1998 we had expanded to four theaters on The Banff Centre campus, and in 1999, we added a theater at the Banff Springs Hotel through a microwave linkup.

Catherine Destivelle graced the Festival stage on opening night of the 1996 Festival. The audience felt they already knew her as a dramatic and intense climber from the many films she had starred in over the years, so they were perhaps surprised by her low-key personal style. But as she talked about the various projects in her life—in a perfectly charming French accent—admiration grew for

(Right) Bernard Abeille,
1999 special guest
(Above, right) 1999 poster

this French alpinist who was as comfortable on a multiday winter solo climb in the Alps as she was on the great European (and North American) stages.

Another guest that year was Alex Lowe. Lowe was widely recognized as America's leading alpinist, but it was his intimate style of storytelling that made his show remarkable. Alex Lowe made a huge impact on the audience in Banff, as well as in the hallways and during his seminar participation. He was understated, friendly, and thoughtful, and he gave as much of his time to people as they felt they needed.

An area of significant growth in the late '90s was mountain environmental and cultural films. The 1997 Grand Prize winner was a stunning natural history film *Puma—Lion of the Andes*. Directed and produced by Hugh Miles, the film represented an incredible commitment by the filmmaker and was beautiful to watch. Miles quietly observed the cats in Chile's Torres del Paine National Park for two years, building trust with the animals in order to bring the images to life on the screen.

Another big winner that year was *The Fatal Game* from New Zealand, a film that tackled an emerging issue of guiding on high mountains. The true story of Everest guide Mark Whetu and his client, the film documented and re-created an unfolding tragedy in an inspiring, yet unsettling way. With the 1996 tragedy on

Mount Everest fresh in everyone's mind, this topic was also the theme of the "Extreme Guiding" seminar, generating much discussion and widely varying opinions.

Mountain legends were here in full force—some on the stage, some in the seminars, and some just to observe. I vividly remember Polish climber Krzysztof Wielicki, Slovenian Silvo Karo, Americans John Roskelley and Alex Lowe, and the Russian Anatoli Boukreev running into each other in the book fair, animatedly exchanging stories and memories from various Himalayan base camps.

British alpinists Doug Scott and Chris Bonington were back as well, and I recall Doug Scott whispering to his companion in the lobby, "Is that Walter Bonatti over there?" It clearly was, and Doug wasted no time in presenting himself to and expressing his admiration for the Italian climber. Bonatti was on the stage Saturday night with his simultaneously translated presentation. He was probably the only speaker in the history of the Festival who not only presented in Italian but also actually finished on time!

(*Above*) Everest—The Death Zone *Director: Liesl Clark* (*Below*) 1999 guest speaker Göran Kropp *on the Summit of Mount Everest*

(Above) Legacy
Director: Peter McAllister
(Right) Mockumentary
Director: Mark Stanger
(Below, right) Mountain
Gorilla—A Shattered
Kingdom
Director: Bruce Davidson

charming Swedish accent and left many in the audience close to rolling in the aisles.

Saturday night was a busy one that year. In one theater, American rock master Henry Barber held a captivated audience in the palm of his hands as he regaled them with stories and film footage from the early days of climbing in the former East Germany. It was part of the continuing "Retro Reels" series. Barber showed important footage of some not-so-famous but accomplished athletes in exotic places at a special moment in history.

In two other theaters, the young and the young-at-heart were getting their adrenaline fix at a new program known as "Radical Rides." Featuring films with a "descent" theme, we were thrilled to find a new audience and a number of young, talented, and excited filmmakers.

And in yet another theater, the program featured a musician; French double-bassist Bernard Abeille gave a spellbinding performance with a film created especially for him. The images of an erupting volcano on Reunion Island, off the coast of Africa, came alive with his original, improvised, and electronically manipulated music.

French director Eric Valli was back again,

what we were looking for. Immediately after the Festival, Cassin and his son headed to the British Columbia coast where they were taken to the gravesite by a group of Roman Catholic clergymen. There, they conducted a moving ceremony, fulfilling a lifelong dream for our special guest.

A relative unknown in North America rolled onto the stage during the opening night of the 1999 Festival—quite literally, as Swedish mountaineer Göran Kropp rode his bike to the podium. Göran was a truly original performer: His incredible achievement of cycling from Sweden to Everest and climbing it solo was almost secondary to his skill as a storyteller. Racing around the stage, his presentation animated with anecdotes and flamboyant gestures, Göran entertained everyone with his

this time with a feature film called *Caravans*, which received its first North American screening. I first heard of this film from Frédéric Fougea, who told me simply that we had to have the film in Banff. Coming from Fougea, I knew it had to be good. The film had only been premiered in France the previous week, and it was a challenge getting a 35-mm print of it. But thanks to a lot of perseverance, ongoing encouragement from Fougea, and finally, the cooperation of the producer, the film arrived on time. It was a brand new print and was proudly accompanied by the executive producer and a representative from the French Consulat in Canada. Everything about the film was magnificent. Filmed in the Dolpo region of Nepal, this story of a salt-trading village featured conflict, leadership, a love story, compelling scenery, impeccable attention to detail, and a haunting musical score. Since all of the other entries in the Festival were documentaries, *Caravans* wasn't in competition, but it was indicative of the growing trend toward big-screen feature-length films based on mountain themes. And it prompted us to look at feature-length film as a competitive category on its own.

But that's for the future. As I close this section of the Festival history, I'm looking ahead and trying to imagine the future of the Banff Mountain Film Festival: What kind of growth will we experience? What direction will mountain films take? What new programming features should we add? What does our audience want, and how can we remain relevant, meaningful, and cherished by the mountain community?

This is an exciting time to be involved with the Festival. There are so many possibilities for the future. I'm lucky to work with a dedicated team, to have willing partners worldwide, to have talented and energetic filmmakers eager to showcase their work, to have a loyal public, and to be situated in this beautiful, protected mountain environment.

As Trina McQueen, Executive Vice President of CTV Inc., said, "I have three things to say about the Banff Festival; it's in a great location, it has great films, and the people are great."

If we can take all of that into the future, the chances are pretty good that someone will be writing the next chapters of this history 25 years from now.

(Above, left)
Ode to Avalanche
Director: Ken Bailey
(Below)
The Mountains of Yesterday
Directors: Jesús Bosque and Guillermo Campo

GLOSSARY

Acclimatize Adapt to a new climate or condition; in climbing most typically associated with the progressive adaptation required for high-altitude peaks.

Aid Climbing Moving up a rock face using fixed or placed protection as a means of progression as well as protection.

Alpine Style A style of climbing mountains in which a typically small team ascends a peak from bottom-to-top in one continuous push, without fixed ropes, carrying all the necessary equipment themselves.

Alpinism The philosophy and practice of climbing high mountains.

Anchor Point at which a fixed rope, rappel rope, or belay is secured to rock, snow, or ice.

Arête Narrow, serrated ridge, usually separating two glacial valleys or adjacent cirques.

Avalanche Snow or ice sliding down a mountain.

Bashie An aid-climbing tool.

Belay To tend the climbing rope, ready to immediately put enough friction on the rope to hold the climber in case of a fall. Belay also refers to the entire system set up to make belaying possible, including the anchor that holds the belayer in place.

Bergschrund ('schrund) A giant crevasse found at the upper limit of a glacier, formed where the moving glacier breaks away from the ice cap.

Big walls A steep cliff or face, vertical or nearly so, that is 1,000 feet or more from bottom to top.

Bivouac (bivvy) A sleeping place in the middle of a route with makeshift shelter.

Bolt An artificial anchor placed in a hole drilled for that purpose.

Bolt ladder A string of bolts found on a climb.

Bouldering Climbing unroped on boulders or at the foot of climbs to a height where it is still safe to jump off.

Buttress The part of the mountain or rock that stands in front of the main mountain face, often flanked on both sides by gullies or couloirs.

Cairn Rocks piled together to mark the summit of a peak or a route on a trail or mountain.

Cam Generic reference to the family of spring-loaded camming devices.

Capsule-style A variation on alpine style (q.v.), in which a climbing party still starts at the bottom and finishes at the top of a mountain without retreat to the base, but which involves progressive forays out of camps on the mountain that move higher as the route is established.

Carabiner (biner, krab) Aluminum alloy ring equipped with a spring-loaded snap gate.

Carpet-bolting The practice of placing numerous bolts on a climb.

Chalk Gymnast's chalk used by climbers to cut the perspiration on their hands in order to better adhere to the rock.

Chockstone A rock wedged in a crack or behind a flake, around which a runner can be threaded and then clipped to a rope for an anchor point.

Chop routes Route on which a leader fall is probably fatal.

Chromoly A strong but very light steel alloy (of chromium and molybdenum) out of which most climbing equipment is made.

Circumambulate To complete a circuit around an entire mountain or massif.

Cirque A deep and steep-walled basin on a mountain usually forming the blunt end of a valley.

Col A low point between two mountain peaks.

Cornice Overhanging snow and ice found on ridges and summits.

Crag Name for a (small) climbing area.

Crampons Spikes or points attached to the bottom of boots that allow a climber to walk and climb on snow and ice.

Crux The most difficult section of a climb or pitch.

Cwm The Welsh word for cirque.

Death Zone The high altitude at which energy expenditure always exceeds possible intake. Deterioration is inevitable and will eventually necessitate descent.

Direct Aid Technique used to climb exceedingly steep and hold-bereft rock, where the gear supports the weight of the climber as he or she ascends.

Dry-tooling An ice-climbing technique where ice axes and crampons are used on rock in sections where the ice is absent or not sufficiently strong.

Enchainments Climbing lots of peaks on the same outing.

Étrier The nylon ladders used in aid climbing (q.v.), clipped into protection and allowing upward progress.

Fixed protection Gear left in place on a climb. Fixed ropes are ropes left in place by a team of climbers.

Flash ascending A climb with no prior knowledge of the route, on the first attempt, with no falls or rests.

Free climb Climbing rock using only hands, feet, and natural holds for forward motion. Ropes and "pro" are only used for protection of the climber and not for progression.

Friends The original spring-loaded camming devices used to protect climbers against a fall.

Glacier A slowly moving permanent mass of ice.

Grade A number denoting the seriousness of a route.

Guide Professional climber hired to take others into the mountains.

Hand jam Slightly masochistic technique where the hand is wedged into a crack.

Hang-dogging Hanging or resting on the rope as one is climbing.

Hardware Technical equipment used by climbers.

Harness Nylon safety webbing sewn to fit the climber's body, into which the rope is tied.

Haul Bag Bag used to drag equipment up a climb.

Headpointing Refers to redpointing traditional or bold routes.

Hexes Six-sided pieces of protection (q.v. "nuts") slotted into cracks in rock.

Hobs Old-style mountaineering boots that had soles studded with rough-headed nails.

Hold-Chipping Artificially enhancing a rock climb through cutting holds where none existed naturally.

Hooks (dim. of skyhooks) Metal hooks hung on edges and nubbins of rock—often precariously—which allow passage across blank areas of aid climbs (q.v.).

Hypoxia Lack of oxygen.

Ice Ax A mountaineering tool two-to-four feet long, pointed at the end with a head consisting of a pick and an adze.

Ice Cap A large, permanent sheet of ice in a mountain or polar area.

Ice Climbing Climbing vertical or overhanging ice formations, often frozen waterfalls.

Ice Screw A protection device for ice climbing. It looks like a large bolt that can be screwed into hard ice.

Iron Railing A permanently fixed metal ladder on a climb (known as a "via ferrata" in Europe).

Jumar A type of rope ascending device.

Klettersteige Fully equipped climbing routes so that hikers or climbers need only attach themselves to the artificial aids and ascend in safety.

Lead Climb To ascend a climb from the bottom up, placing or clipping protection as you go.

Lines Routes or potential climbing routes on a mountain.

Litter A basket used to carry an injured party in a mountain rescue.

Massif A large mountain mass or group of summits.

Mixed Climbing Climbing with a combination of different methods of ascent; e.g., mixed free and aid climbing, mixed rock and ice climbing, etc.

Moraine Rock debris on a glacier, or left behind after the recession of a glacier.

Mountaineering The practice of climbing mountains.

Névé Consolidated granular snow formed by repeated freeze-and-thaw cycles—old snow. Also used to indicate permanent snowfields.

Nut Metal wedge used for protection in cracks.

Off Width A climb too wide to jam, too small to chimney.

On-Sight To ascend a rock climb for the first time, without any prior experience of the climb, without falling or resting on protection.

Overhang Rock (or ice) that is "more than vertical."

Peak Bagging Climbing peaks or groups of peaks in order to complete a set or add a climb to a list of accomplishments.

Picket A metal stake hammered into snow for protection on alpine climbs.

Pitch A section of climb between two belays and no longer than the length of one rope.

Piton (pin) Metal spike hammered into a crack.

Portaledge Hanging platforms on which to sleep.

Porters Individuals hired to carry equipment on a climb, especially on expeditions.

Protection Anchors placed during the climb to protect the leader.

Pulmonary Edema Potentially fatal collection of fluid in the lungs as a result of too-rapid ascent to high altitude.

Pumpy A section of climb requiring explosive physical strength.

Rack The climbing gear carried during an ascent.

Rap-Bolted A rock climb established by descending from the top of a wall or crag, placing bolts (q.v.) wherever desired for protection.

Rappel To descend a rope by means of mechanical brake devices.

Rating A number denoting the technical difficulty of the climb, generally based on steepness of the rock, size, and difficulty of the holds, etc. In North America the Yosemite Decimal System (YDS) begins at 5.0 and proceeds upward to 5.14, increasing with difficulty.

Redpoint Climbing a route without resting on the rope or using artificial holds, after previously having practiced the moves.

Retro-Bolting Replacing existing, old bolts (q.v.) on a climb with newer, and most often safer, bolts.

Rock Blade Type of piton.

Rock Climbing A branch of climbing focused on ascending rock walls.

Runners Accessory cords or nylon webbing used to attach the climbing rope to pieces of protection and natural features on a climb.

Run-Out Long distances between protection on a climbing route, creating a potentially dangerous situation for the lead climber.

RURP Realized Ultimate Reality Piton; a thin, postage stamp-sized piton (q.v.)

Scree Debris that collects at the base of mountains due to rockfall.

Siege Style Ascent of a wall or peak using fixed ropes involving several upward pushes, with retreats to the base to re-equip.

Serac A block or tower of ice on a steep glacier or in an icefall.

Slab Large smooth rock face inclined between 30 and 60 degrees.

Sling A long nylon runner (q.v.).

Smearing Foot technique where a big part of the climbing shoe is used to generate as much friction as possible.

Snow Bridge A temporary covering of a crevasse by snow.

Solo Climbing Climbing alone, though not necessarily without the protection of a rope.

Spindrift Avalanche Blowing snow falling in an avalanche formation.

Sport Climbing A branch of rock climbing with a primarily gymnastic—rather than risk—focus.

Stoppers (Nuts) Metal wedges used for protection on rock.

Test Piece A particularly challenging climb.

Traditional Route A climb requiring the placing of protection (cams, nuts, etc. in cracks, pockets, and other natural features) by the climber herself.

Tricounis Nailed mountaineering boots (q.v. hobnails).

Verglas Thin coating of ice on rock.

THE BILL MARCH
SUMMIT OF EXCELLENCE AWARD

THE AWARD

The Summit of Excellence Award is perhaps the most significant tribute of the Banff Mountain Film Festival and is presented annually to an individual who has made a significant contribution to mountain life in the Canadian Rockies. It is dedicated to the memory of Bill March, a widely respected mountaineer, author, and educator, who led Canada's first successful Everest climb in 1982.

1987 – BRUNO ENGLER
"Photographer"

Legendary mountain guide and photographer, Bruno is renowned as one of the Canadian Rockies' great storytellers and enduring characters. In his long career, he has guided famous mountaineers Frank Smythe, Tony Cromwell, and Georgia Engelhard, and he has undertaken cinematography and location/mountain safety work for Disney, Universal Studios, and most North American television networks.

1988 – JIM DAVIES
"Rescue Pilot"

Jim Davies is a pioneer of helicopter rescue in the Canadian Rockies who, with alpine specialist Peter Fuhrmann, designed the vertical sling-rescue system now used extensively in the mountain national parks. From 1966 until 1990, he participated in over 2,000 rescues of stranded and injured alpinists, for which he received international recognition from the helicopter industry.

1989 – HANS GMOSER
"Heli-skiing"

The father of heli-skiing and heli-hiking in western Canada, Hans's many achievements include the first ascent of Direttissima on Yamnuska and the first guided climb of Mount Alberta. In the higher ranges, he led early ascents of Mounts Logan and McKinley. Hans is a Member of the Order of Canada and an Honorary Member of the International Federation of Mountain Guides.

1990 – PAT MORROW
"Seven Summits"

Pat is an adventure photographer recognized by many as the first to climb the Seven Summits, reaching the highest peak on each continent. For this achievement, he received the Order of Canada in 1987. He worked as photographer or filmmaker on 21 high-altitude expeditions and as photographer for the feature films *K2*, *Seven Years in Tibet*, and *The Vertical Limit*.

1991 – DON FOREST
"Mountaineer"

At 59 years of age, Don Forest became the first person to climb all fifty-six 11,000-foot (3,353-meter) peaks in the Canadian Rockies and subsequently added all seventeen of the 11,000 foot peaks in the Purcell and Selkirk Ranges. However, his proudest achievement is his ascent of the West Peak of Mount Logan, just days after his 71st birthday.

1992 – JON WHYTE
"Historian"

Banff-born Jon Whyte had a lifelong passion for the celebration of local mountain culture. A prolific writer and award-winning poet, he wrote or contributed to more than 20 books and was responsible for publishing the classic *Canadian Rockies Trail Guide*. After his death, Jon was honored posthumously for his commitment to history and his refined sense of mountain place.

1993 – ROGER VERNON
"Filmmaker"

Cinematographer Roger Vernon's expertise has taken him to mountains around the world to work on such films as *The Search for Mallory and Irvine* and *The Vertical Limit*. He was a cameraman for alpine events in the official film of the 1988 Olympic Winter Games in Calgary and assisted with such locally filmed features as *Unforgiven*, *Legends of the Fall*, and *The Edge*.

1994 – LLOYD "KIWI" GALLAGHER
"Emergency Services Coordinator"

In two highly successful careers, "Kiwi" worked as a guide and manager with Canadian Mountain Holidays (CMH) and participated in more than 500 rescue missions in Kananaskis Country, a 4,000-square-kilometer recreation area in the Canadian Rockies. He was awarded the National Search and Rescue Secretariat's "Outstanding Achievement Award for Search and Rescue in Canada."

1995 – BRIAN GREENWOOD
"Climber"

Brian is a Rockies legend and an inspiration to modern climbers who struggle to follow routes he pioneered in the 1960s. His name is synonymous with classics such as Yamnuska's *Belfry*, *Corkscrew*, and the popular *Red Shirt*. But it was during the first ascents of serious alpine routes like the *North Face* of Mount Temple and the *East Face* of Mount Babel that he really established his reputation.

1996 – TIM AUGER
"Park Warden - Rescue Specialist"

For over 25 years, Tim Auger has worked in the Park Service in the Canadian Rockies, while refining the helicopter sling-rescue system, developing rescue pilot standards, and researching avalanche-probing methods. As a climber, he made early ascents at Squamish Chief and contributed to the birth of waterfall climbing in Canada.

WHYTE
MUSEUM
of the Canadian Rockies
Exhibitions • Archives • Heritage

"As an organization dedicated to fostering communication, growth, and vision in the mountain community,
the Whyte Museum is honored to share with The Banff Centre for Mountain Culture and the
National Geographic Society in the development of this important book.
It is a pleasure to participate in a project that is dedicated to documenting the visions and achievements of this unique
global community and to bringing the people together at the Banff Mountain Summit to celebrate these milestones."

—DOUGLAS LEONARD, EXECUTIVE DIRECTOR

CRAIG RICHARDS, renowned Canadian landscape and portrait photographer, makes his home in the Canadian Rockies of Alberta. As head of photography at the Whyte Museum of the Canadian Rockies he has for over 20 years supported its mandate to preserve and celebrate the cultural history of the region.

These portraits are the result of a six-month blur of activity, defined by a demanding schedule, rigorous conditions, and a myriad of challenges. Craig Richards requested that each climber bring an item that embodied his or her experience, and they did—from climbing gear to stories and music.

When you look at these portraits you witness the culmination of Richards's longtime love affair with the spirit of the mountains. You see his technical discipline, his storytelling—and above all his ability to capture the essence of these legends without losing the mystique that such individuals conjure.

Craig Richards at work on the portrait of Kurt Diemberger.

1997 – SHARON WOOD
"Mother - Mentor - Mountaineer"

Sharon Wood is the first Canadian woman to achieve Climbing Guide status in the Association of Canadian Mountain Guides. Her crowning achievement was her ascent of Everest's West Ridge from Tibet in 1986. She is the first North American woman and the sixth woman in history to reach the top of the world.

1998 – JOHN MARTIN
"Climber - Mountain Lover"

John Martin is one of the most prolific contributors to sport climbing and mountain exploration in the Canadian Rockies. He has climbed over 460 different peaks, creating more than 100 first ascents and 60 new routes. In addition, he has established over 500 rock-climbing routes and is co-author of *Sport Climbing of the Canadian Rockies* (1995).

1999 – GUY LACELLE
"Climber"

Guy Lacelle is one of the world's leading ice climbers, having established or repeated many of the most extreme ice routes in the Canadian Rockies. He climbs almost exclusively alone and in remote locations, his only companion being his faithful dog, Sam. This extraordinary level of commitment, combined with a refusal to indulge in self-promotion, has made Guy an unsung hero in the mountaineering community.

2000 – CHIC SCOTT
"Mountaineer - Guide - Writer"

Pioneer of epic ski traverses, including a 21-day, 217-mile traverse from Jasper to Lake Louise, Chic Scott is author of *Ski Trails in the Canadian Rockies* (1992). In addition, he made the first winter ascents of Mounts Assiniboine and Hungabee. He is founder of the Canadian Himalayan Foundation, an originator of the Banff Mountain Film Festival, and Honorary Member of the Association of Canadian Mountain Guides.

—Profiles by John Amatt

THE BANFF CENTRE FOR MOUNTAIN CULTURE

Mountains are powerful touchstones of nature and spirit. Mountains evoke stories that inspire, ignite, and incite. The Banff Centre for Mountain Culture (CMC) gathers and shares these stories and images around the world.

The CMC is committed to offering an international mountain cultural network and forum. It supports leading-edge pursuit of mountain cultural studies through its grants program. The CMC hosts a variety of mountain events and celebrations around the world. It is creating a mountain resource centre through its digital film archive and book collections. It has a global outreach program that reaches millions of viewers on six continents.

PROGRAMS OF THE BANFF CENTRE FOR MOUNTAIN CULTURE

Banff Mountain Film Festival: a three-day, forty-film competitive event each November in Banff, founded in 1976

Best of the Banff Mountain Film Festival World tour: takes the films to 100,000 people in more than 15 countries

Banff Mountain Film Festival network programming brings the Banff experience to millions of viewers

Banff Mountain Book Festival: a five-day annual celebration of the best in mountain literature

Banff Mountain Book Festival Speaker's Tour: takes speakers from the Book Festival to cities across North America

Banff Mountain Photography Competition: an international competition attracting entries from around the world

Grants Program: supports projects that interpret the adventure, environment and inspiration of the mountains

Mountain Adventure Vacations: adventures for the body and mind

Seminars and Speakers: issues, adventures and information from leaders in the mountain community

Banff Mountain Summit: a millennium project, bringing together this century's top mountain personalities

Banff Centre for Mountain Culture Archives: the resource centre for mountain films, books and photos

Banff Mountain Communities: the creation of working partnerships among mountain people to research, explore and resolve mountain issues

CONTACT INFORMATION

Banff Centre for Mountain Culture
Mail: Box 1020, Stn. 38,
    Banff, Alberta T0L 0C0
    Canada
Email: cmc@banffcentre.ab.ca
Web site: www.banffcentre.ab.ca/CMC
Telephone: 403-762-6369
Fax: 403-762-6277

ACKNOWLEDGMENTS

We are grateful to many who believed in this project and contributed to it in words, ideas, and images. First we thank the remarkable characters who offered us a window to their world through the essays. The flexibility and support of The Banff Centre and the Whyte Museum of the Canadian Rockies was crucial. The fact-checking efforts of Geoff Powter were key, as were the images provided by the filmmakers and photographers whose work was featured. As Kevin Mulroy of National Geographic embraced this project, his publishing and design team, especially Carol Norton, Marilyn Gibbons, and Johnna Rizzo, took it to another level, beyond our wildest dreams. Special thanks as well to Colin Ferguson, Paul Ford, Peter Jeune, Erna Kelly, Samantha Kelly, Ann Krcik, Katherine Millet, Marc Ledwidge, Alan McDonald, Giancarlo Palisi, Chris Purcell, Daniele Redaelli, Albert Rondina, Anne Ryall, Linda Ryall, Kelly Stauffer, and Myles Zarowny. The financial support of our sponsors helped make this dream a reality. And finally, the ongoing, unceasing yet enthusiastic determination of project coordinator Paula Rondina was truly inspiring.
—*Bernadette McDonald, John Amatt, and Craig Richards*

PHOTOGRAPHY CREDITS

All portrait photography appearing on pages 8-220 by Craig Richards, © The Banff Centre for Mountain Culture and The Whyte Museum of the Canadian Rockies, Banff.
All photographs appearing on pages 226-251 are courtesy The Banff Centre for Mountain Culture, unless otherwise noted below.
Pp. 2-3, Baiba Morrow; 4-5, Galen Rowell/Mountain Light; 14-15, Vittorio Sella; 19, Pierre Lemire; 27, Barry C. Bishop; 30-31, William Thompson; 40-41, Galen Rowell/Mountain Light; 50, Bill Hatcher; 56-57, Pat Morrow; 61, Martyn Williams; 78-79, Craig Richards; 89, Wade Davis; 97, Galen Rowell/Mountain Light; 100-101, Galen Rowell/Mountain Light; 118-119, Barbara Cushman Rowell/Mountain Light; 129, courtesy The Banff Centre for Mountain Culture; 140-141, Craig Richards; 158-159, Gordon Wiltsie; 180-181, Galen Rowell/Mountain Light; 185, Barry C. Bishop; 200-201, Galen Rowell/Mountain Light; 211, Salkeld Collection; 217, NGS Image Collection; 228 (lower), Leo Dickinson Adventure Archive; 236 (upper right), Ron Kauk/Mountain Light; 237, Guy Martin-Ravel; 256, Erik Decamp.

COPYRIGHT INFORMATION AND CIP DATA

Copyright ©2000 The Banff Centre for Mountain Culture. All rights reserved.
Library of Congress Cataloging-in-Publication Data

Voices from the summit.
  p. cm.
This book is a collection of articles about climbing that was publish to celebrate 25 years of the Banff Mountain Film Festival.
ISBN 0-7922-7958-1
1. Mountaineering. 2. Banff Mountain Film Festival. I. National Geographic Society (U.S.) II. The Banff Centre for Mountain Culture.

GV200. V65 2000
796.52'2--dc21   00-042161

Into the Unknown—A Shaksgam Odyssey by Kurt Diemberger ©2000 by Kurt Diemberger

The Banff Centre for Mountain Culture gratefully acknowledges the following sponsors for their support of this project: